ADAM SMITH and
Modern Political Economy
BICENTENNIAL ESSAYS ON *THE WEALTH OF NATIONS*

ADAM SMITH and
Modern Political Economy
BICENTENNIAL ESSAYS ON *THE WEALTH OF NATIONS*

Edited by GERALD P. O'DRISCOLL, JR.

The Iowa State University Press / Ames, Iowa, U.S.A.

Composed and printed by
The Iowa State University Press
Ames, Iowa 50010

First edition, 1979

Library of Congress Cataloging in Publication Data
Main entry under title:

Adam Smith and modern political economy.

    "Ten of the eleven papers . . . were delivered at the University of California at Santa Barbara, between early January and early March 1976 as the Harry Girvetz Memorial lectures."
    Includes bibliographical references and index.
    1. Smith, Adam, 1723-1790 — Addresses, essays, lectures.   2.   Smith, Adam, 1723-1790. An inquiry into the nature and causes of the wealth of nations — Addresses, essays, lectures.   I.   O'Driscoll, Gerald P.
HB103.S6A623   330.15′3   78-10181
ISBN 0-8138-1900-8

Contents

Preface

TEN of the eleven papers that appear in this volume were delivered at the University of California at Santa Barbara, between early January and early March 1976, as the Harry Girvetz Memorial Lectures. Professor Girvetz of the department of philosophy had begun work on this series to commemorate the bicentenary of the publication of *The Wealth of Nations.* After his death, the administration continued the preparations, and Vernon Cheadle, who was then chancellor, pledged most of the necessary funds. The Fred C. Koch Foundation generously provided the remainder and has continued to support this project.

Although Professor Girvetz had already extended invitations to a number of the participants, Professor William Kennedy of the department of economics completed all the arrangements and attended to the many details of such a program. The press of Professor Kennedy's work dictated that another person administer the program while it was in operation and edit the volume in which the papers were to be collected. When I was asked to do this, Iowa State University, my home institution, willingly gave me the time, including permission to spend the winter quarter of 1976 at Santa Barbara.

Professor James Buchanan had been invited to deliver a paper on *The Wealth of Nations* during a weeklong visit to Santa Barbara but was unable to do so. He graciously consented, however, to have his paper included in this volume.

The papers included here are essentially in the same form as when delivered, subject to editing by the publisher and to revision and expansion by the authors in some cases. Unless otherwise stated, all references to Adam Smith's *The Wealth of Nations* are to the 1937 Modern Library edition, and page numbers are given in parentheses or brackets in the text.

I completed work on this book while a Liberty Fund Senior Fellow at the Institute for Humane Studies in Menlo Park, California. This support is gratefully acknowledged. I benefited greatly from the comments of Roger Garrison, Leonard Liggio, Lawrence H. White, Professors David

O'Mahony and Joseph Salerno, and Lyla H. O'Driscoll.

Acknowledgment and appreciation are also expressed to the following:

University of Chicago Press for permission to include Professor Joseph Cropsey's paper, which appears under the same title in *Political Philosophy and the Issues of Politics,* University of Chicago Press, 1977.

Duke University Press for permission to include two papers published in *History of Political Economy* 8(Winter 1976): Professor Henry W. Spiegel's Adam Smith's Heavenly City, and Professor E. G. West's Adam Smith's Economics of Politics.

The Royal Society of Canada for permission to include a later version of Professor Samuel Hollander's paper, published as The Historical Dimension in *The Wealth of Nations* in *Transactions of the Royal Society of Canada* 14(1976):277–92.

Professor Fred R. Glahe of the University of Colorado for permission to include Professor James Buchanan's paper, The Justice of Natural Liberty, which was presented in the Adam Smith Bicentennial Lecture Series held at the University of Colorado and at Ohio University in 1976 and sponsored by the Earhart Foundation. Professor Buchanan's paper has been published in *The Journal of Legal Studies* 5(Jan. 1976), and permission to include it in this volume is acknowledged. The paper also appeared in Fred R. Glahe, ed., *Adam Smith and The Wealth of Nations: 1776–1976 Bicentennial Essays* (Boulder, Colorado: Colorado Associated University Press, 1978).

Introduction

SEVERAL of the authors in this volume note the connection between the two greatest events of 1776 — the publication on March 9 of Adam Smith's *An Inquiry into the Nature and Causes of the Wealth of Nations* and almost exactly four months later the signing of the Declaration of Independence. Recent historical scholarship has demonstrated that the connection between these two events is even closer than heretofore believed. There are at least two distinct yet related connections between these economic and political events. First, there is the more purely intellectual connection; in its own way each event represents the culmination of a common intellectual development. Second, each event was partly influenced by crosscurrents in British politics; and, in turn, each event influenced the future course of British politics. Both connections are developed briefly in this introduction.

Adam Smith, aptly named the father of the school that later came to be known as "classical economics," is often credited with being the father of scientific economics.[1] Though the latter is true in Great Britain, this honor is perhaps overly generous toward Smith and insufficiently so toward the Continental thinkers who preceded him. Smith is at the beginning of a tradition developed and carried on *inter alia* by Thomas Robert Malthus, James Mill, David Ricardo, James Ramsey McCulloch, Nassau William Senior, and John Stuart Mill. But Smith is also one of the later figures in a much earlier tradition, which may be marked as beginning with Richard Cantillon and was nurtured by Quesnay, the Physiocrats, and Turgot (with J. B. Say tracing roots directly back to this older tradition as well as more immediately to Adam Smith).

The extent to which one perceives Smith as a figure bridging two traditions or as the father of scientific economics often depends on one's linguistic and cultural heritage. Adam Smith, nonetheless, clearly plays a crucial role in the history of economics. He was, moreover, a great synthesizer of ideas, many if not most of which were not original. No one before him had succeeded so admirably in putting together so many diverse but essentially correct ideas, weaving them into a coherent whole—a social analysis.[2]

The development of this social analysis, particularly the economic aspect, occurred against the backdrop of eighteenth-century realities. Smith responded to and criticized essentially conservative institutions that continued to dominate and constrain social life, though they did so less in fact than in law. Not an apologist for the status quo, Smith was one of its profoundest critics.

The ideas and thought of the latter half of the eighteenth century were surely as important an influence on Smith as the social conditions and institutions, legal and otherwise, that then prevailed. Here I refer specifically to the liberal ideas that flourished at this time, which were in the context of eighteenth-century realities (and perhaps today's) truly radical ideas. This eighteenth-century liberalism was synonymous with a defense of private property rights and the political autonomy of the individual and with an opposition to state power or control over the lives of citizens, whether economic or political. As the terms are used today in the United States (but almost nowhere else), conservatism and liberalism both combine elements of eighteenth-century liberalism and eighteenth-century conservatism.

The Glorious Revolution of 1688, the overthrow of the Stuart monarchy and the eventual establishment of the Hanoverian succession, dominated eighteenth-century British political thought. Good Whigs supported both the overthrow and the new succession. ("Whig" refers here to those who were mainly concerned with certain principles and to party scarcely at all.) In popularizing Lockean ideas, Independent Whigs[3] such as John Trenchard and Thomas Gordon did not support merely one party or faction; they developed a radical politics.

The central tenets of radical Whiggery can be summarized by quoting the editor of Trenchard and Gordon's work, historian David L. Jacobson: "There could be no binding of the future, no fixed, unalterable pact among generations as to the form of governments." Moreover, "each subject must judge by his own conscience whether the magistrate be good or evil." And finally, "The right to resist was good Whiggery and contrasted sharply with a Tory or High-Church acceptance of the misuse of power."[4]

In number 59 of the famous *Cato's Letters,* Trenchard argued that "Liberty is the unalienable Right of all Mankind." And in number 62, Gordon defined this liberty as "the Power which every man has over his own Actions, and his Right to enjoy the Fruit of his Labour, Art, and Industry, as far as by it he hurts not the Society, or any Members of it, by taking from any Member, or by hindering him from enjoying what he himself enjoys."[5]

This radical Whiggery was transplanted among the colonists in America, where it took root even more firmly than in Britain. As Jacobson notes:

Trenchard and Gordon wrote expressly to justify the Glorious Revolution
and to reject such doctrines as passive obedience to tyrannical government
or the divine right of hereditary monarchs. . . . To a degree equaling that
of the English population of the early eighteenth century, the American colonists accepted and enshrined a legend of 1688-1689 and even of their own
supposed part in overthrowing Stuart tyranny. . . . They could apply the
doctrines of Trenchard and Gordon in their own ways to new situations
throughout the eighteenth century. . . . In "Cato's" praise of tyrannicide
and justification of resistance to the usurpation of power, they could find ra-
tionales for their own continuing resistance to British authority. From
Trenchard and Gordon's attacks upon the doctrine of divine right might be
drawn arguments finally for rejecting the authority of George III. The after-
the-fact defense of one revolution thus easily provided arguments in support
of another and later revolution by a people who, in 1776, believed they had
kept the Whig tradition purer than the old country and that they were, to a
large extent, simply maintaining and continuing the heritage of ideas and
liberties.[6]

The events of the latter part of the seventeenth century and the intellectual and political reactions in that century and the succeeding one
were thus mirrored in the American colonies. Many of the revolutionary
leaders knew the work of Trenchard and Gordon directly; others, like Tom
Paine, knew of it indirectly.[7] A more radical variant of Whiggery thus
came to dominate in the colonies, for Trenchard and Gordon's views often
went beyond the more popular and moderate Whiggery of their English
contemporaries.

While Trenchard and Gordon's writings had demonstrable impact on
events in this country and thus contributed to one of the two events whose
bicentennial we have celebrated, their writings and concerns had similar if
more muted impact in Britain in Adam Smith's time. Smith was barely
born when this work and its influence were at their peak. Yet the objects of
their polemics — Jacobite conspiracies, High-Church domination, public
corruption, the evils of privilege — were all central concerns of Smith, a
notable Rockingham Whig. We know that part of what he found
distasteful about Oxford was its being a center of Jacobite activity, since
this offended his Republican sensibilities. His own views against
establishmentarianism are well known (pp. 740-66, esp. pp. 744-45). The
corruption of the mercantile system was one of his favorite themes; he
made special note of the South Sea scandal (pp. 703-5), an affair that had
likewise been the object of Trenchard and Gordon's attention. Each saw
this affair and its genre as deeply discordant and a source of the people's
justifiable sense of alienation from their government. In its own sphere
The Wealth of Nations is an implicit attack on privilege in all its
manifestations.

Thus the intellectual linkage between *The Wealth of Nations* and the
American Revolution is fairly direct; both were partly the product of essen-

tially the same intellectual influences. Each was the product of essentially revolutionary times. Adam Smith's work attempted to come to grips with the economics of the emergent liberal order. This intellectual connection is strengthened by the direct knowledge of *The Wealth of Nations* that a number of the revolutionary leaders in the colonies had.[8]

The American problem obviously had its impact on Smith, profoundly affecting the political and intellectual environments in which Smith operated. This point has been put forcefully by Professor Bernard Bailyn. Speaking of Britain, Bailyn argued:

> There is nothing accidental in the chronology of the events of 1776: American independence lay logically in the mid-point of that tumultuous year. For the question of Anglo-American relations was not some separate problem that led by political accident to war and to American independence. It was part and parcel of the major domestic issues in Britain — economic, demographic, religious, and above all political and constitutional. No major thinker could free himself from its perplexing embrace. . . . Adam Smith not only included a 125-page chapter on the subject in his *Wealth of Nations* but delayed publication of the book for over a year in an effort to perfect his original draft of that section, which he correctly believed to be a key to all his thinking.[9]

None of this is to suggest that *The Wealth of Nations* is a political tract, though clearly it is both theory and policy oriented. Nor is it intended to cast doubt on the scientific quality of the book, though Smith himself was evidently not self-conscious about its scientific quality.[10] His arguments stand or fall on their intellectual merit and should be analyzed on their own terms as economic, political, and sociological propositions. One cannot, as John Maurice Clark seemed to imply, simply reduce this work to an effect of the social forces of the time without taking cognizance of the *arguments* that Smith presents.[11] To do so would surely be to commit the genetic fallacy. To acknowledge that the background institutions and intellectual developments influenced Smith is surely not to commit oneself to a genetic interpretation of his work.

Nor do I wish to suggest that Smith was a radical Whig, Whig though he was. He would surely have felt uncomfortable with many of the positions taken by radical Whigs. On the question of standing armies, a burning question of the century, his position might be better described as that of a sophisticated Tory than of a Whig (pp. 667–69).[12] But the characteristic concerns of Whiggery were Smith's also. His positions were generally Whiggish, though more moderate than those of Trenchard and Gordon.

In understanding the radical nature of *The Wealth of Nations*, one must recall that the very concept of economics as a system of scientific principles is an affront to those who support or desire unlimited power. Economics suggests that the power of the tyrant as sovereign is somehow inherently limited, as though by the natural laws of physical sciences.

Specifically, the political economy of the eighteenth and nineteenth centuries was anathema to High Tories. The discipline of economics denies the possibility of truly unlimited political power by its assertion of the existence of some economic laws.

To take a nontrivial problem, economics asserts that the sovereign cannot make goods relatively abundant or scarce as he pleases or decrees. He cannot autonomously determine the real scarcities of goods or their costs in terms of other goods merely by arbitrarily assigning them whatever prices he believes they should have. The arbitrary assignment of prices to goods, independent of demand and supply conditions, affects only their public or official exchange ratios, not the actual value of goods to individuals. By such an arbitrary procedure the sovereign can create shortages and surpluses, but not greater or smaller quantities of goods. Such price controls eventually do cause changes in the quantities of the goods available and in their prices, but these derivative changes will be in the *opposite* direction intended by the soverign. It is no wonder that the tenets of Whiggery and commercial liberalism became associated with political economy. In its own sphere, each opposed unlimited political power, though the strictly political and strictly economic arguments remained logically independent.

Economics is also historically the product of a concern for the material or temporal well-being of the mass of mankind. The radical nature of both these facts is often insufficiently realized. It is by no means clear which characteristic of economic science has earned it more opprobrium in the last two hundred years.[13] But *per contra* Professor Stigler, economics as a discipline is almost by its nature anticonservative.[14] For it involves the assertion that in a constantly changing world constant adjustment is necessary, with concomitant wealth gains and losses, if any kind of efficient resource allocation is to be effected. This implies mobility of economic groups and accompanying social change.

In *The Wealth of Nations* Smith provided an economic program for the liberalism of his day, which was largely embodied in Whiggery. In *The Theory of Moral Sentiments* Smith, the moralist, had articulated a system (or formalized what he saw around him) of how men should behave, given the moral freedom to choose. In *The Wealth of Nations,* Smith sought to explain how his "obvious and simple system of natural liberty" would produce the goods (p. 651). And while he emphasized what economists today would call efficiency of this economic system, Adam Smith had a parallel argument defending the system on grounds of justice.[15]

Despite support of various state activities, Smith was generally consistent in his defense of political liberalism and market economy. In a paper not included in this volume, Professor West has argued that Smith was an even stauncher defender of a liberal market economy than was once thought. According to West, what has been traditionally taken as support by Smith for governmental provision of "public works" was in reality support for governmental permission for corporate, but private, provision of these goods—a form of organization usually opposed by Smith. Moreover, the historical context must be remembered: incorporation required an act of Parliament.[16]

Smith's sympathies were with the common man and not particularly with businessmen. Professor Ginzberg makes this point succinctly in his essay. Political and economic liberals of the eighteenth and nineteenth centuries always maintained that the implementation of their programs would produce the greatest benefit for the mass of mankind. This observation brings us, however, to the final point to be considered in this introductory essay.

Having emphasized the historical setting in which Adam Smith wrote, I must consider the question of his relevance in a seemingly different historical situation. This is the question that Professor Rosenberg, in particular, raises. It is a very general question, touching on whether economic theories are true for all time or only in particular historical contexts, having to be modified or abandoned as institutions, laws, and customs evolve. No convincing answer could be developed in the limited space, but I suggest one possible way to resolve this question as it applies to *The Wealth of Nations* in particular.

Abstracting from obvious and in some cases nontrivial differences between the two centuries (such as the British monarchy of the eighteenth century and the American democracy of the twentieth century), I would question whether things are all that different. Licensing, subsidies, quotas, and the like are once again rampant in the land. Many if not most substantial corporations are significantly dependent on the central government for their continued profitability and hence on government favor for their continued existence. Medieval guilds have been initiated anew in certain craft unions. The Statute of Apprenticeship is still with us in substance if not in form.[17] More generally, the same basic problem of scarcity of resources and the necessity of devising institutions to produce and allocate scarce resources is with us now as in the eighteenth century. This reality may explain why we will surely celebrate the two hundred and fiftieth anniversary of the publication of *The Wealth of Nations*.

GERALD P. O'DRISCOLL, JR.
Assistant Professor of Economics
New York University

NOTES

1. See Jacob H. Hollander, The Founder of a School, in John Maurice Clark et al., *Adam Smith, 1776–1926* (Chicago: Univ. Chicago Press, 1928), pp. 22–52. In what follows, compare Sir John Hicks, "Revolutions" in Economics, in Spiro Latsis, ed., *Method and Appraisal in Economics* (New York: Cambridge Univ. Press, 1976), p. 209ff.
2. On this point, see Professor Hayek's discussion in F. A. Hayek, Adam Smith and the Open Society, *The Daily Telegraph*, London, Mar. 9, 1976.

3. The *Independent Whig* was an early publication of Trenchard and Gordon.
4. See the Introduction by David L. Jacobson, ed., *The English Libertarian Heritage* (Indianapolis: Bobbs-Merrill, 1965), pp. xxxviii-xxxix.
5. Ibid., p. xxxvi.
6. Ibid., pp. xviii-xix. The importance of the Glorious Revolution in eighteenth-century colonial political thought has long been noted. For instance, compare Charles Sellers and Henry May, *A Synopsis of American History* (Chicago: Rand McNally, 1963), pp. 56-59. Likewise, textbook writers have long noted the influence of Lockean ideas on the American Revolution. For instance, see R. R. Palmer and Joel Colton, *A History of the Modern World*, 3rd ed. (New York: Knopf, 1965), pp. 285-87; also see Sellers and May, *Synopsis*, p. 57. The newer scholarship has emphasized that these Lockean ideas filtered through popular writers and pamphleteers such as Trenchard and Gordon. This new work has demonstrated the filiation of ideas and made more plausible the rapid spread of Lockean thought among the masses. See the Introduction by Jacobson to Trenchard and Gordon's writings; also see Bernard Bailyn, *The Ideological Origins of the American Revolution* (Cambridge: Belknap Press, Harvard Univ. Press, 1967).
7. See Jacobson, *Heritage* pp. xlviii-lx; and also Bailyn's extensive discussion in *Ideological Origins*.
8. See G. Warren Nutter, Adam Smith and the American Revolution (Washington, D.C.: Am. Enterprise Inst. Repr. Ser., 1976). Melchior Palyi emphasized that the spread of Smith's ideas on the Continent was likewise made possible by the spread of liberal ideas and liberal practice. Smithian ideas reinforced this process. See his Introduction of Adam Smith on the Continent, in Clark, *Adam Smith*, pp. 180-233.
9. Bernard Bailyn, 1776: A Year of Challenge—A World Transformed, *J. Law Econ.* 19(Oct. 1976):465. In general this whole issue, entitled 1776: The Revolution in Social Thought, is an intellectual gold mine.
10. See Jacob H. Hollander, The Dawn of a Science, in Clark, *Adam Smith*, pp. 15-16.
11. See John Maurice Clark, Adam Smith and the Currents of History, ibid., pp. 53-76.
12. I cannot agree with the suggestion that Smith's position on standing armies can be seen as a logical conclusion of his arguments in favor of the division of labor. Cf. Gary Wills, Benevolent Adam Smith, *New York Review of Books* 25(Feb. 9, 1978):41.
13. Professor Ashton once noted that enhanced consumption by the lower classes during the Industrial Revolution was decried by social observers, who at times also argued that this consumption was a sign of increased poverty! These objections included but were not limited to William Cobbett's denunciation of tea drinking. See T. S. Ashton, The Treatment of Capitalism by Historians, in F. A. Hayek, ed., *Capitalism and Historians* (Chicago: Univ. Chicago Press, Phoenix Books, 1963), pp. 31-61, esp. pp. 37-38.
14. Cf. George J. Stigler, The Politics of Political Economists, in *Essays in the History of Economics* (Chicago: Univ. Chicago Press, Phoenix Books, 1965), pp. 51-65.
15. See the essay by Professor Buchanan in this volume. But cf. George J. Stigler, The Economist and the State, *Am. Econ. Rev.* 55(Mar. 1965):2-3; and Jacob Viner, Adam Smith and Laissez-Faire, in Clark, *Adam Smith*, pp. 116-55.
16. See E. G. West, Adam Smith's Public Economics: A Re-evaluation, *Can. J. Econ.* 10(Feb. 1977):1-18.
17. Professor Hughes has recently suggested a historical reason for the similarity of economic institutions and laws in twentieth-century America and eighteenth-century Britain: the transference of common law with its economic controls to the colonies and its absorption into our legal system. See Jonathan R. T. Hughes, *The Governmental Habit: Economic Controls from Colonial Times to the Present* (New York: Basic Books, 1977).

I   Theory and Policy

1

Adam Smith in Theory and Practice

ADAM SMITH'S *The Wealth of Nations* was a revolutionary event in 1776 — an intellectual shot heard round the world. It attacked an economic system prevalent throughout European civilization, both in Europe itself and in the Western Hemisphere colonies. The pervasive and minute economic regulations that encrusted the British economy in the eighteenth century were widely disliked and evaded, as were similar "mercantilist" schemes of economic control in other countries. But while many people chafed or complained, it was Adam Smith who first convincingly demolished the whole conception behind these regulations and in the process established the new field of economics.

Adam Smith not only attacked prevailing economic doctrines and practices, he attacked the political ruling powers,[1] denounced the rising economic class of capitalists,[2] opposed the creation of a British Empire,[3] and invariably sided with the "underdogs" whenever he took sides between rich and poor,[4] between businessmen and their employees,[5] or between masters and slaves.[6] *The Wealth of Nations* is such a classic that it suffers the fate of many classics; it is seldom read, though frequently mentioned — usually in the light of later concerns, rather than in the historical context in which it was actually written. Some modern writers have even tried to make Smith an apologist for the status quo.[7] But no one writes a 900-page book to say how satisfied he is with the way things are going. *The Wealth of Nations* was an attack on the status quo, and no one was more scathing in his denunciations of businessmen than Adam Smith — not even Karl Marx.

If Smith was a revolutionary, what was the nature of his revolution, what is its present status, and how does it compare with other revolutions in other times and places? To answer such questions, it is necessary to consider both the theory and practice of the system that Smith attacked, as well as the theory and practice of Adam Smith himself. It is necessary to

---

Thomas Sowell is Professor of Economics, University of California, Los Angeles.

3

consider the role of *The Wealth of Nations* in the development of economics and its broader role in the social policies of its era and the succeeding two centuries to the present.

THE ERA OF MERCANTILISM

"Mercantilism" is a sweeping label covering a wide range of writings, laws, and policies beginning in various European nation-states in the seventeenth century, still pervasive in the middle of the eighteenth century, and never completely extinguished till the present day. The mercantilist writers were a motley collection of businessmen, pamphleteers, and politicians; and the doctrines they promoted reflected ordinary commonsense conceptions of wealth and of how an economy should function—conceptions not subjected to any of the systematic dissection or dialectic scrutiny characteristic of the medieval scholastics before them or the professional economists after them.

At the heart of mercantilism was a conception of wealth in purely invidious or competitive terms. Wealth, to the mercantilists, was something obtained at the expense of someone else—a differential gain, like winning a race.[8] A whole society could advance its economic interests only "at the expense of other societies." The cardinal rule of mercantilism was to sell more to foreigners than you buy,[9] acquiring gold to cover the balance. It is only "the treasure which is brought to the realm by the ballance of our foreign trade" which constitutes the amount "by which we are enriched."[10]

While the mercantilists exhorted their respective countrymen to buy domestic products rather than imported goods,[11] the goal of an export surplus was pursued by an array of governmental policies as well. These policies included not only direct controls over imports and exports but also innumerable indirect measures, designed to, or alleged to, promote the same result. For example, wages were kept low through maximum wage laws, in order to lower production costs and help domestic producers to undersell foreign competitors in the world market. Prices were controlled to create a consumption pattern suited to the government's desires and beliefs. The children of the poor were assigned to learn occupations in which they were "needed," according to similar criteria. In this atmosphere, special interest groups were able to obtain all sorts of governmental favors, from direct price-fixing to an exclusion of competitors, under the blanket rationale of promoting the national interest through economic controls.

The magnitude and scope of the controls under mercantilism probably exceeded anything seen in the twentieth century, either in capitalist economies or in most socialist economies. In short, Adam Smith arrived on the scene at a time when he could observe the consequences of mercantilism as it existed in practice, rather than seeing only the theory of mercantilism as envisioned by its advocates. But while the mercantilist scheme of regulation was increasingly unacceptable and unenforceable, there was no clear alternative, nor any clear conception of what was wrong with its basic approach. Smith provided both.

The full title of Smith's classic was *An Inquiry into the Nature and Causes of the Wealth of Nations.* It was necessary to begin with the very nature of wealth, for the whole mercantilist philosophy was built on a fundamental misconception of wealth. To Smith, wealth consisted of real goods and services, and a nation was rich or poor according to its annual production in proportion to its population (p. lvii). This changed everything. If wealth was not a fixed stock of gold but a variable flow of goods, there was no need for international contention over the division of the world's gold; for all nations could grow wealthier at the same time by concentrating on making production more efficient. Implicit also in this was Smith's conception of the "nation" as the aggregate of its people and of their well-being as national prosperity. By contrast, mercantilistic concepts of the wealth of a nation tended to amount to the power of the national government in general, and in particular its power to wage war on other national governments.[12] Since power is by its nature relative, mercantilist political goals consisted of strengthening their respective nations against other nations. But Smith rejected the "malignant jealousy and envy" between nations as a basis for policy. He said:

> France and England may each of them have some reason to dread the increase of the naval and military power of the other; but for either of them to envy the internal happiness and prosperity of the other, the cultivation of its lands, the advancement of its manufactures, the increase of its commerce, the security and number of its ports and harbours, its proficiency in all the liberal arts and sciences, is surely beneath the dignity of two such great nations. These are the real improvements of the world we live in. Mankind are benefitted, human nature is ennobled by them.[13]

Smith differed from the prevailing mercantilist doctrine, not only on the meaning of wealth and of national prosperity but on the very idea of what constituted the nation. Implicit in the mercantilist writings and practices was a conception of the nation as the upper classes, the bearers of its culture and property. Thus wages should be kept low to promote the prosperity of the nation. But to Smith wage earners are the great majority of every society, and "no society can be flourishing and happy, of which the far greater part of its members are poor and miserable" (p. 79). This view of the nation as coextensive with its population was by no means universally accepted in Smith's time either in Europe or America; even in the middle of the next century John Stuart Mill could still say, "When they say country, read aristocracy, and you will never be far from the truth."[14]

Egalitarianism is pervasive in Smith. A philosopher is innately no different from a common laborer, though "the vanity of the philosopher is willing to acknowledge scarce any resemblance" (p. 16). Smith deplored the "disposition to admire, and almost to worship the rich and the power-

ful"[15] and observed that the desire for prominence is the purpose "of half
the labours of human life."[16] *The Wealth of Nations* denounced "merchants and manufacturers" whose "mean rapacity" and "monopolizing
spirit" (p. 460) led them "on many occasions" to "deceive and even to oppress the public" (p. 250). Such people "seldom meet together, even for
merriment and diversion, but the conversation ends in a conspiracy against
the public, or in some contrivance to raise prices" (p. 128). Smith had no
higher opinion of "that insidious and crafty animal, vulgarly called a
statesman or politician," whose concerns were always about the short
run — "the momentary fluctuations of affairs" (p. 435). Smith observed:

> It is the highest impertinence and presumption . . . in kings and minis-
> ters, to pretend to watch over the economy of private people. . . . They
> are themselves always, and without exception, the greatest spendthrifts in
> the society. . . . If their own extravagance does not ruin the state, that of
> their subjects never will [p. 329].

But, unlike some other egalitarians, Smith did not sentimentalize "the
people." The mass was no better and no worse than the elite. Wars, for example, were not foisted on the public by evil leaders, but were popular
adventures:

> In great empires the people who live in the capital, and in the provinces
> remote from the scene of action, feel, many of them, scarce any incon-
> veniency from the war; but enjoy, at their ease, the amusement of reading in
> the newspapers the exploits of their own fleets and armies. . . . They are
> commonly dissatisfied with the return of peace, which puts an end to their
> amusement, and to a thousand visionary hopes of conquest and national
> glory, from a longer continuation of the war [p. 872].

In short, to Smith we are all sinners. None is so noble or so wise as to
dictate to others. In contrast to the mercantilist picture of the able
statesman brilliantly planning the economic affairs of the nation,[17] Smith
depicts politicians as dominated and intimidated by special interests, so
powerful that "like an overgrown standing army," they have become
dangerous to the government itself (p. 438).

Mercantilism concentrated on the *transfer* of wealth while Smith and
classical economics in general concentrated on the *production* of wealth.
For the mercantilists imperialism[18] and even slavery[19] were considered acceptable and effective means of promoting national wealth. For Smith
neither was acceptable and neither was effective. While imperialism produced gains for a few businessmen and colonial officials, this was greatly
outweighed by the costs paid by the taxpayers to maintain an empire. To
Smith, "great fleets and armies . . . acquire nothing which can compensate the expense of maintaining them . . ." (p. 325). *The Wealth of Nations* closes with a plea for Britain to put aside thoughts of the glories of an
empire and accommodate "to the real mediocrity of her circumstances" (p.

900). Slavery was for Smith as economically inefficient as it was morally repugnant, and its existence was explained by man's need to "domineer" rather than by economic principles (p. 365).

Smith not only rejected the policies and practices of the mercantilists, their concept of wealth, and of the nation, he also approached the whole problem of order in the world from a different perspective. The mercantilists were part of a long tradition — still with us today — which assumes that there would be chaos in the absence of a premeditated order imposed by the wise few on the foolish many. During the centuries through which this tradition has endured, the basis for the designs of the few has ranged from the divine right of kings to the inspired ideals of revolutionaries, but the various versions of this tradition incorporate similar assumptions about human beings and about the reasoning process. Smith had very modest expectations concerning people and the power of sheer reasoning to impose itself on a complex system of changing relationships. Yet he saw no chaos in the absence of such heroic feats of the intellect and will. Human society evolved its own balances, much like the ecological systems of nature. That balance reflected the desires and experience of the many rather than the inspiration of the few. All general principles were formed from "experience and induction,"[20] not from scholastic abstractions, "artificial definitions," and elaborate technicalities, which were capable only of "extinguishing whatever degree of good sense there may be in any moral or metaphysical doctrine."[21] In short, prosperity and progress would come, not from the brilliance of an elite, but from knowledge and experience that were widely diffused. In this context, the attempt of political "leadership" to impose its schemes on the economy were both uncalled for and harmful:

> The statesman, who should attempt to direct private people in what manner they ought to employ their capitals, would not only load himself with a most unnecessary attention, but assume an authority which could safely be trusted, not only to no single person, but to no council or senate whatever, and which would nowhere be so dangerous as in the hands of a man who had folly and presumption enough to fancy himself fit to exercise it [p. 423].

In a politically uncontrolled economy, the efforts of each to better himself led to that distribution of capital, labor, and land which maximized their respective returns by maximizing the value of the output to the public. Each "intends only his own gain," but in the end he "promotes that of society," though this "was no part of his intention." Each individual "in his local situation" knows the economic potential of his assets and what sort of goods are "likely to be of the greatest value" far better than "any statesman or lawgiver" (p. 423) can know from a distance.

In rejecting mercantilism, Smith rejected more generally one of the broad traditions of western social thought. Years before he wrote *The Wealth of Nations,* Smith denounced the "man of system" who is "enamored of his own ideal plan of government" and who "seems to imagine that

he can arrange the different members of a great society, with as much ease
as the hand arranges the different pieces on a chess-board. . . ." This
rejected a whole way of thinking that went as far back as Plato's
philosopher-king ("of all political speculators, sovereign princes are the
most dangerous")[22] and as far into the future as twentieth-century revolutionaries and dictators.

Smith's preference for market processes over political processes, as a
means of coordinating a complex economy, was not based on any faith
that market processes were perfect. They were merely considered superior
to political processes. Moreover, Smith recognized what economists today
call "external costs"—that is, costs imposed upon third parties outside the
decision-making units that created these costs. Smith's general preference
for "natural liberty" did not prevent him from opposing "the natural liberty of a few individuals, which might endanger the security of the whole
society . . ." (p. 308). He supported both fire regulations and banking
regulations for this reason. Smith also supported government endeavors in
areas where social purposes required it but where private capital seemed
unlikely to be forthcoming.[23] Education was one such area, especially "the
education of the common people" (pp. 736-37).

CLASSICAL ECONOMICS

Adam Smith was not simply a social thinker but the founder of an enduring school, and indeed, of a whole new area of human knowledge and
analysis. Men had written on economics before, not only about contemporary problems but also about general economic principles. There was
even a school of economists in France—the Physiocrats—before *The
Wealth of Nations,* but they were virtually forgotten a decade after they
were in vogue. By contrast, Smith's work became the foundation on which
succeeding generations of economists built. Even warring factions among
later economists—Sismondi versus Say, Malthus versus Ricardo—invoked
his name and cited his work to support their respective positions on theory
and policy. Indeed, anticipations of economic doctrines attributed to later
economists can be found in *The Wealth of Nations:* Say's Law,[24] the
"Ricardian" theory of rent,[25] and the "Malthusian" population theory,[26]
for example. Scholars have pointed out that some of these theories go back
even before Adam Smith, and have questioned his originality on that
basis.[27] But Smith's great treatise, like most landmarks in human thinking,
is in part a synthesis of disparate elements, and its originality lay partly in
the new configuration of preexisting analytical principles and their
organization into a whole new view of the world. In the same way, most of
the principles behind the airplane were well known before the Wright
brothers.

Smith changed the focus of economic thinking from the marketing
emphasized by the mercantilists, to the *production* of goods, and in particular to the costs of production and therefore to economic efficiency. *The
Wealth of Nations* treated the division of labor as the great source of efficiency in production. Each worker, specializing in his own part of the pro-

duction process, would become faster and more adept at his task. Internationally, the division of labor caused each nation to specialize in what it could produce more cheaply. Both domestically and internationally, the division of labor was limited only by the size of the market for the resulting output (Ch. 3). In a small local market the output of one man, devoting himself to one aspect of the production process, may exceed what is salable. A carpenter in a small rural community may do every kind of carpentry and woodwork (p. 17), rather than specialize in one kind of carpentry, as someone in a large city could do. Therefore, limited markets limit the subdivision of productive tasks and thereby limit efficiency. While some limits on the size of markets are unavoidable, due to transportation costs, for example, artificial limits reduce the markets—and therefore efficiency—more than they have to be reduced. These artificial restrictions range from restrictive licenses for entering some occupations to restrictions on the free movement of international trade.

Free international trade promotes low-cost production by "opening a more extensive market" for a quantity of output "which may exceed the home consumption" if the division of labor is carried out as far as the state of technology will permit. The discovery of America enriched Europe, not by the gold found in the new world, but by "opening a new and inexhaustible market" that allowed "new divisions of labour and improvements of art" which "could never have taken place" for lack of a large enough market otherwise (p. 416).

In keeping with Smith's general picture of an order arising from spontaneous interactions, the division of labor was not the result of any premeditated design or "human wisdom" but resulted instead from a natural "propensity to truck, barter, and exchange" goods (p. 13). These exchanges tended to take place at ratios determined by the goods' respective costs of production—*not* out of a sense of fairness, or for any other philosophical reason, but because costs of production determined the respective supply prices, and goods continued to be supplied only when these supply prices were paid. The supply prices of goods were in turn the result (and sum) of the supply prices of the factor inputs that produced these goods— that is, the supply prices of labor, capital, and land.

Demand played a negligible or passive role in this analysis simply because costs were implicitly conceived of as constant with respect to output, despite Smith's discussions of how they varied with the quantity of output—that is, how the division of labor was limited by the extent of the market.[28] Apparently, there were conceived to be different possible levels of constant cost, corresponding to different methods of organizing the production of various discrete quantities of output, as distinguished from the more modern idea of continuously variable costs of production with respect to output. Still, Smith's general discussion of value proceeded as if there were a single cost of production for each good and value corresponded to that cost. "Effectual" demand was the quantity demanded at a price that covered "the" cost of production per unit (p. 56).

The role of supply and demand in Smith became the role of supply

and demand in later classical economics. Supply and demand were universal mechanisms determining the rise and fall of price, whether in the short
run ("market" price) or the long run ("natural" price).[29] However, the level
around which these fluctuations took place was determined by the cost of
production. The *principle* determining price was different from the
mechanism determining price. The principle operated in the long run,
when there was free competition. The mechanism operated at all times,
whether in competitive markets with continuously variable supply, in
monopolistic markets, or in markets with fixed supply. Supply and demand as a mechanism determining value was compatible with any principle of value determination, whether utility or cost of production. Later,
Ricardo would write to Malthus: "You say supply and demand regulates
value. This, I think is saying nothing,"[30] because it is equally compatible
with one theory or another. Looked at another way, to say that price was
determined solely by supply and demand was to say that there was no
determinant principle at work but only a mechanism.[31]

   Smith had not only a *theory* of value but a *measure* of value. While
the theory of the relative value of individual goods had long-run prices
determined by the cost of production, the measure of value attempted to
compare changing aggregate output over time according to the differing
quantities of labor that these various aggregates could command. The
measure of value translated changing mixtures of heterogeneous goods
into a single index of subjective well-being. Assuming the disutility of work
to be constant over time, Smith measured the corresponding utility of
goods by the amount of work that people were willing to endure to obtain
the goods:

> Equal quantities of labour, at all times and places, may be said to be of
> equal value to the labourer. In his ordinary state of health, strength and
> spirits; in the ordinary degree of his skill and dexterity, he must always lay
> down the same portion of his ease, his liberty, and his happiness. The price
> which he pays must always be the same, whatever may be the quantity of
> goods which he receives in return for it. Of these, indeed, it may sometimes
> purchase a greater and sometimes a smaller quantity; but it is their value
> which varies, not that of the labour which purchases them [p. 33].

   Smith's attempt to establish a single index of heterogeneous output,
and to justify that index philosophically, provided later classical
economists with a basis for much confusion. It appeared to Ricardo, for
example, that Smith had two theories of value — one based on cost of production (ultimately labor cost) and another based on labor command.[32]
But a measure of value is not a theory of value. A theory can be right or
wrong, but a measure is definitional and may only be useful or not. No
substantive testable proposition in *The Wealth of Nations* would be different if Smith had chosen a different index of economic well-being. More
generally, Smith's introduction of a measure of value alongside his theory
of value set the stage for a similar duality in later classical economists — and
for later confusions by interpreters.[33] Perhaps the classic case is Marxian

value, where a measure of value by labor time exists alongside a theory of value determined by costs of production (labor and nonlabor).[34]

As a theoretician Smith was eclectic and was little concerned with elegance, with fine points, or with appearances of consistency. Smith disparaged system building, the reduction of doctrines to "scholastic or technical" systems of "artificial definitions, divisions, and subdivisions. . . ."[35] He was very consistent in his use of terms throughout any given chain of reasoning, so that his conclusions were unaffected by his inconsistent use of terms between one set of reasoning and another. Smith's shifting use of terms provided many pitfalls for later classical writers, but Smith himself did not fall into these pits. Thus "real" was sometimes defined in terms of goods and services[36] and sometimes in terms of labor command.[37] Rent was sometimes a residual determined by price,[38] and sometimes a price-determining factor cost[39] — but correctly used in each context. Unlike Ricardo, Smith did not always reason in terms of a one-product agriculture whose land "rent" was a residual but sometimes considered cases in which agricultural land had to be bid away from alternative uses, and therefore where the "rent" in one use became a cost- determining supply price in alternative uses.[40]

As a pioneer in a new field, Smith had the task of establishing a theoretical foundation and a structure of concepts to define the terms of thinking on the subject for those who would follow. At the same time, as a man advocating particular policies in his own time, Smith had to be concerned with the practice as well as the theory of economics. There was no indication in *The Wealth of Nations* of any confusion or conflict between these two roles. Similarly, theoretical analysis was enriched with vast factual knowledge and a gift for striking examples. The arid theoretical system building of Ricardo and the rambling empiricism of Malthus were equally foreign to Adam Smith. This can be seen especially clearly in these three economists' different approaches to wage determination.

Malthus's population theory established the notion of a "subsistence" wage (whether physically or culturally determined) above which population would grow and below which population would decline. Moreover, the rate at which population could grow was also specified as greater than the rate at which food and other subsistence goods could increase, so that a static level of wages and a population, whose observable growth rate must approximate that of the food supply, were corollaries of the Malthusian theory. But despite the vast quantities of statistical and historical data that appeared in the second (and later) editions of Malthus's *Essay on the Principle of Population,* these hypotheses were never tested. The empirical material was used to *illustrate* — not test — the Malthusian doctrine. In Malthus's own words, "The principle object of the present essay is to examine the effects of one great cause."[41] History would "elucidate the manner" in which the population principle operated,[42] not test its validity. *Any* particular population found to exist in any place or time was consistent with the Malthusian theory: "The natural tendency to increase is everywhere so great that it will generally be easy to account for the height at which the population is found in any country."[43] But to "account for" facts *ex post* is not to test a theory.

Ricardo was even more cavalier. He simply *postulated* that wages were at a subsistence level[44] and proceeded to work out the implications of this postulate, in the context of his general theoretical system. He noted in passing that wages were not in fact at subsistence,[45] but this had no effect on his analysis. Indeed, wage determination was not a concern of the Ricardian system. Real wages were important in that system only because diminishing returns in agriculture meant a rising cost of producing a constant real wage, ultimately reducing the profit rate and bringing on the "stationary state." If real wages were also rising over time, the same result followed *a fortiori*.

For Adam Smith real wages were important to explain, in and of themselves, and theories of wages were to be systematically tested against observable facts. He posed several straightforward tests of the subsistence wage hypothesis. The principle behind these tests was that the cost of living varied substantially from time to time and from region to region, and if wages did not vary in the same pattern, then places with the higher money wages and/or lower living costs must have real wages that are above subsistence. Following this approach, Smith found that (1) living costs were higher in the winter (because of fuel needs) while wages were higher in the summer; (2) although "the price of provisions" generally varied from year to year and even from month to month, "in many places the money price of labour remains uniformly the same sometimes for half a century together"; (3) regional money wage differentials exceeded regional cost-of-living differentials; and (4) money wage variations "in place or time" were "frequently quite opposite" to variations in the cost of living (pp. 74–75). In short, to Adam Smith, hypotheses about the general wage level were subject to empirical verification. Such hypotheses were not self-justifying theories, which could only be *illustrated* by facts, à la Malthus, nor mere convenient postulates, as in Ricardo.

Smith's own wage theories were crucial for setting the framework of classical economic policy concerns for the next century. Like Malthus after him, Smith postulated some culturally determined "subsistence" wage, with wages above that level causing population to increase and wages below that level causing population to decrease. Unlike Malthus, Smith did not take the fatal step of postulating the *rate* of population increase, either absolutely or relative to the rate of increase of the food supply. He did recognize that those relative rates determined whether the workers' standard of living rose or fell over time (pp. 69, 71), but for Smith both outcomes were possible. Everything depended on how fast the demand for labor was increasing over time, which in turn depended upon how fast the country was growing. It was not in the richest countries, but in the fastest growing countries, that wages were highest (p. 69). Given that population would grow whenever wages were above the "subsistence" level, any stationary demand for labor would ultimately be supplied at subsistence wages. But as long as economic growth outpaced population growth, wages could remain above subsistence indefinitely. Smith's postulate of a direct relationship betwen wages and population and his theory of wage determination therefore yielded observable predictions that he verified empirically. A growing country like his own had higher wages than a stationary country like China, which he believed to be wealthier. By the same token, England had lower wages than a faster growing country like America, which he believed to be not as rich as England (pp. 70-72)

Because the rate of growth determined whether the bulk of the population of a nation would be economically well off or miserable, the maintenance of the ongoing growth process became the central policy concern to Smith and to later classical economists. This pervasive concern for economic growth dominated every aspect of classical economics — not only its policy positions on such issues as international free trade (especially in grain) or fiscal policy (the growth-dampening effects of a large national debt) (p. 380)[46] — but it also dominated and shaped the choice of theoretical problems and the approach to them. For example, money was discussed in terms of whether or not the quantity influenced long-run economic growth: It did not, according to classical economics, and money was therefore merely a "veil" obscuring the operation of real variables,[47] even though these same classical economists plainly acknowledged the short-run economic consequences of changes in monetary variables.[48] The wide-ranging controversies over Say's law, which raged for more than two decades, were essentially disputes about the effects of thrift on economic growth.[49] Even Ricardo's narrow perception of economics as a study of the functional distribution of income[50] was geared to changes over time in that distribution in response to growth, and how such changes might tend in turn to end that growth. Smith, in short, provided the agenda of classical economics as well as providing many of its basic concepts and theories.

The authority of Smith in later classical economics is shown by the fact that nineteenth-century dissenters from the contemporary classical tradition nevertheless based themselves on *The Wealth of Nations* and often represented themselves as the true followers of Adam Smith opposing heretics now in the ascendancy. Malthus' attack on Say's law argued that supply does *not* always equal demand, when demand means "effectual demand" as Smith defined it[51] — quantity demanded *at cost-covering prices* (p. 56), (with "cost" also implicitly conceived in Smithian terms as *ex ante* supply prices rather than *ex post* factor payments).[52] Sismondi's attacks on the Ricardians' abstract, deductive method,[53] and their virtually exclusive reliance on comparative statics,[54] held up Smith as a methodological model[55] — incorporating both theory and empiricism, employing logic and history. Even Marx considered Smith's theoretical inconsistencies "justified" historically.[56]

THE ENDURING LEGACY

It was suggested at the outset that *The Wealth of Nations* was a revolutionary event. It represented a contemporary intellectual revolution because it attacked a prevailing scheme of thought and practice and sought to root out both the policies and the misconceptions behind those policies. It was therefore more than just a reform. Whether the changes sought were sufficiently far-reaching or fast-paced enough to be called a "revolution" depends upon what is conceived to be a revolution.

The American Revolution, which occurred in the same year as publication of *The Wealth of Nations,* was very different from the French Revolution of the same era. The French Revolution was faster, more violent — and more short-lived. It was based more on abstract principles, on abstract speculation about the nature of man and the potentiality of government as an instrument of human improvement. Smith was much more in the tradition of the American Revolution — more based on historical experience of the limitations of man as he is, of government's shortcomings as actually observed, and above all, a rejection of the idea that anyone has either such wisdom or such nobility as to wield the unbridled power to shape and direct his fellow-creatures. The American political system of checks and balances and the classical economists' consumer sovereignty in the market are both based on a rejection of uncontrolled power for either political or economic leaders. Both systems put in the hands of the mass of ordinary people the ultimate power to thwart or topple those who assume arbitrary decision-making powers.

Most so-called "revolutions" and revolutionaries seek primarily to change the *cast of characters* who are to wield unbridled power, and change the forms and rhetoric accompanying such power. Smith and the founders of the American republic rejected the whole idea of such power being so concentrated and so unchecked. Powerful traditions, going back thousands of years — at least as far back as Plato — advocated such unchecked sovereignty and differed only in determining the persons and the manner of exercising this power, or the principles that they should use as guides. The depth and scope of the rejection of such long-lived and widespread traditions can well be considered revolutionary in the broad history of the human race.

In terms of methods or mechanisms of change, Smith was clearly *not* revolutionary. The man of "humanity and benevolence," he said, will "content himself with moderating" those evils that he "cannot annihilate without violence." If he "cannot establish the right, he will not disdain to ameliorate the wrong." By contrast the doctrinaire will insist on establishing his Utopia "in all its parts" and "in spite of all opposition." Yet it is not clear that the attempt to create change "at all cost" leads to more actual change in the long run. The resistance to such methods may keep the society "in the highest degree of disorder."[57] In the twentieth century especially, we now know that societies will ultimately submit to dictatorship rather than tolerate disorder indefinitely. And though the dictatorship may continue to use the rhetoric and some of the appearances of the revolution, the kind of society actually existing may be a mockery of the original revolutionary doctrine. Certainly Karl Marx did not suffer through years of poverty to produce his doctrine in order that Stalin could send Solzhenitsyn to a prison camp. More generally, such consequences have followed so regularly from revolutionary methods—both before Smith's time and afterward—that it is not at all clear that politically revolutionary methods produce socially revolutionary results, as distinguished from a change in the cast of characters in governments. Therefore Smith's doctrines may have had more long-run revolutionary potential than the doctrines of those who sought shortcuts to power. In history as in travel, shortcuts often end up taking longer to reach the destination. The concentration of power after a revolution is an obvious factor retarding further social changes, while diffused power permits continuing changes of ultimately unlimited magnitude. The America of today is socially vastly different from colonial America. It is not clear that the Soviet Union of today is socially equally different from Czarist Russia, or even that the differences that do exist are in the direction envisioned by Marxian philosophy.[58]

Whether or not Smith's way of thinking can be classified as revolutionary, it continues to be embattled. There are still those for whom chaos seems the only alternative to an imposed economic order. The great ambiguous phrase, "planning" increasingly appears, not only among socialists but among more politically centrist groups alarmed about some actual or possible "crisis." Smith was very skeptical about the alarms of his own time, even more skeptical of those who would save us from disaster, and had great faith in the capacity of society to accommodate. Once informed after a national setback that "the nation is ruined," Smith complacently replied: "There is a great deal of ruin in a nation."[59] As for so-called "planning," Smith was quite clear that planning goes on all the time in a market economy.[60] The only question was whether this planning should be done by individuals intimately familiar with specific economic circumstances and personally liable to lose or gain by the accuracy of their knowledge, or by distant politicians who could not possibly have equal familiarity or equal incentives. To Smith it seemed unlikely that the "artificial direction" given to the economic efforts of society would be better than the direction it would have taken "of its own accord" (p. 421). But here as elsewhere in *The Wealth of Nations,* the question was ultimately not one of theory but of fact.

History showed that governments habitually mismanaged economic affairs,[61] that such mismanagement was difficult to correct (in contrast to the market's swift correction by bankruptcy), and that the whole bias of government projects was toward things that were big and showy rather than useful. A government will often create works "of splendour and magnificence" to be seen by those whose applause will flatter its vanity and promote its political interests but will neglect "a great number of little works" which may have "extreme utility" but present no "great appearance" to "excite . . . the admiration" of passers-by (pp. 686–87). Down through the centuries governments have been prone to operate at a deficit, often using tricky fiscal devices to conceal just how much they were in debt (p. 867). With all his vast historical knowledge, Smith could not find "a single instance" where a government had actually paid off its debts in full. Every instance where a government debt had been liquidated was a liquidation by bankruptcy—either an open bankruptcy or a "pretended repayment" in devalued money. "Almost all states . . . ancient as well as modern . . . have, upon some occasions, played this very juggling trick" (pp. 882–83).

As already noted, Smith had a low opinion of the honesty and integrity of businessmen, but they at least were forced to compete with one another. It is *competition* that forces businessmen to have "good management . . . for the sake of self-defence" (p. 147). A government by definition is a monopoly in certain functions. Extending that monopoly to economic affairs had dangerous consequences in itself, and bringing economic agents, such as businessmen, under the protection of the government's monopoly was double dangerous. The "spirit of monopoly" was high in businessmen who were adept at "sophistry" to justify government protection of their interests. The protectionist doctrine of businessmen "confounded the common sense of mankind" and those who taught this doctrine "were by no means such fools as they who believed it" (p. 461).

Despite Adam Smith's skepticism about people's morality, he made no real effort to urge higher standards of morality. This is all the more remarkable in a man whose first fame came from a book entitled *The Theory of Moral Sentiments,* published almost twenty years before *The Wealth of Nations.* Yet even *The Theory of Moral Sentiments* was not a work of moral exhortation, but instead a cool psychological and social analysis of the origins and mechanics of morality.[62] Some scholars and critics have tried to show a conflict betwen the first book—in which morality was considered to be based ultimately on man's ability to imagine himself in someone else's place—and *The Wealth of Nations,* in which the central mechanism of the economic system was self-interest. But there was no conflict.

The ability to imagine oneself in someone else's place was considered by Smith to be the basis for systems of morality and law. But in neither book did Smith expect people to adhere to such systems without further pressure or coercion and in the face of temptations to take advantage of others. *The Theory of Moral Sentiments* attempted to show the derivation of moral principles. *The Wealth of Nations* attempted to explain actual behavior. There it was clear that it was not from the benevolence of the butcher that we expected meat but from his regard to his own self-interest (p. 14). This did not make him amoral, only self-regarding. In *The Theory of Moral Sentiments* Smith had pointed out that no one is utterly selfless, but he also noted that even the worst of men had some regard for moral precepts and felt some shame when they violated them.[63] Neither book made men devils or angels but only strivers for self-interest held somewhat in check by public opinion, the law, and other representatives of morality. It was not a bad set of assumptions—for economic analysis or any other purpose.

NOTES

1. Adam Smith, *The Wealth of Nations* (New York: Random House, Mod. Lib. Ed., 1937), pp. 435, 329.
2. Ibid., 128, 249–50, 402–3, 429, 438, 579.
3. Ibid., p. 900.
4. Ibid., pp. 172, 683, 686.
5. Ibid., pp. 66–67, 97–98, 249–50.
6. "There is not a negro from the coast of Africa who does not possess a degree of magnaminity, which the soul of his sordid master is too often, scarce capable of conceiving. Fortune never exerted more cruelly her empire over mankind, than when she subjected those nations of heroes to the refuse of the jails of Europe. . . ." Adam Smith, *The Theory of Moral Sentiments,* (New York: Kelley, 1966), Pt. V, Ch. 2, p. 239.
7. "Smith was, to be sure, an unconscious mercenary in the service of the rising capitalist class. . . . Max Lerner, Introduction, Smith, *Wealth,* p. ix.
8. Sir James Steuart, *Works,* vol. 1, *An Inquiry into the Principles of Political Economy* (1767; London: T. Cadell, 1805), pp. 310–12.
9. Thomas Mun, *England's Treasure by Forraign Trade* (1664; New York: Kelley, 1965), p. 5.
10. Ibid., p. 21.
11. Ibid., p. 7.
12. Jacob Viner, Power versus Plenty as Objectives of Foreign Policy in the Seventeenth and Eighteenth Centuries, *World Politics* (Oct. 1948):1–29; reprinted in Jacob Viner, *The Long View and the Short* (Glencoe: The Free Press, 1958), pp. 277–305.
13. Smith, *Sentiments,* pp. 266–67.
14. John Stuart Mill, Speech on the British Constitution, *Autobiography* (London: Oxford Univ. Press, 1949), p. 276.
15. Smith, *Sentiments,* p. 66.
16. Ibid., p. 63.
17. "It is the business of a statesman to judge of the expediency of different schemes of oeconomy, and by degrees to model the minds of his subjects so as to induce them, from the allurement of private interest, to cooperate in the execution of his plan." Steuart, *Works,* vol. 1, p. 4; ". . . nothing is impossible to an able statesman" (ibid., p. 15); the statesman is "constantly awake" on economic matters (ibid., p. 73), and the "great genius of Mr. De Colbert" and the "genius of Mr. Law" show them to be "born statesmen" (ibid., p. 88).
18. Wesley C. Mitchell, *Lecture Notes on Types of Economic Theory* (New York: Kelley, 1949), vol. 1, p. 52.
19. Steuart, *Works,* vol. 1, pp. 50–52, 337.
20. Smith, *Sentiments,* p. 376.
21. Ibid., p. 341.
22. Ibid., pp. 272–73.
23. Smith, *Wealth,* pp. 684, 714–15.
24. Ibid., pp. 321–23, 406–7.
25. Ibid., pp. 144–46.
26. Ibid., pp. 79–80.
27. For example, J. A. Schumpeter, *History of Economic Analysis* (New York: Oxford Univ. Press, 1954), pp. 182–85.
28. Smith, *Wealth,* pp. 17–21, 706.
29. Ibid., pp. 55–56, 62.
30. David Ricardo, *The Works and Correspondence of David Ricardo,* Piero Sraffa, ed. (Cambridge: Cambridge Univ. Press, 1951–55), vol. 8, p. 279.
31. See Thomas Sowell, *Classical Economics Reconsidered* (Princeton: Princeton Univ. Press, 1974), pp. 104–5.
32. Ricardo, *Works,* vol. 1, pp. 12–14.
33. Sowell, *Classical Economics,* pp. 99–103.
34. See Thomas Sowell, Marx's *Capital* After One Hundred Years, *Can. J. Econ. Polit. Sci.* (Feb. 1967):50–74.
35. Smith, *Sentiments,* p. 341.
36. Smith, *Wealth,* pp. 70, 78.

37. Ibid., pp. 30, 33, 159, 247, 248.
38. Ibid., pp. 145-46.
39. Ibid.
40. Ibid., pp. 145, 150, 151, 152, 159; Cf. Ricardo, *Works*, vol. 1, pp. 67-68, 327-37.
41. Thomas Robert Malthus, *An Essay on Population* (New York: Dutton, 1960), vol. 1, p. 5.
42. Ibid., p. 17.
43. Ibid., p. 131.
44. Ricardo, *Works*, vol. 1, p. 93.
45. Ibid., pp. 94-95.
46. Ricardo, *Works*, vol. 1, pp. 187, 247-48.
47. Sowell, *Classical Economics Reconsidered*, pp. 54-55.
48. Ibid., pp. 56-59.
49. Ibid., pp. 69-70.
50. Ricardo, *Works*, vol. 1, p. 5; ibid., vol. 8, p. 278.
51. T. R. Malthus, *Principles of Political Economy* (1832; New York: Kelley, 1951), p. 66.
52. T. R. Malthus, *Definitions in Political Economy* (London: John Murray, 1827), p. 242.
53. J. C. L. Simonde de Sismondi, *Nouveaux Principes d'Économie politique* (Genève-Paris: Edition Jeheber, 1953), vol. 2, p. 283.
54. Ibid., vol. 1, p. 234.
55. Ibid., pp. 63, 69.
56. Karl Marx, *Theories of Surplus Value* (New York: International Publ., 1952), p. 202.
57. Smith, *Sentiments*, pp. 272-73.
58. See Thomas Sowell, Karl Marx and the Freedom of the Individual, *Ethics*, (Jan. 1963): 119-25.
59. John Rae, *The Life of Adam Smith* (London: Macmillan, 1895), p. 343.
60. "Every individual is continually exerting himself to find out the most advantageous employment for whatever capital he can command." Smith, *Wealth*, p. 421.
61. Smith, *Wealth*, pp. 421, 687, 688, 689, 861, 863, 873.
62. "The present inquiry is not concerning a matter of right . . . but a matter of fact." Smith, *Sentiments*, p. 85.
63. Smith, *Sentiments*, pp. 93-96.

2

Adam Smith and Laissez-Faire Revisited

🌿 NATHAN ROSENBERG

IN his book, *Process and Reality,* Alfred North Whitehead stated that the history of Western philosophy can be characterized as consisting of a series of footnotes to Plato. It can be said with even greater accuracy that the history of economics over the past two hundred years can be adequately characterized as a series of footnotes to Adam Smith. *The Wealth of Nations* is a many-faceted book, dealing with a remarkably wide range of issues and attempting at the same time to provide the reader with a grand synthesis of the whole economic universe. As Jacob Viner has stated, "Traces of every conceivable sort of doctrine are to be found in that most catholic book, and an economist must have peculiar theories indeed who cannot quote from the *Wealth of Nations* to support his special purposes."[1]

In fairness to the successors of both Plato and Smith it should be said that the footnotes to the works of these two seminal figures are getting longer and remoter from the original texts. It is therefore proper that we should pay homage to the enduring impact they have had in shaping our thought without at the same time drowning ourselves in expressions of filial piety. A momentary flash of insight is a very different thing from a systematized and integrated body of analysis. Once a new theory has been developed and elaborated, one can always in retrospect find earlier thinkers who seem to have caught glimpses, however fleeting, of some of its components; perhaps this is often an illusion created by the use of a common language. It has been said of the *tableau économique* of Adam Smith's distinguished French contemporary, François Quesnay, that it was really a primitive input-output table.[2] Indeed, once we have mastered the techniques of input-output analysis, it is no difficult trick to go back to the

Nathan Rosenberg is Professor of Economics, Stanford University.

In a few places the author has drawn upon his earlier articles on Adam Smith, especially Some Institutional Aspects of the *Wealth of Nations, J. Polit. Econ.*, Dec. 1960; and Adam Smith on Profits — Paradox Lost and Regained, *J. Polit. Econ.*, Nov.-Dec. 1974. The author also acknowledges indebtedness to that great scholar Jacob Viner. No one with a serious interest in Adam Smith should fail to read the article Viner wrote in celebration of the sesquicentennial of *The Wealth of Nations.* See note 1.

tableau and translate it into more modern terms. Such an exercise is now easy and obvious. But we should not forget that it took almost two hundred years of hard thinking about macroeconomics and a lifetime of intense effort on Leontief's part before that translation could become obvious. To maintain a proper sense of balance in these matters, it is therefore salutary that we should also recall another observation of Whitehead's—that everything of importance has been said before, but by someone who did not discover it.

However, with respect to the subject of this essay, there is little question about the central and decisive role played by Adam Smith. To the extent that it is ever possible to identify a new perspective with the work of a single individual, we identify Smith with laissez-faire. Almost any educated person subjected to a word-association test and asked to identify some historical personage with the term "laissez-faire" would reply, "Adam Smith." What precisely did laissez-faire mean to Adam Smith, and why?

Laissez-faire is a term that arouses strong emotions. It has become heavily laden with ideological freight and in some circles is employed as a term of abuse—suggesting that belief in laissez-faire is regarded as roughly equivalent to describing that economic philosophy as "Neanderthal" or "antedeluvian." I do not intend to defend laissez-faire for a variety of reasons, but perhaps it is sufficient to say that I happen not to believe in it; that is, I do not regard it as anything like an appropriate guide to the complex policy questions of 1976. This statement is perfectly consistent with stating that I might indeed have advocated such a policy in 1776. To say this is merely to recognize that different problems may require different solutions, and the problems we confront today are vastly different from those of Adam Smith's time.

We all know that Smith believed in and advocated a policy of laissez-faire. What is much less understood is why he believed in it. This will be discussed first because his reasons for supporting such a policy are not understood nearly as well as they deserve to be. Second, and more important, many of his arguments continue to be illuminating, relevant, and full of insight even though we may have cogent reasons today for rejecting a policy of laissez-faire. *The Wealth of Nations* contains a profound analysis of social arrangements that retains its value even though we may no longer accept the particular set of antiinterventionist policy conclusions Smith drew from it two hundred years ago.

THE ECONOMY

Adam Smith was one of the earliest and certainly the foremost spokesman for a policy of laissez-faire. The accepted practice is to portray Smith as an advocate of unbridled freedom of action on the part of the business community (some even say "apologist"). And yet this interpretation is, at least on the face of it, difficult to reconcile with the view of businessmen Smith expresses throughout the book. Even the most casual reading of *The Wealth of Nations* will quickly disclose that he is extremely critical of businessmen as a group and rarely misses an opportunity to malign them. Unlike the laboring classes about whom Smith never utters a harsh or hostile word, his attitude toward businessmen is hypercritical and almost pathologically suspicious.

The Wealth of Nations is full of allusions such as the following:

1. "The sneaking arts of underling tradesmen. . . . The mean rapacity, the monopolizing spirit of merchants and manufacturers. . . . The impertinent jealousy of merchants and manufacturers" (p. 406).
2. "The mean and malignant expedients" of merchants (p. 577).
3. "The clamour and sophistry of merchants and manufacturers" (p. 128).
4. Governments, Smith says, have pursued unwise policies because "the interested sophistry of merchants and manufacturers confounded the common sense of mankind" (p. 461).
5. The business communities of both France and England advocate policies "with all the passionate confidence of interested falsehood" (p. 463).
6. With respect to profits, which one would think would be treated as sacrosanct, Smith makes these devastating remarks: "Our merchants and master-manufacturers complain much of the bad effects of high wages in raising the price, and thereby lessening the sale of their goods both at home and abroad. They say nothing concerning the bad effects of high profits. They are silent with regard to the pernicious effects of their own gains. They complain only of those of other people" (p. 98). These comments are the closing sentences of his chapter on profits. Indeed, Smith apparently held these views so strongly that he repeated the statements, almost verbatim, later in his chapter on colonies (pp. 565–66).

How are we to reconcile this virtual torrent of abuse that Smith heaps upon the businessman with the view that he is a spokesman (or an apologist) for the economic interests of the business community? Just what sort of capitalist apologetics is this? How are we to reconcile Smith's view of the scheming, rapacious, monopolizing businessman with his plea for laissez-faire?

Perhaps the first thing to be said is that Smith was a sophisticated man who was both widely read as well as intimately familiar with the operation of his own society. He accepted the fact that he lived in a highly imperfect world, and he was not given to daydreaming about the operation of some ideal future society. Rather, he was deeply concerned with bringing about immediate improvements in his own society. However, he was convinced that such improvements could be made only if they were realistically grounded upon an accurate assessment of the human animal and the factors that shape human behavior. If we want to come to grips with Smith's social analysis and policy recommendations, we need to start with his conception of human behavior.

Smith sees man as being made up of a bundle of both good and bad qualities — using the terms "good" and "bad" here from the point of view, not of a moralist, but of someone who is single-mindedly concerned with the wealth of nations. From this perspective what does Smith perceive as man's good qualities?

1. A propensity to truck and barter. This quality is terribly important to Smith because the division of labor really follows from this propensity. And the division of labor, as Smith tells his readers in the opening pages of *The Wealth of Nations*, is a basic condition for economic improvement.
2. Man's drive to better his condition. This is perhaps, from Smith's point of view, the most powerful and pervasive of all human drives. He speaks of "the uniform, constant, and uninterrupted effort of every man to better his condition . . ." (p. 326).
3. The propensity to save. Man is frugal, or at least most men are — or at least most men are most of the time. There is nothing instinctive about frugality; such behavior is derived from man's desire to better his condition:

> The principle which prompts to save, is the desire of bettering our condition, a desire which, though generally calm and dispassionate, comes with us from the womb, and never leaves us till we go into the grave. In the whole interval which separates those two moments, there is scarce perhaps a single instant in which any man is so perfectly and completely satisfied with his situation, as to be without any wish of alteration or improvement of any kind. An augmentation of fortune is the means by which the greater part of men propose and wish to better their condition. It is the means the most vulgar and the most obvious; and the most likely way of augmenting their fortune, is to save and accumulate some part of what they acquire, either regularly and annually, or upon some extraordinary occasions. Though the principle of expence, [we would now say "extravagance"] therefore, prevails in almost all men upon some occasions, and in some men upon almost all occasions, yet in the greater part of men, taking the whole course of their life at an average, the principle of frugality seems not only to predominate, but to predominate very greatly [pp. 324–25].

4. Prudence. "Though the principles of common prudence do not always govern the conduct of every individual, they always influence that of the majority of every class or order."

What are man's bad qualities? On the liability side of the human ledger there are several qualities that any realistic policy for social change needs to take into account.

1. An inclination to indolence. People, to put it bluntly, are lazy. Men all want to better their condition, but they would also like to do it with the least exercise of effort. "It is the interest of every man to live as much at

his ease as he can . . ." (p. 718). Other undesirable qualities really flow from this. Men are anxious to improve their status with the least possible effort, and this leads to all sorts of chicanery and deception of the public.

2. It follows that men are likely to try to deceive others about their true intentions, to be hypocritical, to conceal private interest under the guise of public interest. Smith was quick to call attention to such misrepresentation and dissimulation. "I have never known much good done by those who affected to trade for the public good" (p. 423).

3. Man has a strong propensity to monopolize, to connive with others to enhance his own income. "People of the same trade" Smith cautions his readers, "seldom meet together, even for merriment and diversion, but the conversation ends in a conspiracy against the public, or in some contrivance to raise prices" (p. 128).

Because of this combination of human qualities Adam Smith is passionately and vigorously opposed to mercantilism. Indeed, one cannot really understand Smith without placing him directly in the historical context of eighteenth-century Great Britain. Smith lived in a world of very extensive government regulations of all kinds, regulations we summarize today in the word "mercantilism" (actually, Smith coined this usage of the word). Mercantilism involved many detailed regulations over the uses to which capital and labor could be put. It included regulations concerning the movement of the precious metals, restrictions upon imported goods (especially manufactured and luxury goods), financial inducements to encourage exports of manufactured products, and restrictions upon the export of raw materials (particularly wool). It included also a host of special rights and exclusive trading privileges to specific individuals and companies. In Smith's view, mercantilism represented the successful attempts of rapacious and monopolizing merchants to exploit the machinery of government to their own purposes. The trouble is not that the merchant class is selfish and acquisitive — those qualities are not unique to merchants — but that mercantilism was a collection of government measures that made it possible for businessmen to achieve their own selfish goals without at the same time advancing the public interest. Mercantilism represented a successful assault of the business community upon a helpless public. "It cannot be very difficult to determine who have been the contrivers of this whole mercantile system; not the consumers, we may believe, whose interest has been entirely neglected; but the producers, whose interest has been so carefully attended to . . ." (p. 626).

The violence of Smith's polemic against mercantilism lay in the fact that it enabled merchants to better their condition in a manner that did not contribute to the nation's economic welfare. As a result of the dispensation of monopoly grants, of the arbitrary bestowal of "extraordinary privileges" and "extraordinary restraints" upon different sectors of industry by the government, the individual merchant was provided with innumerable opportunities to enrich himself without enriching the nation.

Even when legislation is passed with an ostensibly legitimate social purpose in view, the opportunities for profitmaking are likely to be restructured in such a way as to lead to further possibilities for private enrichment and not social enrichment. Thus, with respect to the herring bounty, Smith sardonically observes that "the bounty to the white herring fishery is a tonnage bounty; and is proportioned to the burden of the ship, not to her diligence or success in the fishery; and it has, I am afraid, been too common for vessels to fit out for the sole purpose of catching, not the fish, but the bounty" (p. 486).

In this context Smith's advocacy of laissez-faire represented advocacy of a program that would involve the elimination of special privilege, arbitrary restrictions, and as in the herring bounty, a wasteful use of scarce resources. It was the essence of mercantilism that it provided a very poor linkup with the individual's attempt to better his condition and the promotion of the general welfare. Smith, by contrast, was advocating a new institutional order in which the private pursuit of wealth would be much more likely to advance the public welfare. The system he is supporting is one that, in his view, would make the best possible use of man's good and bad qualities in promoting the wealth of nations. Smith is advocating the competitive order, where all mercantilist restrictions and privileges are eliminated. Man's natural propensity is to monopolize, and he has been able to do so in the past because of the special privileges dispensed to businessmen by the state. If only the state would leave the economic arena and give each individual an equal chance to "better his condition," the public would benefit immensely.

Smith's "invisible hand" had nothing to do with divine guidance. The phrase makes only one unfortunate appearance in *The Wealth of Nations*—unfortunate because it has been so totally misinterpreted. There is absolutely no question, either in the specific context where he used the phrase or in the larger context of the argument of the entire book, but that the invisible hand is the hard hand of competition, which places immense pressure upon individuals to behave in ways that simultaneously promote the public interest as well as the private interest. The great virtue of a competitive marketplace for Smith is that it closes off antisocial forms of behavior in which self-seeking businessmen would otherwise indulge. It is an institutional system, in brief, for disciplining the business community, not for allowing it to do whatever it pleases. A genuinely competitive marketplace is an intensely coercive institution. The hand that guides individual behavior is invisible in the sense that no government official dictates the behavior of individuals—market forces do it.

Adam Smith was no capitalist apologist (although it cannot be denied that such apologists have used—and misrepresented—Adam Smith for their own purposes). On the contrary, his central preoccupation was to prevent businessmen from pursuing their own interests in antisocial ways. Consider what he has to say in a context where he is discussing the behavior of grain dealers, but where "dealers" is then broadened to include the entire business class:

The interest of the dealers . . . in any particular branch of trade or manufactures, is always in some respects different from, and even opposite to, that of the public. To widen the market and to narrow the competition, is always the interest of the dealers. To widen the market may frequently be agreeable enough to the interest of the public; but to narrow the competition must always be against it, and can serve only to enable the dealers, by raising their profits above what they naturally would be, to levy, for their own benefit, an absurd tax upon the rest of their fellow-citizens. The proposal of any new law or regulation of commerce which comes from this order, ought always to be listened to with great precaution, and ought never to be adopted till after having been long and carefully examined, not only with the most scrupulous, but with the most suspicious attention. It comes from an order of men, whose interest is never exactly the same with that of the public, who have generally an interest to deceive and even to oppress the public, and who accordingly have, upon many occasions, both deceived and oppressed it [p. 250].

Those are the closing words of Book 1 of *The Wealth of Nations*.

THE GOVERNMENT

Smith's whole argument is concerned with the need for erecting an institutional order where the businessman pursuing his self-interest will be compelled to advance the public's welfare. This is not something that happens naturally; it has to be carefully arranged and contrived because businessmen tend naturally to work in opposition to the public welfare. Smith is seeking a way to curb the naturally predatory acts of the businessman. The great virtue of a genuinely competitive order is that it does precisely that.

To appreciate Smith's position, it is necessary to remind ourselves of certain historical facts. Smith was writing in a country that not only was still preindustrial but was also in actuality an oligarchy (though it had what was formally a representative system of government). The franchise was extremely limited. Probably no more than 3 or 4 percent of adult males possessed the right to vote. The most common qualification for the vote was the so-called forty-shilling freehold, and only a tiny fraction of the population possessed that much landed property. We need to remember that Adam Smith himself could not vote, nor could his great and illustrious friend David Hume. The unreformed parliament was the instrument of the powerful and the privileged. It would be difficult in the extreme to consider the parliament of Smith's day as a body that was responsive to the popular will. Indeed, it is worth recalling that during the years when Adam Smith was writing *The Wealth of Nations* it was still regarded as a breach of privilege for newspapers even to divulge the contents of parliamentary debates. These prohibitions were evaded by a variety of journalistic subterfuges. Nevertheless, it is some measure of the undemocratic tenor of the times that, when several officials of the City of London publicly supported the right of journalists to report on parliamentary debates, parliament summarily shipped the offending officeholders to the

Tower of London. To be sure, they did not stay in the Tower very long; but one may conjecture that even a very short residency there was sufficient to assure greater compliance with parliamentary wishes.

Moreover, the British government of Smith's day not only was very narrowly based but was also, by general agreement, highly inefficient and corrupt. Seats in parliament were routinely bought and sold, even advertised in newspapers. This forms the essential backdrop for a crucial point about Smith's commitment to laissez-faire; that is, Smith's antigovernment orientation is not a matter of dogma or, if you prefer, principle. He does not argue for some purely doctrinaire reason that government activity in the economic sphere should be absolutely prohibited. Rather, he is making a very practical judgment. He is generally opposed to government intervention because he is so intimately familiar with the failures and abuses of such intervention. His perception of the political system of his own time was such that he was very skeptical of the government's ability to carry out even a small undertaking with honesty and efficiency. At the same time it is plain that where a government does show itself capable of high standards of honesty and efficiency, Smith is by no means unalterably opposed to its participation in economic affairs. For example, in discussing the propriety of a publicly operated bank, his position is a pragmatic one, not one of principle. The governments of Venice and Amsterdam could reasonably undertake such a responsibility, but not the government of England.

> The orderly, vigilant, and parsimonious administration of such aristocracies as those of Venice and Amsterdam, is extremely proper, *it appears from experience,* for the management of a mercantile project of this kind. But whether such a government as that of England; which, whatever may be its virtues, has never been famous for good economy; which, in time of peace, has generally conducted itself with the slothful and negligent profusion that is perhaps natural to monarchies; and in time of war has constantly acted with all the thoughtless extravagance that democracies are apt to fall into; could be safely trusted with the management of such a project, must at least be a good deal more doubtful [p. 770; emphasis added].

Smith, therefore, was a complete realist. He was well aware that in the political environment of his day government intervention was likely to benefit a small privileged group, as it had in the past, rather than the large mass of society. His plea for laissez-faire was not based on the assumption that the business classes could do no wrong or that government should stand idly by regardless of the abuses or antisocial behavior of merchants and manufacturers. He saw clearly that the powers of government had in the past been used to dispense monopolies and special favors to a small privileged group.

In arguing for nonintervention, Smith was pleading for the elimination of all special treatment and privilege. He believed very deeply that laissez-faire would lead not only to greater production but to greater equality as well. It is certainly conceivable (indeed, probable) that he was right, that a laissez-faire policy in Great Britain, strictly adhered to, would have made incomes more equal in the 1770s. Smith's belief that a laissez-faire policy would lead to greater equality in the distribution of income was additionally reinforced by his belief that the natural inherited differences among men had been vastly exaggerated and that existing differences were due primarily to training, family background, and education. In what we have come to call the "nature-nurture" controversy, Smith was unquestionably on the nurture side.

> The difference of natural talents in different men is, in reality, much less than we are aware of; and the very different genius which appears to distinguish men of different professions, when grown up to maturity, is not upon many occasions so much the cause, as the effect of the division of labour. The difference between the most dissimilar characters, between a philosopher and a common street porter, for example, seems to arise not so much from nature, as from habit, custom, and education. When they came into the world, and for the first six or eight years of their existence, they were, perhaps, very much alike, and neither their parents nor playfellows could perceive any remarkable difference. About that age, or soon after, they come to be employed in very different occupations. The difference of talents comes then to be taken notice of, and widens by degrees, till at last the vanity of the philosopher is willing to acknowledge scarce any resemblance.

Nevertheless, Smith concludes, "By nature a philosopher is not in genius and disposition half so different from a street porter, as a mastiff is from a greyhound, or a greyhound from a spaniel, or this last from a shepherd's dog" (pp. 15-16). Clearly, if one believes, as Smith did, that human beings come into the world with very similar endowments and that observed differences among adults are primarily the consequence of different opportunities, one may plausibly conclude that greater equality of opportunity would result in greater equality of incomes. And to Adam Smith laissez-faire most emphatically meant greater equality of opportunity and the elimination of favored treatment to special privileged groups.

Smith is not, therefore, opposed in principle to government intervention. He believes the outcome of such interventions is likely to lead to greater income inequalities and to a poor allocation of the country's resources. But there is nothing in Smith that is inherently opposed to legislation of a protective nature or to restrictions upon the natural liberty of individuals, where such restrictions are likely to advance important social goals. He favors laws restricting the freedom of bankers to issue small notes. His justification for such legal restrictions is, however, extremely illuminating.

> Such regulations may, no doubt, be considered as in some respect a violation of natural liberty. But those exertions of the natural liberty of a few individuals, which might endanger the security of the whole society, are, and

ought to be, restrained by the laws of all governments; of the most free, as
well as of the most despotical. The obligation of building party walls, in
order to prevent the communication of fire, is a violation of natural liberty,
exactly of the same kind with the regulations of the banking trade which are
here proposed [p. 308].

Smith's case for laissez-faire can now be reduced to a crude syllogism.[3]
The major premise is that people are economically motivated, that every
individual is constantly attempting to improve his economic status. "The
uniform, constant and uninterrupted effort of every man [is] to better his
condition." The minor premise, which is extremely important and was
really quite a novel view when Smith presented it, is that each individual is
the best judge of how his own time, labor, or property can best be
employed. "What is the species of domestic industry which his capital can
employ, and of which the produce is likely to be the greatest value, every
individual, it is evident, can, in his local situation, judge much better than
any statesman or lawgiver can do for him" (p. 423). Note that this is a fundamentally egalitarian and antiauthoritarian, antielitist point of view.
Smith strongly rejects all views that allow one group of people, on whatever
pretext, the right to make important decisions affecting the lives of others.
This includes the notion, which Smith regards as outrageous, that government officials should attempt to regulate the consumption habits of individuals.

It is the highest impertinence and presumption . . . in kings and
ministers, to pretend to watch over the economy of private people, and to
restrain their expence, either by sumptuary laws, or by prohibiting the importation of foreign luxuries. They are themselves always, and without any
exception, the greatest spendthrifts in the society. Let them look well after
their own expence, and they may safely trust private people with theirs. If
their own extravagance does not ruin the state, that of their subjects never
will [p. 329].

Finally, since a nation's wealth is simply the sum total of the incomes
of the individuals who compose it, this wealth can be maximized by allowing complete freedom of movement and action to each individual in his
economic pursuits.

It is thus that every system which endeavours, either, by extraordinary en-
couragements, to draw towards a particular species of industry a greater
share of the capital of the society than what would naturally go to it; or, by
extraordinary restraints, to force from a particular species of industry some
share of the capital which would otherwise be employed in it; is in reality
subversive of the great purpose which it means to promote. It retards, instead of accelerating, the progress of the society towards real wealth and
greatness; and diminishes, instead of increasing, the real value of the annual
produce of its land and labour.
    All systems either of preference or of restraint, therefore, being thus

completely taken away, the obvious and simple system of natural liberty establishes itself of its own accord. Every man, as long as he does not violate the laws of justice, is left perfectly free to pursue his own interest his own way, and to bring both his industry and capital into competition with those of any other man, or order of men. The sovereign is completely discharged from a duty, in the attempting to perform which he must always be exposed to innumerable delusions, and for the proper performance of which no human wisdom or knowledge could ever be sufficient; the duty of superintending the industry of private people, and of directing it towards the employments most suitable to the interest of the society [pp. 650-51].

It is important to insist on the qualifications Smith attached to the view that society's economic welfare is maximized when each individual is allowed to pursue his own interests. It is not true under all circumstances but only under a competitive economic order surrounded by appropriate institutions, laws, and incentive systems. Indeed, *The Wealth of Nations* can be read (and should be read) as a systematic critique of human institutions. Given Smith's basic conception of human nature, he subjects the society of his day to a searching examination in terms of success or failure in linking up the individual's pursuit of his self-interest with the promotion of the welfare of other people.

THE CHURCH

As we have seen, the great and overriding virtue of a competitive society, in Smith's view, is that individuals possess no power they can exercise in the antisocial pursuit of their personal goals. But the point is not confined to the economic arena alone. Smith has a powerful distrust of all people in positions of authority and of the almost inevitable tendency of people in such positions to exploit that power for their own selfish purposes. People in general can be relied upon to behave in self-serving ways, and bureaucrats and politicians predictably avail themselves of numerous opportunities for personal enrichment because they are presented with numerous opportunities. Smith is firmly convinced, for reasons going back to his understanding of human motivation, that when power exists it will be employed in ways advantageous to the possessor of the power but disadvantageous to other members of society. To use game-theoretic terminology, the possession of power inevitably leads to the playing of zero-sum games instead of positive-sum games. A great virtue of laissez-faire, then, is that it leads to the elimination (or at least to the minimization) of possibilities for the abuse of power in the economic arena. A common theme running throughout Smith's book is the warning that government interventionism creates a bad system of personal incentives by offering some people both power and opportunities for self-enrichment through zero-sum games. As Smith states: "All for ourselves, and nothing for other people, seems, in every age of the world, to have been the vile maxim of the masters of mankind" (pp. 388-89). In other places he speaks of "the violence and injustice of the rulers of mankind" (p. 460), and the "insolence of office" (p. 718). Elsewhere he refers with obvious sarcasm to "that insidious and crafty animal, vulgarly called a statesman or politician" (p. 435). Indeed, "the avarice and injustice of princes and sovereign states, abusing the confidence of their subjects," is a sad phenomenon that can be found "in every country of the world" (p. 27).

It must be emphasized that, although Smith singles out the rulers of mankind for such reprobation, he does not regard such people as psychologically constituted so that they are different in any way from the rest of mankind. They are different only in their access to the exercise of power. Their special situation and opportunity, not their unique psychological makeup, accounts for their misbehavior. Almost everyone except for a few saintly types may be expected to behave similarly in similar situations. The desire to "get something for nothing" is practically universal. Remember that Smith said of landlords, they "love to reap where they never sowed." Few people, however, seem to realize that this statement is usually quoted incorrectly (as done here) by the omission of a critical qualification. Smith's exact words were: "Landlords, *like all other men,* love to reap where they never sowed . . ." (p. 49; emphasis added).

The proper goal of social policy, then, is (or ought to be) to structure the framework of incentives within which each individual functions so that everyone will, in pursuit of his own interests, behave in a manner that will simultaneously advance the interests of others. This is far from easy and can never be done perfectly, but it represents the direction in which we should attempt to move. In the process we must avoid two pitfalls. The first is the zero-sum game pitfall, which we have just discussed. The other is the creation of a system that relies for its success upon weak incentives rather than strong ones. If we develop institutions that for their success require people to behave out of benevolence instead of self-love, we will almost surely fail. The great virtue of Smith's proposals, as he saw it, is that they required for their success only the operation of self-love, not benevolence. Institutional arrangements that draw upon such a universal quality are likely to function much more effectively than those that require benevolence—a most desirable characteristic, surely, but one in uncommonly short supply. For precisely these reasons, Smith tells us that "man has almost constant occasion for the help of his brethren, and it is in vain for him to expect it from their benevolence only. He will be more likely to prevail if he can interest their self-love in his favour, and shew them that it is for their own advantage to do for him what he requires of them. . . . It is not from the benevolence of the butcher, the brewer, or the baker, that we expect our dinner, but from their regard to their own interest. We address ourselves, not to their humanity but to their self-love, and never talk to them of our own necessities but of their advantages" (p. 14).

It is essential in understanding Smith to appreciate the consistency with which he applied to all spheres the arguments he had developed most extensively in the economic sphere. This is because human behavior in all walks of life flows in a consistent way from these basic psychological impulses in which Smith believed. All men are economically motivated and can be relied upon to respond to the system of incentives in which they find themselves immersed. If, however, material goods are made available to them independently of their own diligence and application, we have no right to be surprised if such diligence and application are not forthcoming. Thus clergymen who belong to wealthy religious orders with independent endowments are typically given to indolence and negligence. They display, as Smith puts it, "those contemptuous and arrogant airs which we so often meet with in the proud dignitaries of opulent and well-endowed churches." If their endowments are sufficiently large, they simply "repose themselves upon their benefices" (p. 762), and do little else. Such situations always have implications not only for the supply of people who already pursue this vocation; high incomes in exchange for small amounts of work also have an allocative effect in drawing people away from other lower paying and more demanding professions. Thus, "After the church of Rome, that of England is by far the richest and best endowed church in Christendom. In England, accordingly, the church is continually draining the universities of all their best and ablest members . . ." (p. 763). On the other hand, in those religious orders that are underpaid, priests are likely to behave in an aggressive way and to exploit the public by too much of the wrong kind of attention—by an excessive zeal in the performance of their duties, which Smith vividly likened to a plundering army: "The mendicant orders derive their whole subsistence from such [voluntary] oblations. It is with them, as with the hussars and light infantry of some armies; no plunder, no pay" (p. 742). It is no surprise that Smith's suggested solution to the problems that arise in the religious sphere, where spiritual leaders possess such great and unusual powers for exploiting public credulity and gullibility, is the elimination of government intervention in support of an established church and greater competition among numerous religious orders.

> The interested and active zeal of religious teachers can be dangerous and troublesome only where there is, either but one sect tolerated in the society, or where the whole of a large society is divided into two or three great sects; the teachers of each acting by concert, and under a regular discipline and subordination. But that zeal must be altogether innocent where the society is divided into two or three hundred, or perhaps into as many thousand small sects, of which no one could be considerable enough to disturb the public tranquillity. The teachers of each sect, seeing themselves surrounded on all sides with more adversaries than friends, would be obliged to learn that candour and moderation which is so seldom to be found among the teachers of those great sects, whose tenets, being supported by the civil magistrate, are held in veneration by almost all the inhabitants of extensive kingdoms and empires, and who therefore see nothing round them but followers, disciples, and humble admirers. The teachers of each little sect, finding themselves almost alone, would be obliged to respect those of almost every other sect, and the concessions which they would mutually find it both convenient and agreeable to make to one another, might in time probably reduce the doctrine of the greater part of them to that pure and rational religion, free from

every mixture of absurdity, imposture, or fanaticism, such as wise men have in all ages of the world wished to see established . . . [p. 745].

Smith, you see, really believed in competition!

THE EDUCATIONAL SYSTEM

Finally, it seems appropriate to close with a brief consideration of Smith's views on the educational establishment. This was a subject on which Smith had some very strong feelings. He had spent several unhappy years at Oxford (Balliol) as a young man, so it was on the basis of personal experience that he derisively observed, "In the University of Oxford, the greater part of the public professors have, for these many years, given up altogether even the pretence of teaching." Again, the reasons are apparent. Like all other people, a teacher's "diligence is likely to be proportioned to the motives which he has for exerting it." Accordingly, the large independent endowments of the great English universities in the eighteenth century had, in effect, all but destroyed the motives for serious effort on the part of the teachers. (We must recall, "it is the interest of every man to live as much at his ease as he can . . ." (p. 718). As a result, the quality of the intellectual life at these institutions declined seriously.

> The improvements which, in modern times, have been made in several different branches of philosophy, have not, the greater part of them, been made in universities; though some no doubt have. The greater part of universities have not even been very forward to adopt those improvements, after they were made; and several of those learned societies have chosen to remain, for a long time, the sanctuaries in which exploded systems and obsolete prejudices found shelter and protection, after they had been hunted out of every other corner of the world. In general, the richest and best endowed universities have been the slowest in adopting those improvements, and the most averse to permit any considerable change in the established plan of education. Those improvements were more easily introduced into some of the poorer universities, in which the teachers, depending upon their reputation for the greater part of their subsistence, were obliged to pay more attention to the current opinions of the world [p. 727].

Indeed, matters had become so bad at the universities that the English upper classes were falling into the habit of sending their sons off for several years of foreign travel after they finished school, as a substitute for attendance at universities. Smith did not approve the practice.

> Our young people, it is said, generally return home much improved by their travels. A young man who goes abroad at seventeen or eighteen, and returns home at one and twenty, returns three or four years older than he was when he went abroad; and at that age it is very difficult not to improve a good deal in three or four years. In the course of his travels, he generally acquires some knowledge of one or two foreign languages; a knowledge, however, which is seldom sufficient to enable him either to speak or write them with propriety.

In other respects, he commonly returns home more conceited, more unprincipled, more dissipated, and more incapable of any serious application either to study or to business, than he could well have become in so short a time, had he lived at home. By travelling so very young, by spending in the most frivolous dissipation the most precious years of his life, at a distance from the inspection and controul of his parents and relations, every useful habit, which the earlier parts of his education might have had some tendency to form in him, instead of being rivetted and confirmed, is almost necessarily either weakened or effaced. Nothing but the discredit into which the universities are allowing themselves to fall, could ever have brought into repute so very absurd a practice as that of travelling at this early period of life [p. 728].

The quality of university teaching had declined for another basic reason. Not only was the teacher's income divorced from his effectiveness as a teacher, the system also disallowed the exercise of consumer sovereignty on the part of the students by presenting the teacher with a captive audience, thus dulling whatever remaining incentive the teacher might have had to present "tolerably good" lectures. Smith offers a masterly analysis that is worth quoting at length:

If in each college the tutor, who was to instruct each student in all arts and sciences, should not be voluntarily chosen by the student, but appointed by the head of the college; and if, in case of neglect, inability, or bad usage, the student should not be allowed to change him for another, without leave first asked and obtained; such a regulation would not only tend very much to extinguish all emulation among the different tutors of the same college, but to diminish very much in all of them the necessity of diligence and of attention to their respective pupils. Such teachers, though very well paid by their students, might be as much disposed to neglect them, as those who are not paid by them at all, or who have no other recompence but their salary.

If the teacher happens to be a man of sense, it must be an unpleasant thing to him to be conscious, while he is lecturing his students, that he is either speaking or reading nonsense, or what is very little better than nonsense. It must too be unpleasant to him to observe that the greater part of his students desert his lectures; or perhaps attend upon them with plain enough marks of neglect, contempt, and derision. If he is obliged, therefore, to give a certain number of lectures, these motives alone, without any other interest, might dispose him to take some pains to give tolerably good ones. Several different expedients, however may be fallen upon, which will effectually blunt the edge of all those incitements to diligence. The teacher, instead of explaining to his pupils himself the science in which he proposes to instruct them, may read some book upon it; and if this book is written in a foreign and dead language, by interpreting it to them into their own; or what would give him still less trouble, by making them interpret it to him, and by now and then making an occasional remark upon it, he may flatter himself that he is giving a lecture. The slightest degree of knowledge and application will enable him to do this, without exposing himself to contempt or derision, or saying any thing that is really foolish, absurd, or ridiculous. The discipline of the college, at the same time, may enable him to force all his pupils to the most regular attendance upon this sham-lecture, and to maintain the most decent and respectful behaviour during the whole time of the performance.

The discipline of colleges and universities is in general contrived, not for the benefit of the students, but for the interest, or more properly speaking, for the ease of the masters. Its object is, in all cases, to maintain the authority of the master, and whether he neglects or performs his duty, to oblige the students in all cases to behave to him as if he performed it with the greatest diligence and ability. It seems to presume perfect wisdom and virtue in the one order, and the greatest weakness and folly in the other [pp. 719-20].

CONCLUSION

It is impossible to appreciate fully the thrust of Adam Smith's arguments concerning laissez-faire until he is regarded as very much, and very self-consciously, a social critic of eighteenth-century society. As we have seen, Smith subjected most of the basic institutions of his day — the economy, the government, the church, the educational system — to searching and far-reaching criticism. The concepts of laissez-faire and consumer sovereignty had some quite radical implications in Smith's time. I do not wish to portray Smith as a radical in any of the twentieth-century meanings of the term, but in eighteenth-century Britain these were distinctly radical ideas, with radical policy implications.

NOTES

1. Jacob Viner, Adam Smith and Laissez-Faire, in J. M. Clark et al., *Adam Smith, 1776–1926* (Chicago: Univ. Chicago Press, 1928), Ch. 5.
2. See A. Phillips, The Tableau Economique as a Simple Leontief Model, *Quart. J. Econ.* (Feb. 1955):137-44.
3. See Wesley Mitchell, *The Backward Art of Spending Money* (New York: Kelley, 1950), p. 85. See also Mitchell's *Lecture Notes on Types of Economic Theory* (New York: Kelley, 1949), vol. 1, Ch. 5.

3

An Economy Formed by Men

🖋 ELI GINZBERG

THE original title of this essay in celebration of the bicentennial of the publication of Adam Smith's *The Wealth of Nations* was "Distributive Justice." After some reflection, it seemed inappropriate in honoring the memory of a man who was a master stylist to resort to a concept that has no currency beyond the academic community and only limited recognition therein. Accordingly, I selected a title drawn from *The Wealth of Nations* itself.

Not only the title of this essay but all the analysis will be based directly on Smith's opus. His views, not mine, warrant attention and reflection. There is a further reason for such a textual approach. It is more than forty years since *The House of Adam Smith*[1] was first published; in the interim I have not stayed abreast of the critical literature on Smith, though I have reread his classic, not once, but many times. I am therefore more at home with *The Wealth of Nations* itself than with comment concerning the author and his works.

It may be helpful by way of orientation to consider the complete title of Smith's work—*An Inquiry into the Nature and Causes of the Wealth of Nations*. He defines his effort as an inquiry, not a theory. Next he emphasizes the causes of wealth, thereby establishing his intention of dealing with a wide array of institutions and forces that illuminate the dynamics of wealth creation. Finally, in sharp differentiation from his predecessors, the mercantilists, his focus is not limited to exploration of conditions that can contribute to the well-being of England alone but covers conditions affecting all nations.

Smith's work has been the principal source of inspiration for the efforts we have been carrying on at Columbia University since prior to World War II, when we first began to delineate what has come to be known as the field of human resources and manpower.[2] The simplest way of establishing this linkage is to recall the comment that Wesley Clair Mitchell made in his

Eli Ginzberg is A. Barton Hepburn Professor of Economics and Director, Conservation of Human Resources, Columbia University.

capacity as chairman of a doctoral committee when my first student offered "human resources" as a field for examination. Mitchell observed that he was pleased to see that economics, which had been rooted by Smith in human resources but deflected by his successors to a preoccupation with commodity trade, was now getting back on the main track. I hope that the bicentennial celebrations of *The Wealth of Nations* will impress those now entering upon the study of economics that Smith's broad-scale historical, comparative, and institutional approach is more apposite to the present and the future than the narrow preoccupations of the applied mathematicians who continue to dominate the discipline.

Let us look more closely at Adam Smith. The stages in this analysis involve a brief recapitulation of how the main-line economists interpret Smith, the critical role of human resources in Smith's analysis, the principal market institutions that mediate this role, and several observations on the relationship between the two bicentennials of 1976—that of *The Wealth of Nations* and the independence of the American colonies.

GENERAL INTERPRETATION

The following seems a fair description of how the economists in the main-line tradition see Adam Smith's work.

1. The individual is the best judge of his own self-interest; and the more freedom the individual has to pursue self-interest within the law, the better off society will be.
2. The more people are able to specialize, the greater the wealth of a nation. The division of labor is the source of increasing productivity. Therefore, the more a society is able to specialize, the greater its wealth potential.
3. The third proposition, closely related to the second, holds that the larger the market, the greater the possibilities for specialization. The more one can enlarge trade between the city and the rural areas and between one country and another, the larger the market and the greater the degree of specialization.[3]
4. Smith believed in a limited role for the state. It should be concerned with defense, justice, and public works; all other economic activity should be in the private sector.

These four propositions can be reformulated: the larger the market, the more the specialization, the less the involvement of government in economic affairs, the greater the output. This is the dominant view, but a "vulgar" interpretation of Adam Smith's central thesis.

It is not only tendentious but downright wrong to lift analytic formulations and policy prescriptions out of context and to apply them uncritically to another era. We must recall that industry for Adam Smith was represented by a pin factory of ten workers. It is twice wrong to quote only part of a hallowed text—that which suits one's interpretation and prejudice. Smith was no absolutist and warned against simplistic assumptions concerning the behavior of men in the market or the appropriate role of the state in economic affairs. Specifically, he noted that "man is of all sorts of luggage the most difficult to be transported" (p. 75), clearly a constraint on developing an optimal division of labor and specialization. One of my earliest studies in the manpower arena centered on the long-term unemployed in South Wales in the 1930s. Despite job prospects that were much better in the Midlands than in the valleys, it was exceedingly difficult to encourage even young people to move the distance, which was less than two hundred miles![4]

True, Smith was skeptical of the ability of government to play a constructive role in economic affairs, but not to a point of insisting on the theorem of maximum freedom for the individual. In discussing laws to restrain the issuance of small bank notes, he observed:

> Such regulations may, no doubt, be considered as in some respect a violation of natural liberty. But those exertions of the natural liberty of a few individuals, which might endanger the security of the whole society, are, and ought to be, restrained by the laws of all governments, of the most free, as well as of the most despotical [p. 308].

Much as Smith was convinced of the value of broadening the market to increase productivity and output, he questioned whether he could persuade his fellow countrymen of the wisdom of such action. His skepticism was expressed in these terms: "To expect . . . that the freedom of trade should ever be entirely restored in Great Britain, is as absurd as to expect an Oceania or Utopia should ever be established in it" (p. 437). The fact that Great Britain opted for free trade in 1844 reflected the dominance of new forces that did not emerge until long after Smith's death.

These few quotations should help to warn the uninitiated about their need to be on guard against interpreters who present Smith as a dogmatist. That, above all else, he was not. After all, he did not hesitate to recommend that the state require the study of science and philosophy "to be undergone by every person before he was permitted to exercise any liberal profession . . ." And he further recommended an increased frequency and gaiety of public diversions "to amuse and divert the people by painting, poetry, music, dancing; by all sorts of dramatic representations and exhibitions . . . [to] dissipate . . . the melancholy and gloomy humour which is almost always the nurse of popular superstition and enthusiasm" (p. 748).

In his search for the good (more correctly, the better) society, Smith does not hesitate to argue against his own theoretical principles in stipulating that the leadership should be forced to undergo specific instruction in science and philosophy. In rising above the dominant culture of Calvinist Scotland, he advocated state-supported amusements as a method of controlling the passions of the common people. What we find here and throughout his work is the sacrifice of general theory in favor of specific pragmatic goals. For Smith, general principles were guides, not dogmas.

THE ROLE OF HUMAN RESOURCES

The realism of Smith is reinforced by consideration of our second theme — his treatment of the human resource factor in political economy. We tend to forget that Smith was a close friend and admirer of the French intelligentsia who were the principal architects of the Revolution. In more recent years, the American academic world has been wracked by dissension over claims advanced by the neo-Galtonians that blacks are intellectually and genetically inferior to whites. Here is Smith's clear-cut position on the relative roles of heredity and environment:

> The difference between the most dissimilar characters, between a philosopher and a common street porter, for example, seems to arise not so much from nature as from habit, custom, and education. When they came into the world, and for the first six or eight years of their existence, they were, perhaps, very much alike, and neither their parents nor playfellows could perceive any remarkable difference. About that age, or soon after, they came to be employed in very different occupations. And the difference of talents comes then to be taken notice of, and widens by degrees, till at last the vanity of the philosopher is willing to acknowledge scarce any resemblance [pp. 15-16].

Such an extreme environmentalist view of human ability, which postulates a rough equality of potential among all people and ascribes the differences in their later performance to relative opportunities to acquire skills and competences, goes a long way to explain why Smith urged state action with respect to education.

> The public can impose upon almost the whole body of the people the necessity of acquiring those most essential parts of education, by obliging every man to undergo an examination or probation in them before he can obtain the freedom in any corporation, or be allowed to set up any trade either in a village or town corporate [p. 738].

It might be well in the present context to recognize that Smith the moral philosopher saw benefits from public support of education beyond the gains in productivity that attracted the attention of Smith the economist.

> A man without the proper use of the intellectual faculties of a man is, if possible, more contemptible than even a coward, and seems to be mutilated and deformed in a still more essential part of the character of human nature. Though the state was to derive no advantage from the instruction of the inferior ranks of people, it would still deserve its attention that they should not be altogether uninstructed. The state, however, derives no in-

considerable advantage from their instruction. The more they are instructed, the less liable they are to the delusions of enthusiasm and superstition, which, among ignorant nations, frequently occasion the most dreadful
disorders. An instructed and intelligent people besides, are always more decent and orderly than an ignorant and stupid one [p. 740].

Having studied in Heidelberg, Germany, in the late 1920s, I cannot resist
the temptation to point out that a relatively well-educated people is not
immune to the scourge of fanaticism. Witness Hitler. But this important
exception does not vitiate, at least in my view, Smith's insight about the
relation of education to political stability.

Let us shift the focus slightly. Of late, considerations of worker alienation have been very much to the fore. Let us review how Smith dealt with
the issue:

In the progress of the division of labour, the employment of a far greater
part of those who live by labour, that is, the great body of the people, comes
to be confined to a few very simple operations, frequently to one or two. But
the understandings of the greater part of men are necessarily formed by
their ordinary employments. The man whose whole life is spent in performing a few simple operations, of which the effects too are, perhaps, always the
same, or very nearly the same, has no occasion to exert his understanding, or
to exercise his invention in finding out expedients for removing difficulties
which never occur. He naturally loses, therefore, the habit of such exertion,
and generally becomes as stupid and ignorant as it is possible for a human
creature to become [p. 734].

A considerable scholarly effort has been directed recently to an attempted
reconciliation of Smith's pessimistic assessment of what the division of
labor implies for the life of the laborer and his insistence that such division
is the foundation for productivity gains and economic growth.[5] In my view,
all efforts at reconciliation have failed and will continue to do so. The best
I can offer is the observation that Smith was a preindustrial economist with
prescience about the shortcomings of large-scale manufacturing, a condition that he could imagine even before it had arrived.

The gap that separated Smith from his predecessors and contemporaries is nowhere better illustrated than in his views about the wage
structure. The leaders of the mercantilist school saw high wages as a
disincentive to work, but Smith did not. He argued against the mercantilists and the entrenched theory that the lower the wage rate, the better for the country. We still have some exponents of that doctrine. They
explain the high rates of youth unemployment in the United States as the
direct consequence of a minimum wage. Smith's thought on wages follows:

The wages of labour are the encouragement of industry, which, like every
other human quality, improves in proportion to the encouragement it receives. . . . Some workmen, indeed, when they can earn in four days what

will maintain them through the week, will be idle in the other three. This, however, is by no means the case with the greater part. Workmen, on the contrary, when they are liberally paid by the piece, are very apt to over-work themselves, and to ruin their health and constitution in a few years. A carpenter in London, and in some other places, is not supposed to last in his utmost vigour above eight years. Something of the same kind happens in many other trades, in which the workmen are paid by the piece . . . [pp. 81–82].

Since Karl Marx's doctrine of class interest and class struggle has had such a potent influence on modern societies, it is interesting to consider how Smith dealt with the same subject.

But though the interest of the labourer is strictly connected with that of society, he is incapable either of comprehending that interest, or of understanding its connexion with his own. His condition leaves him no time to receive the necessary information, and his education and habits are com-monly such as to render him unfit to judge even though he was fully in-formed. In the public deliberations, therefore, his voice is little heard and less regarded . . . [p. 249].

Without entering into the merits of these contradictory views, it may suf-fice (considering the earlier reference to Hitler) to point out that, at least in 1933, the workers in one major industrial country failed to choose in terms of their self-interest.

The selected quotes provide an overview of Adam Smith's assessment of the critical dimensions of the human resource factor. In his view every human being is born with considerable potential, much of which goes to waste because of lack of developmental opportunities. He was deeply con-cerned about the individual and the social costs of undereducation. He was worried about the fact that economic pressures and the individual's desire to accumulate wealth would lead many workers to destroy their health through overwork. And he was restive that the work in which many en-gaged would stunt their intellect and warp their emotions, thereby under-mining the strength of the nation.

THE MARKET

We shift to the third dimension of this analysis—how Smith saw the market and the principal institutions that helped to shape its performance. We will consider his views of property, monopoly, security, and na-tionalism.

On property, Smith says: "As soon as all the land . . . has become private property, the landlords, like all other men, love to reap where they never sowed . . ." (p. 49). Landlords are monopolists, and like all monopolists, they "love to reap where they never sowed." The rich land-lord at the end of feudal times sought to convert the rent due him from produce and labor to money because "where he can spend the greatest revenue upon his own person, he frequently has no bounds to his expence, because he frequently has no bounds to his vanity, or to his affection for his own person" (p. 391). Smith saw capital accumulation as the major precondition for economic development, but he had little good to say about many of the accumulators. His acerbic views about the engrossers of property paralleled his criticism of monopolists.

Smith's concern about the evils of monopoly went beyond the unjustified rewards that accrued to the man who was able to rig the market. A still more untoward consequence of monopoly was the ineffective management that in Smith's view was the likely concomitant of an entrepreneur's being sheltered from the cold winds of competition. In his words: "Monopoly . . . is a great enemy of good management . . ." (p. 147). He elaborated this view in dealing with the great landlords: the great proprietor was seldom the great improver. And in Smith's view there was little prospect for sustained economic progress without improvements in agricultural productivity.

All for ourselves, and nothing for other people, seems, in every age of the world, to have been the vile maxim of the masters of mankind [pp. 388-89]. The monopolists, by keeping the market constantly under-stocked, by never fully supplying the effective demand . . . raise their emoluments . . . greatly above their natural rate [p. 61].

Smith placed great emphasis on security of person and property as a cornerstone for economic progress. The following quotation alone establishes Smith as a *political* economist. The failure of the developed nations to appreciate this linkage between public security and private enterprise led them to advance to the recently liberated nations huge sums, much of which have been wasted because these nations could not secure their domestic tranquility.

Commerce and manufactures can seldom flourish long in any state which does not enjoy a regular administration of justice, in which the people do not feel themselves secure in the possession of their property, in which the faith of contracts is not supported by law, and in which the authority of the state is not supposed to be regularly employed in enforcing the payment of debts from all those who are able to pay. Commerce and manufactures, in short, can seldom flourish in any state in which there is not a certain degree of confidence in the justice of government [p. 862].

While much of Smith's opus was directed to pointing out the shortcomings of British policy, he never lost sight of the comparative advantage of Great Britain over its Continental rivals (particularly Spain and France) by virtue of the strength of its constitution. "That security which the laws in Great Britain give to every man that he shall enjoy the fruits of his own labour, is alone sufficient to make any country flourish . . ." (p. 508).

Further insight into the sensitivity of Smith to the political element in economic life is revealed by his treatment of nationalism. Unlike his successor, Karl Marx, who saw the speedy erosion of national interests, Smith believed that it was difficult to exaggerate the power of nationalism in public imagination and in the actions of governments. "But though empires, like all the other works of men, have all hitherto proved mortal, yet every empire aims at immortality" (pp. 781-82). To propose that Great Britain should voluntarily give up all authority over her colonies would be to propose in Smith's view "such a measure as never was and never . . . will be adopted, by any nation in the world" (pp. 581-82).

Much as it went against his grain, for he viewed international commerce as beneficial to both parties, Smith had no illusion about the emotions that shaped the policies of both Great Britain and France in their relations to one another: "Being neighbours, they are necessarily enemies. . . . Mercantile jealousy is excited, and both inflames, and is itself inflamed, by the violence of national animosity" (p. 463).

The thrust of this analysis has not been to deny that Smith saw great virtues in the competitive market but to emphasize his awareness of property, monopoly, and nationalism—which could and did distort the outcomes.

THE AMERICAN REVOLUTION

In this celebration of a double bicentennial, I would like to call attention to Adam Smith's views of the American colonies and their likely future.

> In what way, therefore, has the policy of Europe contributed either to the first establishment, or the present grandeur of the colonies of America? . . . It bred and formed the men who were capable of achieving such great actions, and of laying the foundation of so great an empire; and there is no other quarter of the world of which the policy is capable of forming, or has ever actually and in fact formed such men. The colonies owe to the policy of Europe the education and the great views of their active and enterprising founders; and some of the greatest and most important of them, so far as concerns their internal government, owe to it scarce any thing else [p. 556].

After Smith had established so clearly the indebtedness of the American colonists to their British heritage, how did he explain their state of rebellion? The economist turns psychologist to find the answer:

> Men desire to have some share in the management of public affairs chiefly on account of the importance which it gives to them. Upon the power which the greater part of the leading men, the natural aristocracy of every country, have of preserving or defending their respective importance, depends the stability and duration of every system of free government. In the attacks which those leading men are continually making on the importance of one another, and in the defence of their own, consists the whole play of domestic faction and ambition. The leading men of America, like those of all other

countries, desire to preserve their own importance. They feel, or imagine, that if their assemblies, which they are fond of calling parliaments, and of considering as equal in authority to the parliament of Great Britain, should be so degraded as to become humble ministers and executive officers of that parliament, the greater part of their own importance would be at an end [pp. 586-87].

Smith carries conviction on many fronts—as historian, economist, and psychologist—but nowhere are his great gifts of analysis more visible than in his concluding observation in *The Wealth of Nations*. He offers his compatriots advice to let the American colonies go free:

The rulers of Great Britain have, for more than a century past, amused the people with the imagination that they possessed a great empire on the west side of the Atlantic. This empire, however, has hitherto existed in imagination only. It has hitherto been, not an empire, but the project of an empire; not a gold mine, but the project of a gold mine; a project which has cost, which continues to cost, and which, if pursued in the same way as it has been hitherto, is likely to cost, immense expence, without being likely to bring any profit; for the effects of the monopoly of the colony trade, it has been shewn, are, to the great body of the people, mere loss instead of profit. It is surely now time that our rulers should either realize this golden dream, in which they have been indulging themselves, perhaps, as well as the people; or, that they should awake from it themselves, and endeavour to awaken the people. If the project cannot be completed, it ought to be given up. If any of the provinces of the British empire cannot be made to contribute towards the support of the whole empire, it is surely time that Great Britain should free herself from the expence of defending those provinces in time of war, and of supporting any part of their civil or military establishments in time of peace, and endeavour to accommodate her future views and designs to the real mediocrity of her circumstances [pp. 899-900].

We have every reason to believe that a hundred years hence, there will be a tercentenary celebration of *The Wealth of Nations*. That is the measure of Smith's genius.

NOTES

1. Eli Ginzberg, *The House of Adam Smith* (New York: Columbia Univ. Press, 1934). Reprinted with a Foreword by Octagon Books, New York, 1964.
2. Eli Ginzberg, *The Human Economy* (New York: McGraw-Hill, 1976) makes this linkage explicit both on the dedicatory page and by the quotations from *The Wealth of Nations* used to introduce each of the five books.
3. In this connection, I recall a visit to a large farm not too far from Calcutta that could be reached only by a foot path from the main road. The missing piece of road made it impossible for the owner to sell his surplus in the city, and he therefore was forced to operate his farm as a self-contained unit.
4. Eli Ginzberg, *Grass on the Slag Heaps: The Story of the Welsh Miners* (New York: Harper, 1942).
5. Robert Lamb, Adam Smith's Concept of Alienation, *Oxford Economic Papers*, vol. 25, July 1973.

4

Adam Smith on Human Nature and Social Circumstance

🍃 LOUIS SCHNEIDER

TWO centuries have elapsed since the publication of *The Wealth of Nations* and somewhat longer since the appearance of Adam Smith's other central work, *The Theory of Moral Sentiments*. During this time Smith has been pondered and repondered, and one might think that virtually every line of these major writings and his several minor ones had been weighed and in some sense tested. It is a witness to Smith's stature and significant place in the history of thought that we constantly come back to him, and it is always possible that a new time will discover in him new and engaging perspectives. But we must also be prepared for inevitable review of much that has been said about him previously. This essay is designed to achieve a relative comprehensiveness (although we do not focus on sympathy) on the matter of Smith's views on human nature and its social and economic outcomes, the social constraints within which it operates, and the wider social contexts by which it is influenced (to all of which we mean to allude with the title phrase, "human nature and social circumstance"). It is further hoped that this essay may usefully bring together cogent statements on Smith's work from major modern commentaries.

Of concern here will be rationality and its limitations and the meaning of these for a wider social order. Then, in relation to rationality, a certain incompleteness in Smith's thought will be considered. Thereafter, the concern will be with social and economic harmony, and, finally, with the shaping of motives by situations.

It is well to add two comments before proceeding with Smith on rationality. First, I hold firmly to the thesis (shared with numerous modern commentators, although not undisputed by others) that there is no serious discrepancy between the basic outlook of *The Wealth of Nations* and that of *The Theory of Moral Sentiments*. One modern student remarks, "The view that the central doctrine of one is inconsistent with that of the other is without foundation."[1] Since this occasion highlights *The Wealth of Na-*

Louis Schneider is Professor of Sociology, University of Texas, Austin.

tions, copious citation will be made from that work, but certainly not to the neglect of what I regard as complementary statements from *Moral Sentiments.*

Second, I refuse to be inhibited by what seems to be a widespread horror of reading an author in terms that depart from what he presumably had in mind. If we want to know how Adam Smith conceived things, it is important to try to discover just that. We must not read present-day economic or sociological analysis into him. But it may be that, as Paul Samuelson has remarked, there is a worse sin than reading present-day analysis into earlier writers.[2] This is the sin of "not recognizing the equivalent content in older writers because they do not use the terminology and symbols of the present."[3] Adam Smith says much that may be translated into later language conveniently and without distortion, and the position taken here is that it is historicist foolishness to deny this. I do not wish to do violence to Smith's views nor to inflate the significance of something of present-day interest he may have referred to in passing, but a spade is surely a spade still, even if Germans call it a *Spaten.*[4]

FROM RATIONALITY AND ITS LIMITATIONS
TO SOCIAL AND ECONOMIC ORDER

The theme or matter of human rationality in Adam Smith's work has a certain complexity, and we must approach it with some patience. It has often been observed that Smith did not place great reliance on man's rationality and did not count on reason as a human faculty (here referred to as "rationality") that would serve in a major way to organize social and economic life. But this is a very broad, loose statement.

Granted that human rationality is for Smith a frail reed, it is still well not to forget that he conceded something to it. Human beings do have some rational faculty. They have capacity to comprehend, intelligence, insight, and foresight. Self-interest is after all a most significant reality for Smith and intimately associated with a certain endowment of human rationality. Economic agents have at least a commonsense sort of rationality about their interests. They are also likely to possess a modicum of relevant knowledge. They know which side their bread is buttered on — within limits but genuinely, nevertheless. This sometimes becomes quite explicit. Slave labor is ultimately "the dearest of any," for "a person who can acquire no property, can have no other interest but to eat as much, and to labour as little as possible." Whatever work such a person does in excess of what will buy his own maintenance "can be squeezed out of him by violence only, and not by any interest of his own" (p. 365). Smith contrasts metayers (sharecroppers) and slaves:

[Metayers], being freemen, are capable of acquiring property, and having a certain proportion of the produce of the land, they have a plain interest that the whole produce should be as great as possible, in order that their own proportion may be so. A slave, on the contrary, who can acquire nothing but

his maintenance, consults his own ease by making the land produce as little
as possible over and above that maintenance [p. 366].

Only the obvious imputation of rationality by Smith is important for present purposes. He would undoubtedly have thought that he and even the
least sensible of those he knew would have acted in the ways indicated had
they been slaves or metayers.

It would seem also that individuals can be trusted to possess insight
into what is in their interest better than others who might be tempted to be
insightful for them. Smith tells us that the individual in his local situation
can judge better than the statesman or lawgiver what is economically to his
advantage or how he should employ his capital.[5] For his part, the
statesman or lawgiver would evidently be the more inadequate, the larger
the number and variety of individuals whose economic activity he might
seek to direct to the end of general ecomomic welfare. The statesman
tempted to be thus oversupervisory would assume an authority with which
no person and no organization could be trusted and which would "nowhere
be so dangerous as in the hands of a man who had folly and presumption
enough to fancy himself fit to exercise it" (p. 423). The aspiration to
superintending the industry of private people with a view to effecting
general welfare, indeed, "must always be exposed to inumerable delusions"
and "no human wisdom or knowledge could ever be sufficient" for it (p.
651).

This plainly bears on the subject of laissez faire, but that would be a
distraction; instead we note the curious character of these arguments as
they relate to human rationality. What Smith concedes with one hand he
withdraws with the other. Broadly, men have a commonsense rationality
and perceptiveness about their own interests; but at the same time, a
strong limitation on the scope of rationality in economic affairs is imposed:
for the sovereign's rationality in economic matters is severely restricted,
and any presumptions he might exhibit in this sphere would be mistrusted
by Smith.

We already confront a transition. If we begin by emphasizing a
limited but *real* rationality, we soon will emphasize, following Smith, a
real but *limited* rationality. Men generally tend to act with very narrow
ends in view. Their reason (that is, their rationality as a faculty) ordinarily
operates within strict limits even within the economic sphere, in regard to
what they envisage as aims. The owner of capital seeks his own welfare,
and considerations appertaining to the economy as a whole "never enter
into his thoughts" (p. 355) as he does so. They never (or rarely) enter his
thoughts partly because he is powerfully motivated to think in terms of his
own interests and partly because his insight and penetration do not in any
case extend to a comprehension of the economy as a whole.

Let us consider four related points. We will look more closely into the
matter of man acting with limited ends in view. Then we may attend to the
point that deliberately undertaken actions often have outcomes that tran-

scend any calculation man may have made or any foresight he may have had. Thereafter, we consider the operation of the cunning of reason in Smith's work. (When we speak of this, the sense of "reason" no longer has to do with rationality as faculty.) And finally, in the present framework it will be appropriate to say something about unanticipated order or system as the outcome of human purposive action. These four matters are so closely connected that their separation may even seem a bit forced, but it is nevertheless helpful in comprehending Adam Smith.

What is involved in the matter of acting with limited ends in view was beautifully suggested in what might be called "the watch passage" in *The Theory of Moral Sentiments:*

> The wheels of the watch are all admirably adjusted to the end for which it was made, the pointing of the hour. All their various motions conspire in the nicest manner to produce this effect. If they were endowed with a desire to produce it, they could not do it better. Yet we never ascribe any such desire or intention to them. . . .[6]

The wheels of the watch of course have no purposes at all; an analogy with men with their quite narrow purposes is clearly intended. If the wheels of the watch succeed in a "pointing of the hour" (what one might call the "great end" of the watch in Smith's teleological style), so too men will often in societies and economies inadvertently achieve or bring about "great ends," although they deliberately pursue only decidedly limited ones. (Inevitably, we begin to move toward the second of the four matters mentioned above.)

Even when Smith does allow (as he does just before the watch passage) that men may actually have certain "great ends" deliberately in view, he stresses human concentration on action that works intermediately toward those great ends:

> With regard to all those ends which, upon account of their peculiar importance, may be regarded . . . as the favourite ends of nature, she has . . . not only endowed mankind with an appetite for the end which she proposes, but likewise with an appetite for the means by which alone this end can be brought about, for their own sakes, and independent of their tendency to produce it. . . . [Reference is now made to "the great ends" of self-preservation and the propagation of the species.] But though we are in this manner endowed with a very strong desire of those ends, it has not been entrusted to the slow and uncertain determinations of our reason, to find out the proper means of bringing them about. Nature has directed us to the greater part of these by original and immediate instincts.[7]

A sentence then immediately follows that, in its denial of human reflection upon the tendency of actions undertaken in very limited perspective to work toward "beneficent" larger outcomes, is entirely in the spirit of the later watch passage:

Hunger, thirst, the passion which unites the two sexes, the love of pleasure, and the dread of pain, prompt us to apply those means [which actually lead to the "favorite ends"] for their own sakes, and without any consideration of their tendency to those beneficent ends which the great Director of nature intended to produce by them.[8]

The impulses associated with self-interest clearly work in the same way in the economic sphere. Human rationality, once more, at least ordinarily, does not extend to a comprehension of very important larger social and economic "ends" or outcomes of action. If in *The Theory of Moral Sentiments* we are told that the wheels of the watch could not succeed better than they do in the pointing of the hour were they endowed with a desire to effect that pointing, what could be closer to this than the well-known statement in *The Wealth of Nations* that "by pursuing his own interest he [the individual] frequently promotes that of the society more effectually than when he really intends to promote it" (p. 423)?

But if men act with limited aims or ends in view, it is a certainty that their purposive social and economic action will often bring results they never contemplated, as Smith was obviously very well aware. A contemporary sociologist has made familiar to social scientists the rather long but useful phrase, "the unanticipated consequences of purposive social action."[9] Adam Smith never employs just this phrase, but what it points to interests him again and again. It also interested other members of the eighteenth-century Scottish school of social scientists doing work stimulated by older moral philosophy, for example, Adam Ferguson and John Millar. More or less in Smith's time alone it was of great interest to Vico, Bernard Mandeville, and the Joseph Priestley who delivered *Lectures on History and General Policy* at the nonconformist academy of Warrington. Indeed, so salient a matter as "unanticipated consequences of purposive social action," which has played so large a role in the philosophy of history and social science, has expectably attracted much attention before and must again. Adam Smith's preoccupation with the idea is too large for us to handle casually; it plays far too significant a role in theoretical constructions in his main works.

It needs to be kept clearly in view that Smith's notion of human nature is inseparable from his social and economic thought. They belong together in such intimacy as to suggest the virtual inevitability of the conjunction of the components of "human nature and social circumstance." Man's endowment with rational faculty is such as to allow him only limited foresight of the effects of carrying out within social (or economic or political) frameworks his various aims. For Smith, the limitation is clearly unavoidable. It is inseparable from the nature of men and women. If they were different in this respect, human society and economy would certainly be different. In this sense the character of society and economy is of course deeply connected with human nature.

How then does the matter of unanticipated consequences come up in Smith? Near the very beginning of *The Wealth of Nations* we find the avowal that the division of labor is not initially the outcome of "any human wisdom, which foresees and intends that general opulence to which it gives occasion." Rather, the division of labor grows out of a human propensity to truck, barter, and exchange "which has in view no such extensive utility" (p. 13).[10] (It is possible to distinguish unanticipated from unintended or even unrecognized consequences, but our usage here in this respect will be deliberately loose.)

There is so much to be noted in this connection, even with the limitations we must impose, that abrupt shifts of illustration may be allowed. In the sphere of banking the operations of the Ayr bank "seem to have produced effects quite opposite to those which were intended by the particular persons who planned and directed it." Indeed, ironically, in the long run it would seem," the operations of this bank increased the real distress of the country which it meant to relieve; and effectively relieved from a very great distress those rivals whom it meant to supplant" (pp. 299, 300). In connection with his discussion of the manner in which the commerce of the towns "contributed to the improvement of the country," Smith observes that "a revolution of the greatest importance to the public happiness was . . . brought about by two different orders of people, who had not the least intention to serve the public." Neither of these orders "had either knowledge or foresight of that great revolution which the folly of the one, and the industry of the other, was gradually bringing about" (pp. 391-92).

Another example of the same general phenomenon may suggest how pervasive the notion of unanticipated consequences was in Smith's outlook: "The tendency of some . . . regulations to raise the value of timber in America, and thereby to facilitate the clearing of the land, was neither, perhaps, intended nor understood by the legislature. Though their beneficial effects, however, have been in this respect accidental, they have not on that account been less real" (p. 547). An example outside the economic sphere will suggest the same pervasiveness. The sect called Independents (Smith writes), "a sect no doubt of very wild enthusiasts," proposed to establish, at the end of the civil war in England, free sectarian competition without governmental or political commitment to any particular sect.

From Smith's point of view this would have been an admirable parallel in religion to competitive conditions he wished to see obtain in the economy. Had this happy scheme prevailed in the religious sphere, "though of a very unphilosophical origin, it would probably by this time have been productive of the most philosophical good temper and moderation with regard to every sort of religious principle" (p. 745). This is a speculative projection of unintended consequences, but it is clearly quite seriously set forth. It throws in an interesting paradox by suggesting that "a sect of very wild enthusiasts" might have brought about most "philosophical" and rationally desirable results. (The paradox is incidentally strongly reminiscent of Mandeville's whole style of thought.) Given the animus he reveals in the passage devoted to this matter, Smith

may be said to be arguing roughly on the line that the juxtaposition and
the interaction of numerous particular fanaticisms would result in diminu-
tion of fanaticism for the community as a whole (as the juxtaposition of
self-interests on the market might have another kind of felicitous outcome). "The teachers of each little sect, finding themselves almost alone,
would be obliged to respect those of almost every other sect . . ." (p. 745).
Religious "monopoly" is as harmful as the economic kind.

It is well to remind ourselves lastly of a famous instance of unanticipated consequences in *The Theory of Moral Sentiments:*

> They [the rich] are led by an invisible hand to make nearly the same
> distribution of necessaries of life which would have been made had the earth
> been divided into equal portions among all its inhabitants; and thus,
> without intending, without knowing it, advance the interest of the society,
> and afford means to the multiplication of the species.[11]

Having seen that men act with limited ends in view and having considered unanticipated consequences, we turn to the third of our four
related points, which has to do with the cunning of reason. This is closely
connected with the invisible hand but helps to make the meaning of the
latter more graphic, and to speak in terms of the cunning of reason is to
sharpen our apprehension of Smith's position in intellectual history. We
turn first to *The Theory of Moral Sentiments.*

We know that men are with some frequency, in Smith's view, led to
realize "larger ends" indirectly, through being attracted to something that
itself simply leads to larger ends. Smith contended that riches bring the
rich only a very modest increment of satisfaction beyond what might be
had without them. But the economy and the society have great need for
the energy and industry of the rich or of those who have distinctive traits
that in time will make them rich. How are the rich enticed to engage their
energies in the interest of general welfare? The general answer Smith gives
is that men are intrigued by the spectacle of the order and beauty of the
complex operations set in motion to attend to the requisites of the rich.
Thus:

> We are . . . charmed with the beauty of that accommodation which
> reigns in the palaces and economy of the great; and admire how every thing
> is adapted to promote their ease, to prevent their wants, to gratify their
> wishes, and to amuse and entertain their most frivolous desires. If we con-
> sider the real satisfaction which all these things are capable of affording, by
> itself and separated from the beauty of that arrangement which is fitted to
> promote it, it will always appear in the highest degree contemptible and
> trifling. But we rarely view it in that abstract and philosophical light. We
> naturally confound it in our imagination with the order, the regular and
> harmonious movement of the system, the machine or economy by means of
> which it is produced.[12]

"It is well," Smith adds, "that nature imposes upon us in this manner." For "it is this deception which rouses and keeps in continual motion the industry of mankind."[13] The invisible hand is at work. The rich are "usefully" induced to advance the interest of the society, precisely by an illusion, a seduction, an enticement. It may just as well be said that the cunning of reason is at work. For that cunning consists in alluring humans to work toward objects that have a mediating function and (with dim human knowledge, at best, that this is occurring) actually subserve "larger ends" or "the favourite ends of nature" (in the language of Smith's early work). Men follow their own passions and interests, in the limiting case wholly unaware that these find their place in a chain that stretches to points never imagined in a limited human envisagement of "links" (which in turn were not recognized by humans as being links in a chain at all). If we drop the teleological and theological vocabulary from all this, we are left with what many scholars have regarded as one of the most fundamental insights or perspectives in the social sciences.[14]

It bears stress that the cunning of reason clearly could not operate as presumed and would not "need" (!) to do so if man's own rationality were not so limited in the first place. We know that it would not have been uncharacteristic for Adam Smith to observe that all around it is better that it should be so. But in any case the cunning of reason underlines once more the narrow scope of human rationality.

Able modern commentators have suggested the affinity of Smith's thought to the notion of the cunning of reason. Thus one of Wilhelm Hasbach's notable treatises on the development of economic thought has this to say:

> Man produces and saves, in order to acquire wealth for himself, but without his knowledge or will he indirectly advances the material condition of the whole society. He is a tool in God's hand.
>
> To clarify Smith's meaning, I remind the reader of the intention of nature, of the cunning of reason, which plays so prominent a role in German philosophy, most grandiosely since Hegel.[15]

Overton H. Taylor takes up the invisible hand passage in *The Theory of Moral Sentiments* and rehearses Smith's view that the desire of an able and ambitious person for riches makes him inadvertently do things that are economically most useful. Taylor paraphrases Smith thus: "The goal of his selfish ambition is a chimera with which cunning 'nature' lures him into serving others better than he serves himself."[16] If Taylor did not have a Hegelian model in view, his language at any rate is sufficiently suggestive of one.

We may adduce a final and longer relevant statement that will appropriately indicate the fourth matter that we wish to discuss. In his monograph on the state of nature and the natural history of civil society, Hans Medick comments:

> Smith reveals society as an objective context of activity which not only guides the comportment of the individual by way of moral and aesthetic standards of conduct but lays down the consequences of this comportment beyond the subjectively oriented intentions of the individual, which are dictated by self-interest. This happens as if behind men's backs. The individual striving after wealth in a society differentiated according to status and property appears as "cunning of reason," through which socially interconnected action shows itself as economically productive in a measure that was in no way intended by the actor. Through social stimulation of the artificial need for wealth the individual is incited to economic actions which in their results in terms of productivity exceed all his consumption capacities and therefore finally lead to a higher level of need for the totality of the members of the society. This grounding of the Smithian "philosophy of wealth" in a theory of society as an objective, self-directing context of activity was described by Smith by the image of the "invisible hand."[17]

Medick's statement plainly intimates an unanticipated order or system resulting from human purposive action. Society becomes "an objective context of activity." It constitutes an order or system that constrains the individual, and it is at the same time one that comes out of individual actions (whether they are by individuals or groups or organizations). And certainly what is true of society is true of economy. This recognition of social or economic order or system on Smith's part has been noted by numerous students. Viner goes so far as to say that "Smith's major claim to originality, in English economic thought, at least, was his detailed and elaborate application to the wilderness of economic phenomena of the unifying concept of a co-ordinated and mutually interdependent system of cause-and-effect relationships. . . ."[18] Glen R. Morrow correctly discerned in Smith's work what he called "an effort to think of the social order as a genuine organic unity, with principles of structure and functioning which maintain themselves independently of the wills of individuals."[19] Schumpeter proposes concisely that Smith held that "free interaction of individuals produces not chaos but an orderly pattern."[20]

It has also been noticed that Smith's work has some strong affinities with modern functional analysis in sociology. Smith was obviously clear on the distinction between subjective intent of action and its objective effect within a larger context or system, as he was aware of unintended "beneficent" contributions of individual actions to larger orders or systems and of sheer systemic interdependencies in social and economic phenomena. To note Smith's cognizance of these "functionalist" points is not to do violence to his thought, nor to deny he was a moral philosopher with a normative outlook on society, economy, and policy. It is not to suggest that being in his own way alert to order or system, he was thereby blind to change.[21] It is not to neglect or thrust aside the circumstance that various social arrangements could in some respects work excellently toward general welfare and in others work very deleteriously — a notable example being the division of labor, with its simultaneous enhancement of productivity and degradation of the labor force.[22]

In connection with the argument, stretching from limitations of rationality through unanticipated consequences and the cunning of reason to order or system, we would unequivocally affirm that the representation given of Smith's thought holds for *each* of his two main works— *The Wealth of Nations* and *The Theory of Moral Sentiments.*

It is rather curious that Medick should observe that "one must certainly acknowledge the correctness of A. L. Macfie's view that the importance of the 'invisible hand' principle for the total intention of Smith's social philosophy has been overestimated." Medick himself adds at once that Macfie's view "should not mislead us into denying altogether the . . . value of Smith's metaphor."[23] The importance of this arises from what we perceive as the crucial role of the notion of the invisible hand in *The Wealth of Nations* (as well as in the earlier work). In the model of society and economy, involving limited rationality and so on through order or system, the importance of the invisible hand "principle" would be hard to overestimate. We contend that the relative paucity of invisible hand phrasing in *The Wealth of Nations* is of minor importance. In any case, that volume contains at least three relevant references. There is the central invisible hand passage, where Smith writes of the individual's being "led by an invisible hand to promote an end which was no part of his intention" (p. 423). There is the prior, cognate statement:

> Every individual is continually exerting himself to find out the most advantageous employment for whatever capital he can command. It is his own advantage, indeed, and not that of the society, which he has in view. But the study of his own advantage naturally, or rather necessarily leads him to prefer that employment which is most advantageous to the society [p. 421].

If Smith does not actually say "invisible hand" here, it is of purely verbal significance that he does not; and the same is true of the following assertion that appears later:

> Without any intervention of law . . . the private interests and passions of men naturally lead them to divide and distribute the stock of every society, among all the different employments carried on in it, as nearly as possible in the proportion which is most agreeable to the interest of the whole society [pp. 594-95].

The invisible hand thus intervenes or mediates between limited self-interest and general welfare. It effects an *Ausgleich,* a balancing or smoothing out as it works within an economic or social scheme to co-ordinate human actions and make them come out a certain way without human intention. Smith was not so naive as to think that the invisible hand is omnipresent and omnipotent or that it is at work under any social or economic circumstances at all. What is central here is that it refers to what one may call *conversion mechanisms*— which operate precisely (with particular reference to the economic sphere) to convert private interest into public welfare and which have an indispensable place in the model, stretching from limitations of rationality to order or system (on which we have been insistent). Hollander illustrates well enough what is meant by a conversion mechanism and at the same time gives special credit to Smith for his treatment of the particular mechanism illustrated.

> The crucial mechanism in the process of adjustment which assures that the prices of commodities will in fact be "continually gravitating" or "constantly tending towards" their respective cost prices is the tendency toward an equality of the returns to labour, capital and land respectively in different activities. The harshest critics of Smithian value theory concede that his treatment in this regard represents a substantial achievement. For Smith explicitly recognized that resources are transferred individually from less to more remunerative uses until an equality across the board is achieved. . . .[24]

This mechanism has its evident starting point in the striving for advantage on the market. Smith could not foresee various theoretical refinements and highly sophisticated questions bearing on what Hollander thus suggests. His awareness of conversion mechanisms nevertheless provides a powerful constituent in the theoretical structure of *The Wealth of Nations*. In the sense of our interpretation, as the invisible hand refers to conversion mechanisms and fits as it does into the model from limited rationality on, it becomes utterly inadequate to conceive of the invisible hand (as some economists have done)[25] as being equivalent to self- interest. Aside from being inadequate or simply wrong, such an equating obscures fundamental theoretical similarities between *The Wealth of Nations* and *The Theory of Moral Sentiments*. (It is still possible that Smith was too optimistic about the invisible hand, even if he was not hopelessly naive about it.)

LIMITATIONS OF RATIONALITY AND A CERTAIN INCOMPLETENESS IN SMITH'S THOUGHT

Near the beginning of this essay reference was made to a certain incompleteness in Smith's thought, which has to do with the matter of rationality. Attention to this will bring us a little closer to a rounded treatment of Smith on human nature and social circumstance.

Not only does man (for Smith) have limited rationality in the sense of an intrinsically limited insight and foresight but further constraints on his rationality are created by the pressure of various motivations that diminish economic rationality in particular. This actually raises some problems of analysis of rationality in its economic contexts that cannot be faced here in their full complexity. But we note some relevant tendencies in Smith's thought. That he himself thought he discerned constraints on economic rationality arising from motivational sources other than inherent limitations of human capacity to see and foresee is beyond question. Among the most important of these motivational sources is that represented by vanity.

Vanity had caught Smith's attention early, and he evidently devoted considerable thought to it. He asks, in *The Theory of Moral Sentiments,* whence arises "that emulation which runs through all the different ranks of men, and what are the advantages which we propose by that great purpose of human life which we call bettering our condition?" He answers, "To be observed, to be attended to, to be taken notice of with sympathy, complacency, and approbation are all the advantages which we can propose to derive from it. It is the vanity, not the ease, or the pleasure, which interests us. . . ."[26] That this point struck Smith forcibly is suggested by the repetition we find in *The Wealth of Nations:*

> With the greater part of rich people, the chief enjoyment of riches consists in the parade of riches, which in their eye is never so complete as when they appear to possess those decisive marks of opulence which nobody can possess but themselves. In their eyes the merit of an object which is in any degree either useful or beautiful, is greatly enhanced by its scarcity, or by the great labour which it requires to collect any considerable quantity of it, a labour which nobody can afford to pay but themselves [p. 172].

Smith sees numerous social and economic phenomena he did not particularly admire or approve, but his peculiar outlook often allows them a sort of redemption because, even if they do not appear admirable, they perform some beneficent or useful "function" within a larger social or economic order, as we know. This is the sort of outlook with which he may approach vanity, riches, or the like. This was plain in *The Theory of Moral Sentiments* in any case. We recall how Smith there derives a general beneficence from a sort of aestheticism that makes attractive to one aspiring to riches the elaborate and idle machinery that caters to the desires of those who are actually rich. One may suspect from Smith's tone that he himself regarded this aestheticism as rather imbecilic. One might then think that this is the end of the matter and perhaps enjoy the contemplation of the ironic contrast (for Smith), whereby a vanity or an ostentation (or a "pointlessly" elaborate apparatus of want satisfaction) has useful social or economic effects. But we are not really at the end of the matter, for there is a strong hint that Smith also discerns a more powerful economically irrational element in vanity in particular and in the propensity of the rich to conspicuous consumption than this would suggest. Vanity and luxury may be economically damaging immediately *and* at the same time fail of a redeeming function in a larger economic context. A certain inconsistency or at any rate incompleteness in Smith's thought thus appears.

It is argued in *The Wealth of Nations* that "the high rate of profit seems every where to destroy that parsimony which in other circumstances is natural to the character of the merchant. When profits are high, that sober virtue seems to be superfluous, and expensive luxury to suit better the affluence of his situation" (p. 578). We are then told that the lapse of sober parsimony and attentiveness on the part of the members of higher economic strata affects the workman also, with further consequent economic damage. "If his employer is attentive and parsimonious, the workman is very likely to be so too; but if the master is dissolute and disorderly, the servant who shapes his work according to the pattern which his master prescribes to him, will shape his life too according to the example which he sets him" (p. 578).

All this occurs in the midst of one of Smith's critiques of monopoly and when he is not concerned with a general assessment of the functions of riches or affluence. Yet it seems fair to recognize a tendency on Smith's part to see luxury as "expensive," as breaking down "economic virtues" of parsimony and attentiveness, and thereby of ultimately diminishing wealth. The tone about "luxury" is now not the same as when it was conceived (as evidently it was in *The Theory of Moral Sentiments*) to redound to the general benefit. Assuming the rationality of productivity and accumulation as goals, high profits can apparently have an economically irrational effect by way of their destruction or mitigation of "economic virtues." And it also seems clear that high profits need not spread general economic benefit. "Have the exorbitant profits of the merchants of Cadiz and Lisbon augmented the capital of Spain and Portugal? Have they alleviated the poverty, have they promoted the industry of those two beggarly countries?" (p. 578). Apparently, for Smith, to ask these questions was to answer them. On the motivational side, the desire for wealth can actually interfere with the thrust of the "economic virtues." Man's rationality would then appear to be mitigated not only because his vision and foresight and grasp of social or economic wholes or systems are limited but also because "properly" productive and "soberly" accumulative propensities are blocked and inhibited by vanity and the attraction of "luxury."

Is there perhaps a radical disjunction between *The Theory of Moral Sentiments* and *The Wealth of Nations*? And was Smith indeed grievously inconsistent? It seems more sensible to contend that his scheme of thought was incompletely worked out. There is something to be said for *both* his perspectives on vanity, riches, and luxury. But a really thoroughgoing analysis of human rationality and its limitations, together with its social ann economic effects and correlates, Smith did not in the end give us, despite his ingenious work on this line.

It is possible that Smith did not give the ideally full analysis he might have partly because he was torn between two inclinations. On the one hand, there was an aversion to conspicuous consumption and "luxury" and the impairment of the "economic virtues," which provoked a negative inclination. On the other hand, there was Smith's perception of the possibility of a rich economic development of what psychologists have called functional autonomy, which provoked a more positive inclination (although Smith still had his suspicions of wealth and the wealthy).

Where functional autonomy of motives comes about, one pursues an object for one set of motives but produces a result that brings into play another new set of motives, which are then followed.[27] If men strive for gain or wealth with a view to employing it for originally quite delimited wants, it is still nevertheless true that wants can strongly expand once accumulation is sufficient to permit it (and when cultural barriers are removed). One strives for gain for one use or reason, but once gain is present in sufficient quantity it occasions new strivings for different uses or reasons. This may result in highly creative endeavors and the generation of remarkable new commodities and services (although it may also get entangled with vanity or conspicuous consumption and corrupt industry, frugality, and the like).

This is not really a very airy speculation. It remains close to things we can read in Smith's two main books. But it is true that Smith is no great friend of personal wealth or its appurtenances (except of course as he may treat it in terms of the invisible hand). He writes readily of "the sober and industrious poor" (p. 823), but he has no parallel phrase suggestive of sympathy or compassion for the rich. Even when he writes of what we would today call social status or rank, which so easily attaches to wealth, his tone is not especially amiable. "Place," meaning status, is described by him as "that great object which divides the wives of aldermen." The language strikes one as at least mildly sardonic; then Smith goes on to say of "place" that it is "the end of half the labours of human life; and is the cause of all the tumult and bustle, all the rapine and injustice, which avarice and ambition have introduced into this world."[28]

HUMAN NATURE AND SOCIAL AND ECONOMIC HARMONY

With this somewhat larger view of Smith on the subject of rationality achieved, it is appropriate to consider him on the subject of human nature and social circumstance on another front—that of harmony in social and economic matters.

There is appreciable optimism in Adam Smith (particularly in the first of his two major books), but it is by no means unmixed with a certain pessimism. One need not penetrate far beneath the surface of those books to ascertain that in both Adam Smith is much concerned with the matter of processing and training or domesticating a creature about whom one cannot be unqualifiedly optimistic. Overton H. Taylor was struck by the contrast between Smith's view of humanity as set out in *The Theory of Moral Sentiments* and Freud's more somber one—if somber is not too euphemistic a term.[29] Yet even if one grants the relatively optimistic nature of *The Theory of Moral Sentiments,* there is still the patent suggestion that, after all, humans are potentially rather unruly creatures whom societies must hold within bounds.

How, then, are humans to be held within bounds so that a harmonious or orderly society may be possible? The use of the term "orderly" as a synonym for "harmonious" at this juncture has to do, not immediately with systemic interdependencies or the like, but with standards and arrangements whereby aggression is restrained or conflict and outright murder and the like are kept within strict limits. On the problem of harmony or order suggested in this sense, Smith addresses what has sometimes been called the Hobbesian problem.[30]

Man might be a volatile, extremely passionate, unreservedly self-interested being, puffed up with notions of his own importance. But the impartial spectator is present to control these tendencies. This is one of the great themes of *The Theory of Moral Sentiments*. The impartial spectator of one's actions and reflections exercises a crucial moderating influence. The story is familiar to the most casual reader of Smith. One wants to punish cruelly the relatively minor dereliction of another who has done a small damage to one's self. The spectator is there to indicate that social approbation of one's punitive tendency is likely only when it is very much softened. The really great triumph of the spectator is that he does not remain "external." He is very likely to be made part of the self. In language now often used, he is "internalized." Man carries "society" within himself, constitutes as part of his own self the broad generalized standards, judgments, and sentiments of others. The impartial spectator, Adam Smith's own treatment encourages us to say, has as his inner counterpart "the man within the breast."[31]

Here the connection of human nature with social circumstance is very evident. Human nature is not even conceivable on the terms on which it is actually encountered without the existence of the impartial spectator. Smith's social psychology already shows much sophistication. What we call conscience has important foundations in the impartial spectator. And it must at times go back to such foundations: "The man within the breast, the abstract and ideal spectator of our sentiments and conduct, requires often to be awakened and put in mind of his duty by the presence of the real spectator."[32] In important ways human nature is evoked by society, and it is sustained by society. One may even argue reasonably that, granted that conscience can exhibit highly individual elements and operate with its own distinctive norms (as Smith granted), the individuality and individual norms are still likely to have social roots or references. This seems to be the burden of the statement by a student of Adam Smith who remarks that "the love of self-approbation, which is in fact the same as the love of virtue, is still founded on an implied reference to the verdict of persons external to ourselves, and thus the 'still small voice' of conscience resolves into the acclamations of mankind."[33] If this statement should be judged too strong (and much depends on how one interprets it), it still makes a useful point.

It is neither necessary nor feasible to go to into detail here on the relation of the impartial spectator and conscience. Does the impartial spectator stand precisely for "the common consensus of the attitudes of the group," as Bitterman averred?[34] Does the spectator embody a norm "only in the sense of an average standard that emerges from the interplay of ordinary spectators and agents," as Campbell asserts?[35] How then does ideality, or ideal ethical judgment that in some sense transcends group norms, arise? These questions are beyond our present scope; it suffices to recognize the forthright contribution to the problem of harmony or order that Smith makes on the sociopsychological side, whatever we may decide about various particulars of his relevant conceptions.

In regard to what is necessary for social harmony or order, again, Smith does hold in *The Theory of Moral Sentiments* that society may subsist "from a sense of its utility" and without mutual love and affection. "Society may subsist, though not in the most comfortable state, without beneficence," but justice it must have, for "the prevalence of injustice must utterly destroy it."[36] Certainly, various social arrangements are possible on a basis of justice alone, but it is probably best not to press Smith too far on the matter and ask whether "a whole society" such as that of a large nation could really subsist with justice alone. Let us not strain his meaning, which is perhaps clear enough for his purposes at the point in *The Theory of Moral Sentiments* where he introduces these observations. What is important is that it seems unlikely, on Smith's general analysis, that powerful foundations for justice without support from the impartial spectator could exist.

But what about *The Wealth of Nations?* It may seem true that the impartial spectator is not in the premises of that book. Bitterman observes, "In the *Wealth of Nations* the impartial spectator puts in no appearance, unless perhaps Smith cast himself in that role."[37] (Bitterman adds that the ethical assumptions are essentially the same in Smith's two main works. And again Bitterman writes that "the disinterested spectator does not put in an appearance in the economic treatise" (although he now comments that "there is the same regard for common sentiment").[38]

In *The Wealth of Nations* the specific job of social psychology that Smith undertook in *The Theory of Moral Sentiments,* in the sense of seeking to trace group influences on the morality and conscience of the individual, is not continued. How then does he handle the matter of harmony, order, or control? Plainly, Smith did not favor unimpeded play for self-interest. A problem of harmony or order is just as much confronted in *The Wealth of Nations* as it is in *The Theory of Moral Sentiments.* A by no means altogether promising human nature must be subjected to social controls. That Smith did not favor unrestricted play of self-interest is one of the best known features of his work in *The Wealth of Nations.* Three things may be considered in this connection.

First, Bitterman's qualification to his own contention that the impartial spectator does not appear in the economic treatise has been noted ("unless perhaps Smith cast himself in that role"). This is not an unreasonable qualification or suggestion. And in this sense there certainly are echoes of the impartial spectator in *The Wealth of Nations.* Essential evidence for the point is given in Smith's numerous strong reservations about merchants and manufacturers. These men complain about the high wages that elevate prices, but not about the untoward effects of high profits. "They are silent with regard to the pernicious effects of their own gains." Who has not read or heard Smith's observation that "people of the same trade seldom meet together, even for merriment and diversion, but the conversation ends in a conspiracy against the public, or in some contrivance to raise prices"? Again, the dealers in any branch of manufacture in effect wish "to levy, for their own benefit, an absurd tax upon the rest of their fellow-citizens" (pp. 98, 128, 250). This is a mere sampling of such statements, for they recur frequently in *The Wealth of Nations* (e.g., pp. 428-29, 434, 438, 460-61, 565, 578). We may take it as a certainty that when Smith made the statement, "All for ourselves, and nothing for other people, seems in every age of the world to have been the vile maxim of the masters of mankind" (pp. 388-89), the more dubious ways of merchants and manufacturers were not far from his thought.[39]

Whether or not we wish to say in view of all these critical remarks that Smith himself is the impartial spectator in *The Wealth of Nations,* it seems fair to assert that he envisaged the possible results of social criticism of those who sought to disadvantage the public by monopoly or restraint of trade. Smith was entirely willing to make normative judgments on the economic order. No one with excessive scruples about such judgments could have written as he did about "pernicious effects of their own gains" or "an absurd tax" or "the vile maxim of the masters of mankind." If he is critical of these "masters," he is also capable of asking what he conceives to be justice for the "lower ranks of the people" — "It is but equity . . . that they who feed, cloath and lodge the whole body of the people, should have such a share of the produce of their own labour as to be themselves tolerably well fed, cloathed and lodged" (p. 79).

If the phrase "impartial spectator" is not used in *The Wealth of Nations,* the spectator *is* still on the premises. (Perhaps the largest concession one could make to Smith's failure to use the phrase in his later work is to speak of the *implicit spectator* there.)[40] It is simply not to be expected that the moral philosopher would cease to be at work in Smith when he turned to economic matters.[41]

It is quite accurate to contend that it is indeed control of economic appetite which Smith seeks. He wants restraint, not repression. There is justice in Macfie's observation, "To Mandeville, passions are evil. To Smith, they are natural, but to be duly restrained."[42] Mandeville's moral rigorism (assuming he really adheres to it) is not acceptable to Smith, nor is an older disposition to threaten the desire to make a buck with hell and damnation. The enterprise of buying and selling is not in itself an ineffable danger to the soul. The implicit spectator is critical only of certain kinds of excesses.

Second, there is the control or restraint exercised because the operations of the market economy are to take place within a government framework that establishes justice. "Every man, as long as he does not violate the laws of justice, is left perfectly free to pursue his own interest his own way. . . ." (p. 651). According to what Smith called "the system of natural liberty," the sovereign had three duties to perform — to protect a society from violence and invasion from other societies; to build and maintain certain public works; to provide "an exact administration of justice" or to protect all from injustice and oppression, as far as possible (p. 651). Unbridled assertion of self-interest would evidently be checked; and the checking could combine with social criticism, so that properly hedged and bounded self-interest might work toward general benefit.

Third, we come again to the invisible hand. Government administration of justice, aided by the force of social criticism, modifies the power of deep impulses of human nature that carry a large potential of selfishness and scorn for mankind. (We accept here Smith's premises and raise no question about the "real sources" of selfishness.) With movement away from monopoly, we must move toward perfect competition and equilibrium prices. The ordinary material of self-interest changes into the golden metal of general welfare by the familiar paradoxical action of the invisible hand. Moreover, intimate connection of two senses of "order" is suggested. For the order that is synonymous with harmony and the result of legal and other norms or standards also produces a "factual" order. It does so in the sense of creating uniformities and predictabilities in conduct insofar as there is actual conformity to standards. It does so in the sense of preparing the way for emergence of a scheme that takes up minuscule human intentions and actions, shaping them by a kind of juxtaposition and synthesis into a larger systemic whole.

All this unquestionably has an "ideal" aspect. Smith knew very well that things do not always work out thus. To say that he envisaged problems of harmony does not entail the preposterous view that he saw no social or economic conflict or disorder. His preoccupation with harmony or order arose out of a clear perception of disharmonies and a sense for potential disturbances. Certainly, the notion of class conflict was not foreign to him. Some also may be embarrassed by the evidence he would appear to give of partiality toward what he called "the martial spirit" (see, e.g., p. 738).

SOCIAL SITUATION AND MOTIVE

These remarks were begun with observations of Smith's need to be understood in a larger context than that of his economics alone; indeed, his economics is not properly understandable without considering a larger context. A final look at certain of Smith's sociological views will be in accordance with the spirit of the prior observations and will once again connect human nature and social circumstance, as we consider relations between situation and motive.

Man's intimate involvement in society and the inseparability of human nature therefrom are certainly indicated in the theory of the impartial spectator, but in Smith's view involvement in society runs further. For Smith sees motivation in the broadest terms (and much of habit and perception) as bound up with social circumstance.

For present purposes we utilize somewhat loose terms like "institution" or indeed the convenient broad term "social situation" to refer generally to social circumstances "surrounding" the individual and shaping his motivations, habits, or perceptions. Economists have been partial to "institution," and this is understandable in view of the "sociological" bias of so-called institutionalists in economics. Nathan Rosenberg touches on the major theme of this portion of our remarks on Smith on human nature and social circumstance when he refers to Smith's concern with whether human institutions were so contrived or structured as to move self-interest to work for the general welfare.[43] Rosenberg recognized Smith's perception of the nexus between situation and motive and referred to the aptly illustrative passage in *The Wealth of Nations* where Smith, after criticizing self-aggrandizing behavior on the part of servants of the East India Company, comments:

> I mean not . . . to throw any odious imputation upon the general character . . . of the East India Company, and much less upon that of any particular persons. It is the system of government, *the situation in which they are placed,* that I mean to censure; not the character of those who have acted in it. *They acted as their situation naturally directed,* and they who have clamoured the loudest against them would, probably, not have acted better themselves [pp. 605–6; emphasis added].

Human beings have their potentials, and potentials of one kind or another are made actual by surrounding circumstance, saliently including social circumstance. Men may be encouraged to seek their self-interest in a way conformable to general welfare, or they may not. It is not that there is indefinite or unrestricted malleability, and we believe Smith assumes strong common components of human nature for all mankind. Discussing certain demographic phenomena, he writes, "The laws of nature are the same everywhere, the laws of gravity and attraction the same, and why not the laws of generation?"[44] Had it not been for his particular preoccupation of the moment, he might as well have said, "and why not the laws whereby motives are evoked, habits formed, and perception influenced?" But within a common framework of human nature, variations are certainly possible, and social situations influence them profoundly. The influence of custom alone on mankind is great.

One pertinent set of observations in *The Theory of Moral Sentiments* may be noted before we return to *The Wealth of Nations.* Contrasting the civilized with those he called savages and barbarians, Smith remarks, "The general security and happiness which prevail in ages of civility and politeness afford little exercise to the contempt of danger, to patience in enduring labour, hunger, and pain." And a little farther on: "Among savages and barbarians it is quite otherwise."[45] The discussion that follows shows Smith's sensitivity to the connection of the situation of the "civilized" person and the "savage" or "barbarian" with the character and propensities of each. Smith even writes, "The different *situations* of different ages and countries are apt . . . to give different characters to the generality of those who live in them. . . ."[46] (Emphasis added.)

Consider something from a quite different context. Smith observes:

> To improve land with profit, like all other commercial projects, requires an exact attention to small savings and small gains, of which a man born to a great fortune, even though naturally frugal, is very seldom capable. The *situation* of such a person naturally disposes him to attend rather to ornament which pleases his fancy, than to profit for which he has so little occasion [p. 364; emphasis added].

Or we may once more refer to Smith on the subject of slavery. It is the slave's social and economic situation that explains his motivation as a worker. As stressed before, in Smith's conception the slave reacts rationally to his situation; but it is precisely to his *situation* that he so reacts. Referring to a pertinent passage in which Smith speaks of habits in relation to social situation, we find him comparing merchants with country gentlemen in respect to improving land—when merchants develop an interest on these lines. As we might expect, Smith argues that the merchant concerned with land improvement is the better improver: "The habits . . . of order, economy and attention, *to which mercantile business naturally forms a merchant,* render him much fitter to execute, with profit and success, any project of improvement" (p. 385). (Emphasis added.)

Consider perhaps the most striking relevant example of all. Now we deal with situational constraints that shape perception, consciousness, or understanding. We come in this context to Smith's famous conception of the adverse side of the division of labor—its effects upon the common people:

> In the progress of the division of labour, the employment of the far greater part of those who live by labour, that is, of the great body of the people, comes to be confined to a few very simple operations, frequently to one or two. *But the understandings of the greater part of men are necessarily formed by their ordinary employments.* The man whose whole life is spent in performing a few simple operations, of which the effects too are, perhaps, always the same, or very nearly the same, has no occasion to exert his understanding . . . [p. 734; emphasis added].[47]

It is hoped that it will not be anticlimactic, in view of the importance of Smith's speculations on the unhappy side of the division of labor, to allude briefly, in this array of cases, to a last item—that represented by professors, for they also act responsively to their situations. This was the clear conviction of a one-time professor of moral philosophy at the University of Glasgow, who observed that "in every profession, the exertion of the greater part of those who exercise it is always in proportion to the necessity they are under of making that exertion" (p. 717).

The nexus of social situation and motivation holds for Adam Smith's early occupation too, and he does not hesitate to say so. Greater integrity hath no man. Or was Adam Smith highly motivated to give expression to a disgruntlement with the teaching he had received as a youth at Oxford, which indeed he suggests in *The Wealth of Nations?*

CONCLUSION

Much of the considerable work that Adam Smith accomplished can be glimpsed through a view of his notions regarding human nature and social circumstance. What we see is not invariably satisfying; we must be particularly wary in Smith's case lest his appearance be distorted. It is notorious that he has been too readily twisted by many eager to apologize for a status quo, just as (in my view) he has been too readily seen by others as having strong affinities with Marxism. But if one tries to see Smith in as honest and unprejudiced a fashion as possible, perhaps it is well to say something like this: Of course he has his limitations. His is not the most powerful analytical mind that has appeared in economics or social science at large. It would be futile to turn back to him on the notion that one would thereby find shining remedies for the numerous shortcomings of the social sciences now sharply (even too sharply) proposed by their critics. "New and engaging perspectives" (as said in beginning) one might find in him, but resounding answers to the problems of the social sciences today: hardly. Yet when this is acknowledged, much about Smith still suggests the master builder. He still stands up as a figure eminently worth revisiting, for his achievement is such as to kindle or rekindle in those who return a faith in the social science enterprise itself.

NOTES

1. Overton H. Taylor, *Economics and Liberalism* (Cambridge: Harvard Univ. Press, 1955), p. 92. In connection with arguments about the mutual consistency of Smith's two major works, it is worth having Mossner's reminder: "Let us not forget that Adam Smith had seen through the press the Fourth edition of the *Theory of Moral Sentiments* in 1774 and, after the publication of the *Wealth of Nations* in 1776, the Fifth in 1781 and the Sixth, that greatly revised and enlarged edition, in 1790. Clearly, the ethical values of the first book were in his mind until the very end." (Only the ethical values?) See Ernest C. Mossner, *Adam Smith: The Biographical Approach* (Glasgow: Univ. Glasgow Press, 1969), p. 17. Our approach to Smith and our bias that *The Wealth of Nations* and *The Theory of Moral Sentiments* are basically quite consistent rest also on the easily supported notion that these books are portions of a larger work of social science that Adam Smith never completed and that would have had something of a unitary character. The relationship of the two actually completed portions to one another is expressed thus by Meek: "The more narrowly economic views of the *Wealth of Nations* have usually been emphasized at the expense of the general sociological system of which they were essentially a part. The elements of that sociological system can, indeed, be easily enough detected in the *Wealth of Nations* . . . but for a more complete outline of it we have to go to Smith's *Glasgow Lectures* and to his *Theory of Moral Sentiments.*" See Ronald L. Meek, *Economics and Ideology and Other Essays* (London: Chapman and Hall, 1967), p. 35. (Smith's *Lectures* are given only incidental attention in this essay but we would still subscribe to Meek's statement by and large.) Or one may say that the ultimately unitary character of Smith's main works would be suggested by their emergence from the common matrix of moral philosophy and natural law. Among older writings on this subject, Hasbach remains outstanding. See Wilhelm Hasbach, *Untersuchungen über Adam Smith und die Entwicklung der Politischen Oekonomie* (Leipzig: Duncker and Humblot, 1891). Somewhat closer to our own day, Small is characterized by his special insistence that political economy for Smith was to be approached and understood against a background of moral philosophy and general sociological thought. See Albion W. Small, *Adam Smith and Modern Sociology* (Chicago: Univ. Chicago Press, 1907). A sense of the larger philosophical and social-science contexts of Smith's views in such areas as the economic has again been conveyed by Hans Medick, *Naturzustand und Naturgeschichte der bürgerlichen Gesellschaft* (Göttingen: Vandenhoeck and Ruprecht, 1973).

2. Paul Samuelson, Review of Hla Myint, *Theories of Welfare Economics, Economica* 16(Nov. 1949):371-74.

3. I am indebted for the reference to Samuelson's review made by Samuel Hollander, *The Economics of Adam Smith* (Toronto: Univ. Toronto Press, 1973), p. 14.

4. In intellectual history, also, it would be arbitrary to overlook the sometimes very significant consequences of men's ideas, which they did not themselves anticipate.

5. Grampp observes that "if he [Smith] was at all optimistic, it was only in thinking that the economic man — as frail as he was in understanding and frailer still in execution — still knew his interests better than his governor could know them, and in thinking that the economy would be better off if each individual looked after his interests in his own way" This possibly attributes too much "pessimism" to Smith, but that is incidental here. William D. Grampp, Adam Smith and the Economic Man, *J. Polit. Econ.* 56(Aug. 1948):336.

6. Adam Smith, *The Theory of Moral Sentiments* (New York: Kelley, 1966), p. 126.

7. Ibid., p. 110.

8. Ibid. German writers in the nineteenth century were keenly aware and appreciative of Smith's views as indicated in these quotations from *The Theory of Moral Sentiments*. Note the very pertinent and apt lines, quoted from Schiller and Goethe in Richard Zeyss, *Adam Smith und der Eigennutz* (Tübingen: H. Laupp'schen Buchhandlung, 1889), p. 115; and in Hasbach, *Untersuchungen*, p. 3. Schiller celebrates natural impulses (hunger and love) that maintain the mechanism of the world "before" philosophy can do so; Goethe affirms or approves "innocent drives," given by nature, which often irresistibly lead man to happy circumstances where "understanding and reason" cannot.

9. Robert K. Merton, The Unanticipated Consequences of Purposive Social Action, *Am. Sociol. Rev.* 1(Dec. 1936):894-904.

10. Note the parallel statement that "we cannot imagine" the division of labor to be "an effect of human prudence," in Adam Smith, *Lectures on Justice, Police, Revenue, and Arms,* E. Cannan, ed. (Oxford: Clarendon Press, 1896), p. 168. The matter of interest to us is just the having "in view" of "no such extensive utility," while to derive the division of labor from the "propensity" Smith appeals to is much too simple. See Robert M. MacIver, *Social Causation* (Boston: Ginn, 1942), pp. 315-16.

11. Smith, *Sentiments,* pp. 264-65.

12. Ibid., p. 263.

13. Ibid.

14. Just how important the teleological and, particularly, theological element here was to Adam Smith is notoriously a vexed question. One significant example of a statement on the matter that clearly seems to lean toward the view that Smith took the teleological and theological overtones of "the invisible hand" seriously is provided by Jacob Viner, *The Role of Providence in the Social Order* (Philadelphia: Am. Philosoph. Soc., 1972), pp. 81-82. An example of a quite different statement is provided by J. Ralph Lindgren, *The Social Philosophy of Adam Smith* (The Hague: Martinus Nijhoff, 1973), p. 148. Lindgren argues that Smith "embellished" *The Theory of Moral Sentiments* with phrases such as "the Director of Nature" by way of a "rhetorical strategem" designed to enlist assent for his views or "to obscure the unorthodoxy of his religious convictions." Bitterman argues that there is no direct evidence to connect the term, "invisible hand," in *The Wealth of Nations*, with the deity "since the preceding and following discussion proceed in purely economic terms." But in *The Theory of Moral Sentiments* the invisible hand reference is immediately followed by a sentence that refers to Providence. See Henry J. Bitterman, Adam Smith's Empiricism and the Law of Nature: II, *J. Polit. Econ.* 48(Oct. 1940):719. Our second guess is that the Adam Smith of *The Theory of Moral Sentiments* was only mildly pious and the Smith of *The Wealth of Nations* even less so. One must concede, however, that Smith did use pious language in *Sentiments*. We can often say justifiably that the core of his argument could be restated without the apparatus of piety, but it does not necessarily follow that the possibility of doing this would have appealed to Adam Smith.

15. Wilhelm Hasbach, *Die Allgemeinen Philosophischen Grundlagen der von François Quesnay und Adam Smith begründeten Politischen Oekonomie* (Leipzig: Duncker and Humblot, 1890), p. 153.

16. Overton H. Taylor, *A History of Economic Thought* (New York: McGraw-Hill, 1960), p. 70.

17. Medick, *Naturzustand,* p. 229.

18. Jacob Viner, *The Long View and the Short* (Glencoe: Free Press, 1958), p. 213.

19. J. M. Clark et al., *Adam Smith, 1776–1926* (New York: Kelley, 1966), pp. 171–72. Cf. also Glenn R. Morrow, *The Ethical and Economic Theories of Adam Smith* (New York: Kelley, 1969), pp. 41–43.

20. Joseph A. Schumpeter, *History of Economic Analysis* (Oxford: Oxford Univ. Press, 1954), p. 185. We have deliberately avoided use of the term "natural" or "natural order" in the present context. It is notorious that Adam Smith's own use of the word "natural" could be confusing. Thus: "Adam Smith misused the word 'natural.' Sometimes it meant in accordance with reason, sometimes in the natural course of things, sometimes corresponding to human nature, sometimes obvious, sometimes customary—and with this the task of a Smithian philology is still not exhausted." See Hasbach, *Grundlagen der Politischen Oekonomie*, p. 87.

21. He had much interest in social change, as indicated by his presentation of the rudiments of a theory of social evolution in *The Wealth of Nations*, p. 653ff. and in his *Lectures*, p. 14ff. That our representation of Smith's work is entirely compatible with the interest in social evolution and "progress" he also had is well indicated by Duncan Forbes, "Scientific Whiggism": Adam Smith and John Millar, *Cambridge J.* 7(Aug. 1954):643–70, esp. 651.

22. See p. 63. On the affinity of Smith's work with functional analysis, see Louis Schneider, ed. *The Scottish Moralists on Human Nature and Society* (Chicago: Univ. Chicago Press, 1967), Introduction; and T. D. Campbell, *Adam Smith's Science of Morals* (Totowa, N. J.: Rowan and Littlefield, 1971), esp. pp. 69–79.

23. Medick, *Naturzustand*, p. 231.

24. Hollander, *Economics of Smith*, p. 120. We must not be understood to wish to confine the meaning of conversion mechanisms to mechanisms that convert self-interest into public good within an economic context, but this point will not be discussed further.

25. For example, Bitterman, Adam Smith's Empiricism: II, p. 719.

26. Smith, *Sentiments*, pp. 70–71.

27. Smith's sense for functional autonomy is pointed out by Lindgren, *Social Philosophy*, pp. 40, 75. Note the suggestiveness in this connection of these comments in *The Theory of Moral Sentiments*; "Bring him [man] into society, and all his own passions will immediately become the causes of new passions. He will observe that mankind approve of some of them, and are disgusted by others. He will be elevated in the one case, and cast down in the other; his desires and aversions, his joys and sorrows, will now often become the causes of new desires and new aversions, new joys and new sorrows: they will now, therefore, interest him deeply, and often call upon his most attentive consideration" (pp. 162–63).

28. Ibid., p. 80.

29. Taylor, *History*, p. 72.

30. See Talcott Parsons, *The Structure of Social Action* (New York: McGraw-Hill, 1937) p. 89ff. Given the concern of this essay with this problem, it is worth remarking that, whatever the merits of the recent argument by Giddens that Parsons' stress on the high importance of the problem in the work of outstanding modern sociologists (especially Durkheim) is unjustified and actually nourishes a "myth," I do not see how there can be any doubt whatever about the centrality of the problem for the thought of Adam Smith. See Anthony Giddens, Classical Social Theory and the Origins of Modern Sociology, *Am. J. Sociol.* 81(Jan. 1976):703–29.

31. Thus: "The *representative* of the impartial spectator, the man within the breast." (Emphasis added.) Smith, *Sentiments*, p. 314. Smith's social psychology has aroused interest far outside the ranks of economists and philosophers. For a significant comparison of Smith with Freud on certain points, and going beyond the noting of a general contrast such as that by Overton H. Taylor, see R. F. Brissenden, Authority, Guilt and Anxiety in the *Theory of Moral Sentiments, Tex. Stud. Lang. Lit.* 11(Summer 1969):945–62. A comparison of Smith's work with that of others, such as the social psychologist George Herbert Mead, can be equally illuminating.

32. Smith, *Sentiments*, p. 216.

33. J. A. Farrar, *Adam Smith* (New York: G. P. Putnam's Sons, 1881), p. 77.

34. Henry J. Bitterman, Adam Smith's Empiricism and the Law of Nature: I, *J. Polit. Econ.* 48(Aug. 1940):487–520.

35. Campbell, *Science of Morals*, p. 137.

36. Smith, *Sentiments*, pp. 124-25.
37. Bitterman, Smith's Empiricism; I, p. 520.
38. Bitterman, Smith's Empiricism: II, p. 728.
39. One should still not be misled about Smith's judgments on merchants and manufacturers, granted all the passion of his criticism of them. Smith *can* stress, as in his *Lectures*, that commerce and probity have certain connections. "A dealer," he observes, "is afraid of losing his character and is scrupulous in observing every engagement. When a person makes perhaps twenty contracts in a day, he cannot gain so much by endeavouring to impose on his neighbours, as the very appearance of a cheat could make him lose." Again: "When the greater part of people are merchants, they always bring probity and punctuality into fashion, and these, therefore, are the principal virtues of a commercial nation." See Smith, *Lectures*, pp. 253-55.
40. Zeyss suggests that one might summarize Smith's views on the morality of conduct in the "practical" imperative: "So act that the impartial spectator is able to sympathize with the motive and with the tendency of your action." See Zeyss, *Adam Smith*, p. 52. Our argument would be that this imperative is, at the least, clearly implied even in *The Wealth of Nations*.
41. For example, see August Oncken, *Adam Smith and Immanuel Kant* (Leipzig: Duncker and Humblot, 1877), pp. 35-36.
42. A. L. Macfie, *The Individual in Society: Papers on Adam Smith* (London: Allen and Unwin, 1967), p. 81.
43. Nathan Rosenberg, Some Institutional Aspects of the *Wealth of Nations*, *J. Polit. Econ.* 68(Dec. 1960):557-70.
44. Smith, *Lectures*, p. 83.
45. Smith, *Sentiments*, p. 297.
46. Ibid., p. 296.
47. Cf. Smith, *Wealth*, pp. 734-36, 127; and *Lectures*, pp. 255-57. For all the interest in Smith's views on the sociopsychological effects of the division of labor, they are only briefly developed by him. Smith's student John Millar offers some elaboration in *An Historical View of the English Government*, vol. 4 (London: J. Mawman, 1818), pp. 138-61.

II Intellectual and Historical Background

5

Historical Dimension of
The Wealth of Nations

🍃 SAMUEL HOLLANDER

ECONOMIC THEORY AND HISTORY

Since the publication of the *Principles of Political Economy* in 1817, it has been common to read of a sharp breakaway by Ricardo from Smithian methodology. An early statement of the contrast discerned is by Simonde de Sismondi, who compared Smith's view of political economy as *"une science d'expérience"* with Ricardo's speculations.[1] Statements to much the same effect appear in two important new works on classical economics.[2]

The presumed contrast between Smithian and Ricardian procedures is frequently related to Smith's place within the Scottish historical school (a group that includes Adam Ferguson, William Robertson, and John Millar), whose members, it is said, "were concerned to base their social and economic generalizations on firm historical facts, and were opposed to abstract speculation and conjecture."[3] More generally, it has been observed that "the idea of the progress of society can be described as the historical frame of reference of the *Wealth of Nations.*"[4] There is no comparable dimension in Ricardo's *Principles.*

On our reading of the primary literature, the sharp contrast between a Smithian empirical-historical approach and a Ricardian hypothetical-deductive approach is invalid. Ricardo's procedures were derived from a pattern formulated by Smith.

Smith's main objective in *The Wealth of Nations* was the formulation of a reform program on the basis of an analytical model of the operation of a capitalist exchange economy. More specifically, he wished to demonstrate the adverse effects upon development of distortions in resource allocation due to a variety of contemporary policies and institutions that remained in force without the justification they might once have had. At the same time he also isolated contemporary institutions that had a favorable effect on growth. The understanding of the *origins* of such in-

---

Samuel Hollander is Professor of Economics, University of Toronto, Canada.

stitutions could only be appreciated in terms of a historical account; here we discern a fundamental function of the historical dimension of *The Wealth of Nations.* Smith engaged not merely in description of the historical record as he understood it — particularly the transition from an agricultural system (entailing a *service* nexus) to a mixed system (entailing a *money* nexus) — but also in interpretation. Both the theme and the principles involved in its interpretation — namely, a materialistic conception of history and a general notion of the temporal priority of agriculture over commerce during the course of "normal" development — were characteristic of the Scottish historical literature. But two points require emphasis. The historical analysis is best viewed as a digression; since the recommendations for the reform of actual institutions and policies (the statement of which constitutes the prime objective of *The Wealth of Nations*) are based upon a rather precise analytical model of the "progress of society" applicable to a competitive capitalist exchange economy. The model of development used in this context is a classic example of hypothetical-deductive theorizing and cries out for mathematical formulation. (A second prime example of such method in *The Wealth of Nations* is the theory of value and distribution, which is in some respects even more important from the point of view of its influence on nineteenth-century thought.) At the same time it must be emphasized that there is no clash between the stadial sequence discerned by the Scottish historical school (aspects of which are to be found in *The Wealth of Nations*) and that entailed in the Smithian analytical model, although the latter is designed for the analysis of economic process in the final stage and stands on its own feet independent of the Scottish procedures.[5]

Inquiry into the origins of contemporary institutional arrangements was one major function of the historical investigation in *The Wealth of Nations.* A second function concerns the behavioral axiom. The theoretical models of *The Wealth of Nations* were based squarely on the behavioral assumptions characterizing "economic man," for the proposition that self-interest is the governing motive throughout time and space as far as it concerns man in his economic affairs is Smith's fundamental axiom. But the scope for the various constituent elements incorporated within "self-interested" motivation varies considerably according to the institutional framework, and for this proposition Smith sought evidence from the record. Smith went to great lengths to build up, from both contemporary and historical evidence, the self-interested patterns of behavior for which there is scope in a capitalist exchange society. The essence of his position turns upon an environmental approach to behavior, and this too is characteristic of the Scottish historians. The effort to provide a sound empirical basis for at least certain aspects of the premise can be easily documented.

In what follows we develop in some detail the nature of the historical dimension of *The Wealth of Nations.* Particular attention will be paid to the perspectives characteristic of the Scottish historical school. The basis for Smith's premise of self-interest is discussed by the author elsewhere.[6]

THE HISTORICAL DIMENSION

Two of the fundamental propositions discerned in the literature as common to the Scottish historical school are that the mode of subsistence existing at any time determines the legal and institutional framework and that a causal connection exists between property relationships and the nature and degree of government authority. These propositions combined with a standard position regarding the uniformity of the human constitution (in which self-love coupled with an environmental approach to behavior plays a large role) were applied in an investigation of historical progress. The focus of the investigation was the nature of social progress, envisaged in terms of the development of the productive forces through four main stages — an initial primitive stage of hunting succeeded by stages of pasturage, agriculture, and commerce (the exchange economy) — generating a process of constant change in civil society.[7]

There is much new evidence regarding the extent of Smith's contribution to the historical-sociological tradition.[8] Nevertheless, although it is true that characteristics of the Scottish approach may be detected in *The Wealth of Nations,* and in some specific contexts are even the focus of attention, the work as a whole is not governed by the tradition.[9]

In the first place, the transfer from a simple or "rude" to a complex or "civilized" economy involving private property in land and the accumulation of stock is glossed over at key junctures. This approach does not suggest a keen interest in the early stages of the Scottish developmental sequence. For example, it is sometimes implied that the advantages of specialization and the necessary capital accumulation to support division of labor were potentially available in the simple economy: "Had this [simple] state continued, the wages of labour would have augmented with all those improvements in its productive powers, to which the division of labour gives occasion" (p. 64). At the same time Smith asserts that "this original state of things, in which the labourer enjoyed the whole produce of his own labour . . . was at an end . . . long before the most considerable improvements were made in the productive powers of labour, and it would be to no purpose to trace further what might have been its effects upon the recompence or wages of labour" (p. 65). Smith was by no means consistent regarding the proposition that it is only in the modern economy that the division of labor is applied, thus necessitating capital advances (p. 259).

The early stage is rapidly passed over and the nature of the transition is not examined carefully. Apart from the discussion in Book 5, the notion of a hunting stage is used largely as a fiction for analytical purposes rather than for its own sake as part of a treatment of historical development; the key historical facts relating to the institution of wage labor dependent upon the capitalist employer (as distinct from self-employed or independent labor) are not brought conspicuously to the reader's attention. Thus the fundamental fact, noted by Smith in Book 1, that "in every part of Europe, twenty workmen serve under a master for one that is independent . . ." (p. 66) is not accounted for, except perhaps by implication — and this despite a rather harsh evaluation of the system (reminiscent of Josiah

Tucker).[10] It would appear in fact that Smith's preoccupation was with the operation of an existing capitalist exchange economy—with the fourth stage, so to speak, of the stadial sequence, or more accurately a late period (or even the final period) of the fourth stage.[11]

Our conclusion is reinforced by reference to Book 3 itself, which is preoccupied with the transfer from an agricultural to an exchange economy, entailing the transition from a service nexus (dependency) wherein the authority of the dominant class derives from ownership of the means of subsistence to a cash nexus (independency), a theme truly characteristic of the historical school.

The temporal priority of agriculture, a theme consistent with the position of the Scottish historians, is justified briefly:

> As subsistence is, in the nature of things, prior to conveniency and luxury, so the industry which procures the former, must necessarily be prior to that which ministers to the latter. The cultivation and improvement of the country, therefore, which affords subsistence, must, necessarily, be prior to the increase of the town, which furnishes only the means of conveniency and luxury. It is the surplus produce of the country only, or what is over and above the maintenance of the cultivators, that constitutes the subsistence of the town, which can therefore increase only with the increase of this surplus produce. . . . If human institutions had never thwarted those natural inclinations, the towns could no-where have increased beyond what the improvement and cultivation of the territory in which they were situated could support; till such time, at least, as the whole of that territory was completely cultivated and improved.
>
> According to the natural course of things, therefore, the greater part of the capital of every growing society is, first, directed to agriculture, afterwards to manufactures, and last of all to foreign commerce. This order of things is so very natural, that in every society that had any territory, it has always, I believe, been in some degree observed. Some of their lands must have been cultivated before any considerable towns could be established, and some sort of coarse industry of the manufacturing kind must have been carried on in those towns, before they could well think of employing themselves in foreign commerce [pp. 357, 360].

But what must also be noted of the above extracts is the insufficient groundwork they provide for the "natural course of things."[12] Smith does not spend much time laying out the basis for the normal stadial sequence, and we cannot be sure that he had in mind in the present context a well-founded theory of the progress of society.[13] In any event, as we shall now see, in Book 3 he was largely concerned with the actual historical record, which entailed a distorted pattern of development, and sought for hypotheses to explain the record as he read it.

The breakdown of feudalism entailing a master-slave relation, (a primary issue in Book 3) and the growth of a metayer system are accounted for largely in terms of the self-interested behavior of landlords faced by altered objective conditions (rendering them increasingly unwilling to accept the inefficient slave system) coupled with pressure from the sovereign. The inefficiency of slave labor (compared with that of a metayer system) is in turn accounted for in terms of the effect of property ownership and income upon effort (pp. 365–67). A second fundamentally important historical phase is the transition from a metayer organization to one of tenant farming. While the sharecropper was induced to cultivate well with the stock provided by the landlord (in sharp contrast with the slave), it was not in his interest to save and invest his own capital since the landlord shared the produce (p. 368).[14]

The change in objective circumstances with which landlords were faced, according to Smith's account, involved the growth of manufacturing and commerce in the towns where the system of "villainage and slavery" was initially abolished in consequence of the self-interested action of the sovereign, who sought allies against the lords (p. 375). Much is then made of the relatively rapid development of the towns in consequence of the effects of "order and good government" upon effort (p. 379).

The effect of the growth of manufactures and foreign commerce to which we have alluded was the creation of a market for agricultural produce in exchange for luxury goods. Landlords were now motivated to increase their rents by way of altered tenure systems, even if it meant the surrender of some of their personal power: "What all the violence of the feudal institutions could never have effected, the silent and insensible operation of foreign commerce and manufacturers gradually brought about" (p. 388). An institutional framework came into being wherein the great proprietors were "insignificant," and "a regular government was established in the country as well as in the city, nobody having sufficient power to disturb its operations in the one, any more than in the other" (p. 391).[15]

Now the priority of the agricultural stage and the substitution of a cash for a service nexus (in effect the transition from the agricultural stage) are discussed by various members of the Scottish historical school such as John Millar and also by Sir James Steuart.[16] Nevertheless, the undermining of the authority of the great landlords by foreign commerce and manufactures is an insight attributed explicitly by Smith to Hume alone.[17] Moreover, and this is the point we wish to emphasize in particular, Smith's concern in *The Wealth of Nations* is with the distorted pattern of events that had occurred, that is to say the dependency of agricultural development upon the prior expansion of manufacturing and commerce, rather than the normal relationship: "It is thus that through the greater part of Europe the commerce and manufactures of cities, instead of being the effect, have been the cause and occasion of the improvement and cultivation of the country" (p. 392).[18] At least for Smith, the progress of society was certainly not inevitable, as implied by some accounts of the Scottish tradition.[19] It will also be observed that much is made of the "fortuitous" role played by individuals, particularly the "sovereigns," in contributing to the distortion of the natural stadial order; there is, in brief, no simple one-way relation from the mode of subsistence to institutions and governmental forms.[20]

Furthermore, there is much "reading back" into the historical record patterns of behavior envisaged in contemporary society, thus belying to some extent accounts of the historical school that emphasize a preoccupation with the real facts of history. Despite the overwhelming significance of the breakdown of feudalism, Smith himself conceded that "the time and manner . . . in which so important a revolution was brought about, is one of the most obscure points in modern history" (p. 367).[21]

It is appropriate to refer at this point to Dugald Stewart's celebrated description of "theoretical or conjectural history" (which is identified also with Hume's "natural history" and the French *histoire raisonnée*): "When we cannot trace the process by which an event *has been* produced, it is often of importance to be able to shew how it *may have been* produced by natural causes. . . . [The] mind is not only to a certain degree satisfied, but a check is given to that indolent philosophy, which refers to a miracle, whatever appearances, both in the natural and moral worlds, it is unable to explain."[22] Stewart's account may well be relevant as a description of Smith's procedures in Book 3 of *The Wealth of Nations.*[23]

Quite apart from the validity of the term "conjectural" history as a description of Smith's Book 3, the relative disinterest therein with the earlier stages of the Scottish stadial sequence and the preoccupation with the distorted pattern of development insofar as the later stages are concerned, imply that the incorporation of the materials into *The Wealth of Nations* was designed with an eye upon something other than the account of major historical transitions in terms of the standard stadial model. His objective is, in fact, clarified in an introductory note to the third and fourth books:

> In all the great countries of Europe, however, much good land still remains uncultivated, and the greater part of what is cultivated, is far from being improved to the degree of which it is capable. Agriculture, therefore, is almost every-where capable of absorbing a much greater capital than has ever yet been employed in it. What circumstances in the policy of Europe have given the trades which are carried on in towns so great an advantage over that which is carried on in the country, that private persons frequently find it more for their advantage to employ their capitals in the most distant carrying trades of Asia and America, than in the improvement and cultivation of the most fertile fields in their own neighbourhood, I shall endeavour to explain at full length in the two following books [p. 355].

Smith thus chose to incorporate the historical materials of Book 3 (older than most of *The Wealth of Nations*) into his general study to throw light upon contemporary institutions. History had left its mark on the modern states of Europe: "The manners and customs which the nature of their original government introduced, and which remained after that government was greatly altered, necessarily forced them into . . . [an] unnatural and retrograde order" (p. 360).

Smith had particularly harsh words for the law of primogeniture and the system of entails (archaic remnants of the feudal period), which encouraged the maintenance of great estates, the proprietors of which were notoriously poor improvers (p. 361ff.). The impediments constraining the creation of small estates had also reduced the supply of land offered for sale so that the price of land was extremely high, "a monopoly price" (pp. 392–93).[24] In England itself the distortions were less severe. The security of long leases characteristic of the English system of tenant farming (the origins of which Smith explains at length) and the independence and respect enjoyed by the class of farmers had profoundly influenced the national growth rate, compared at least to that of Continental Europe; it was "the laws and customs so favourable to the yeomanry, [which] have perhaps contributed more to the present grandeur of England, than all their boasted regulations of commerce taken together" (p. 369). But even in the English case, and certainly in the Scottish, there was much to be done to clear away the institutional debris. For example, while "the common law of England . . . is said to abhor perpetuities, and they are accordingly more restricted there than in any other European monarchy . . . even England is not altogether without them. In Scotland, more than one-fifth, perhaps more than one-third part of the whole lands of the country, are at present supposed to be under strict entail" (p. 363).[25] Thus, while British agriculture had "no doubt" advanced since the reign of Elizabeth—when the legislature began to be "peculiarly attentive to the interests of commerce and manufactures"—it had followed "slowly, and at a distance, the more rapid progress of commerce and manufactures," and the cultivation of "the far greater part," of the country remained "much inferior to what it might be" (p. 393). Yet agricultural progress might have been much slower: "What would it have been, had the law given no direct encouragement to agriculture besides what arises indirectly from the progress of commerce, and had left the yeomanry in the same condition as in most other countries of Europe" (p. 394)?

There is, we conclude, historical dimension to *The Wealth of Nations,* in some respects characteristic of the Scottish historical school. The historical work is interesting in its own right but (as far as Smith's objectives in *The Wealth of Nations*) mainly because it strengthens the understanding of the contemporary exchange economy. This observation applies to the institutional arrangements Smith fought to have disbanded and to those institutions favorable to growth, the roots of both of which were to be found in past ages. (It also applies, it may be shown, to the analysis of the relationship between the constant behavioral motive of "self-interest" and the institutional and legal framework within which the "economic man" operates.)

Yet once the basic framework relevant for a capitalist exchange system had been constructed, the historical scaffolding was no longer formally essential and could be removed. We refer now to Smith's use of an analytical model of investment priorities over time in making his case for the abandonment of various institutional arrangements. This conclusion is further reinforced by the Smithian analysis of the theory of value-and-distribution as applied to contemporary policy issues. Here the historical dimension fades away completely. Nor is this surprising, for the Scottish historical writers had little to offer on the mechanisms at work within an already well-developed capitalist exchange economy.

THE FOUNDATION OF SMITH'S REFORM PROGRAM

The model of investment priorities turns upon the fundamental proposition regarding profit-maximizing behavior on the part of the capitalist ("the consideration of his own private profit"), which Smith actually states (too hastily on his own grounds) to be "the sole motive which determines the owner of any capital to employ it either in agriculture, in manufactures, or in some particular branch of the wholesale or retail trade" (p. 355).[26] Precisely in this context we find the most celebrated statements of the operation of economic man (and the consistency of private and public interests).[27] It is on the basis of this behavioral assumption regarding profit-maximizing motivation—taking for granted a capitalistic form of environment combined with assumptions relating to the changes over time in the productive factor base (relating particularly to the land-labor and the capital-labor ratios)—that Smith constructed his rather sophisticated theory of the secular pattern of development.[28]

Smith's primary concern was, we believe, the economic development of contemporary Britain (defined in terms of real national income per capita); his objective, it would appear, was to demonstrate that reliance upon the operation of the competitive mechanism of resource allocation within a suitable institutional framework would assure the maximization at any time of the national income generated by community resources. Society could thereby most effectively provide the means for a rapid rate of capital accumulation (and thus satisfactory living standards for the common people) and allow for the financing of government services. The argument proceeds in terms of a model of economic process, that is to say a mutually interdependent system of cause and effect relationships, appropriate for a capitalistic form of organization.[29] The analysis extends far beyond a demonstration of the nonchaotic nature of the competitive price mechanism in a static context, for it encompasses the effects of differential factor proportions upon the pattern of activity and applies the principle to the issue of investment priorities over time. Smith's system can thus be construed as a model of capitalistic economic process in a developmental context designed to elucidate the interrelations between apparently disparate variables upon the basis of a small number of fundamental principles.

But the model was not devised for its own sake (although doubtless it satisfied an aesthetic taste, the *esprit de rationalité* of which so much is made in the "Essay on Astronomy"). The model was used to interpret the observed differentials between the growth rates and patterns of resource allocation of the North American colonies and those of various European countries.[30] It also served for prediction of the probable future course of

American development under alternative imperial regulations. The main function of the entire construct, however, was to provide an ideal pattern against which actual European and British progress could be measured and thus to discern the steps required to correct divergencies from the norm. The analysis of investment patterns in an established exchange system characterized by capitalistic institutions provides the model of the "progress of society" used as the basis for the "very violent attack . . . upon the whole commercial system of Great Britain," as Smith himself describes *The Wealth of Nations.*[31]

We do not intend to suggest that Smith contributed nothing in *The Wealth of Nations* to the materialist conception of history characteristic of the Scottish school. His account of the breakdown of feudalism and the development of a commercial system (the materials of Book 3) rules out any such extreme position. Moreover, Book 5 is in part devoted to what Smith referred to as the general principles of law and government and the revolutions they had undergone in different periods of society. Our proposition relates to the conceptual framework accounting for secular development patterns used as the basis for recommendations regarding policy reform, Smith's predominant concern. This is provided, not by a structure such as the four stages theory, but by the model we have outlined above, which takes for granted capitalistic institutions and a fully developed exchange system and proceeds to outline "the natural progress of opulence" within such a framework.[32]

NOTES

1. G. Sotiroff, ed., *Nouveaux Principes d'Economie Politique,* vol. 1 (2nd ed., 1827; Geneva: Edition Jeheber, 1951), pp. 69-70.
2. D. P. O'Brien, *The Classical Economists* (Oxford: Oxford Univ. Press, 1975), p. 67. For a detailed account of Smithian procedure along these lines see Henry J. Bitterman, Adam Smith's Empiricism and the Law of Nature: I, *J. Polit. Econ.* 68(Aug. 1940):487-520, esp. 500-502. Bitterman maintains that "Adam Smith's methodology was essentially empirical, deriving its inspiration from Newton and Hume, in contrast to the rationalistic method of the natural-law school of thought" (ibid. p. 497). See also Thomas Sowell, *Classical Economics Reconsidered* (Princeton: Princeton Univ. Press, 1974), pp. 113-14.
3. O'Brien, *Classical Economists,* pp. 66-67. See also A. L. Macfie, *The Individual in Society* (Glasgow: Allen and Unwin, 1967), pp. 29-30. Here very great weight is placed upon the philosophic, historical, and sociological dimensions of Smithian economics—a "synthetic," in contrast to the modern or "analytical," approach. Those writing in the Scottish tradition "are not concerned with logical processes or sequences, or the framing of abstract hypotheses and their analysis to their utmost limits. They wish to build a force which controlled it," and Smith devoted only a fraction of *The Wealth of Nations* to economic analysis as such (ibid., pp. 29-30). Similarly, "The whole Scots sequence cleaves to actual events, to historical and institutional relations growing between them, and to individual experiences that support and develop the argument. But such individual factors do not lend themselves to mathematical or purely deductive logical treatment. . . . The Scottish philosophical and the mathematical methods do not blend" (ibid., p. 23).
4. Duncan Forbes, "Scientific" Whiggism: Adam Smith and John Millar, *Cambridge J.* 8(Aug. 1954):648: "The idea of the progress of society can be described as the historical frame of reference of the *Wealth of Nations*—a fact that seems to have been ignored in the long debate as to how far Smith's method is really deductive or empirical. This is especially clear not only in Book 3 (the natural progress of opulence), which as W. R.

Scott has shown, is the oldest part of *The Wealth of Nations,* traceable back to the Edinburgh lectures, but also in Book 5 (revenue), in which Smith shows how the expense of
defence, justice, public works and institutions, education etc. varies in the different
stages of society. . . ."
5. There is no clash between Smithian economic method as here conceived and Smith's
approach to the notion of the progress of society incorporated within the stadial conception insofar as the latter constitutes an effort to apply Newtonian methodology to history,
whereby we "lay down certain principles, primary or proved, in the beginning, from
whence we account for the several phenomena, connecting all together by the same
chain." Cf. A. S. Skinner, Adam Smith: An Economic Interpretation of History in *Essays
on Adam Smith,* A. S. Skinner and T. Wilson, eds. (Oxford: Oxford Univ. Press, 1975),
p. 169. See also A. W. Coats, Adam Smith and the Mercantile System, ibid., pp. 224-25.
6. Samuel Hollander, Adam Smith and the Self-Interest Axiom, *J. Law Econ.* 20(Apr.
1977):133-52.
7. In this summary paragraph we rely largely upon the splendid accounts given by R. L.
Meek and A. S. Skinner. Cf. R. L. Meek, *Economics and Ideology and Other Essays*
(London: Chapman and Hall, 1967), pp. 34-50; R. L. Meek, Smith, Turgot, and the
"Four Stages" Theory, *Hist. Polit. Econ.* (Spring 1971):9-27; A. S. Skinner, Economics
and History—The Scottish Enlightenment, *Scott. J. Polit. Econ.* (Feb. 1965):1-22. See
also Skinner, Adam Smith: Economic Interpretation, p. 154ff.
8. Meek's discussion of the "four stages" theory draws upon a newly discovered set of
student's notes taken of Smith's early Glasgow lectures (and emphasizes intellectual
developments proceeding in France similar in many respects to those in Scotland).
(Smith's early preoccupation with the progress of society is discussed by Cannan in his account of the lecture notes available to him. Cf. his introduction to *The Wealth of Nations,* p. xxxiiiff.) The "stages" theory, as here described, envisaged development "as proceeding through four normally consecutive stages, each based on a particular 'mode of
subsistence'—viz., hunting, pasturage, agriculture, and commerce. To each stage there
corresponded different ideas and institutions relating to property; to each there corresponded different ideas and institutions relating to government and in relation to each,
general statements could be made about the state of manners and morals, the social
surplus, the legal system, the division of labour, etc" (Meek, "Four States" Theory, p.
10).
    Meek's account of the early lectures tends to confirm the weight given to the
materialist conception of history in Dugald Stewart's memoir. For Stewart refers to a
report of Smith's Glasgow lectures that emphasized his endeavor—following
Montesquieu—"to trace the gradual progress of jurisprudence, both public and private,
from the rudest to the most refined ages, and to point out the effects of those arts which
contribute to subsistence, and to the accumulation of property, in producing corres-
pondent improvements or alterations in law and government. This important branch of
his labors he also intended to give to the public; but this intention, which is mentioned in
the conclusion of *The Theory of Moral Sentiments,* he did not live to fulfil." Dugald
Stewart, *Biographical Memoir of Adam Smith,* Sir W. Hamilton, ed. (1793; repr. New
York: Kelley, 1966), p. 12.
    But the report of the lectures recorded by Stewart refers also to *The Wealth of Na-
tions:* "In the last part of his lectures, he examined those political regulations which are
founded, not upon the principle of *justice,* but that of *expediency,* and which are
calculated to increase the riches, the power, and the prosperity of a State. Under this
view, he considered the political institutions relating to commerce, to finances, to ec-
clesiastical and military establishments. What he delivered on these subjects contained
the substance of the work he afterward published under the title of *An Inquiry into the
Nature and Causes of the Wealth of Nations"* (ibid.).
    In his Preface to the sixth (1790) edition of *The Theory of Moral Sentiments,* Smith
himself refers to his promise in the first edition (1759) to make a study "of the general
principles of law and government, and the different revolutions they had undergone in
the different ages and periods of society." This task he had undertaken, he writes, in *The
Wealth of Nations* as far as policy, revenue, and arms were concerned (but he had not
achieved his objective in the matter of jurisprudence). See John Rae, *Life of Adam Smith*
(1895; repr. New York: Kelley, 1965), p. 426.
9. The point we now emphasize is that the observations regarding *The Wealth of Nations* by

Stewart, and Smith himself, discussed in note 8, describe particular sections of Books 3 and 5. (The significant references to the first two "stages" — hunting and pasturage and their determining influence on governmental forms — will be found in Book 5. For a detailed textual account of the stages of hunting and pasturage as developed in Book 5 see Skinner, Adam Smith: Economic Interpretation, pp. 156-68.) But in the book as a whole the governing theme of the developmental process runs along different lines.

10. "Nothing can be more absurd, however, than to imagine that men in general should work less when they work for themselves, than when they work for other people. A poor independent workman will generally be more industrious than even a journeyman who works by the piece. The one enjoys the whole produce of his own industry; the other shares it with his master. The one, in his separate independent state, is less liable to the temptations of bad company, which in large manufactories so frequently ruin the morals of the other" (pp. 83-84).

It may also be noted that Smith had very little to say on the distinction between the merchant and the capitalist employer of wage labor.

There are, however, references in The Wealth of Nations, Book 3, Chapter 4, to the "dependency" of landless individuals upon the authority of a land-owning class controlling the means of subsistence. Thus the landowner is "surrounded with a multitude of retainers and dependants, who having no equivalent to give in return for their maintenance . . . must obey him, for the same reason that soldiers must obey the prince who pays them" (p. 385). And a contrast is drawn between this form of dependency and the "independency" of laborers in an exchange system. In this sytem although the wealthy consumer "contributes to . . . the maintenance of them all, they are all more or less independent of him, because generally they can all be maintained without him" (p. 389). See also the reference to "our present sense of the word Freedom" (p. 375).

11. Smith's general preoccupation with the analysis of the capitalist economy is emphasized in the accounts by Skinner in his Introduction to The Wealth of Nations (Harmondsworth: Penguin, Ltd. 1970), pp. 12, 42-43, 75-76; Adam Smith and the Role of the State (Glasgow: Univ. Glasgow Press, 1974), pp. 6, 20; and Adam Smith: Economic Interpretation, p. 168. See also R. L. Meek, The Rise and Fall of The Concept of the Economic Machine (Leicester: Leicester Univ. Press, 1965), pp. 6-7, and Meek, Social Science and the Ignoble Savage (Cambridge: Cambridge Univ. Press, 1976), p. 220.

R. L. Meek and A. S. Skinner, The Development of Adam Smith's Ideas on the Divison of Labour, Econ. J. 83(Dec. 1973):1094-1116, provides further evidence to the same effect. For it would appear that Smith "purged" the discussion of division of labour in Book 1 of The Wealth of Nations of various "sociological" illustrations that appear in earlier formulations (ibid., p. 1108n). In one omitted passage "Smith explicitly established a connection between mode of subsistence, size of community, and division of labor, illustrating the point in terms of three distinct economic types (hunting, pasturage, and agriculture)" (ibid., p. 1109). The authors do not consider Smith's decision to omit the passage to be an improvement; be that as it may, the decision suggests that the themes were of secondary importance as far as The Wealth of Nations was concerned.

12. Some complications inherent in the notion of agricultural priority are briefly alluded to in the following extract: "The town, indeed, may not always derive its whole subsistence from the country in its neighbourhood, or even from the territory to which it belongs, but from very distant countries; and this, though it forms no exception from the general rule, has occasioned considerable variations in the progress of opulence in different ages and nations.

That order of things which necessity imposes in general, though not in every particular country, is, in every particular country, promoted by the natural inclinations of man" (p. 357).

13. Smith also refers to the relatively low risk supposedly attaching to agricultural investment — an observation that seems more appropriate for an advanced economy than for that presumably characteristic of the early period with which he (formally) seems to have been dealing: "Upon equal, or near equal profits, most men will chuse to employ their capitals rather in the improvement and cultivation of land, than either in manufactures or in foreign trade. The man who employs his capital in land, has it more under his view and command, and his fortune is much less liable to accidents, than that of the trader . . . " (pp. 357-58). Relevant also is the assertion that "as to cultivate the ground

was the original destination of man, so in every stage of his existence he seems to retain a predilection for this primitive employment" (p. 358) because of the nonmonetary advantages of country life, that is, the beauty of the countryside, the tranquillity of mind promoted, the independency—no doubt introspective considerations that reflect the good press for agriculture at the time. (The extracts appear to neglect the "normal" stadial sequence that gives priority to the hunting and pasturage stages.)

14. Reference to capitalistic farmers is apparent here, but nothing is said of the employment of wage labor.

15. In this context of "economic determinism" we find a basic summary of the role of self-interest and the unintended consequences of self-interested behavior (pp. 391-92). For a veritable catalogue of instances of "the law of the heterogeneity of ends"—the unintended consequences of behavior—in *The Wealth of Nations* and other writers of the day see Forbes, "Scientific" Whiggism, pp. 653-58.

16. Cf. Skinner, Economics and History, p. 10ff.

17. "Mr. Hume is the only writer who, so far as I know, has hitherto taken notice of it." (p. 385). Skinner, Adam Smith: Economic Interpetation, p. 165n, has observed that since Steuart, Ferguson, Millar, and Kames had all written to the same effect by 1776, Smith's citation of Hume above "provides further evidence as to the age of this section (Book 3) of the work."

   However, it should be noted that Smith left a role for the feudal law in the decline of the authority of the great landlords, for he envisaged it as attempting "to moderate the authority of the great allodial lords" (p. 388). But it was *insufficiently* effective.

18. Cf. also "But though this natural order of things must have taken place in some degree in every such society [that has any territory], it has, in all the modern states of Europe, been, in many respects, entirely inverted. The foreign commerce of some of their cities has introduced all their finer manufactures, or such as were fit for distant sale; and manufactures and foreign commerce together, have given birth to the principal improvements of agriculture. The manners and customs which the nature of their original government introduced, and which remained after that government was greatly altered, necessarily forced them into this unnatural and retrograde order" (p. 360).

   An observation by Stewart, *Biographical Memoir*, pp. 60-61, is also relevant: "What the circumstances are, which, in modern Europe, have contributed to disturb this order of nature, and, in particular, to encourage the industry of towns, at the expense of that of the country, Mr. Smith has investigated with great ingenuity, and in such a manner, as to throw much new light on the history of that state of society which prevails in this quarter of the globe."

19. Skinner (Economics and History, p. 7) refers to the emphasis given by the Scottish historians "to the historically inevitable development of productive forces. . . ." In his Introduction to *The Wealth of Nations*, p. 40, this notion is apparently attributed to Smith himself. But see Skinner, Adam Smith: Economic Interpretation, p. 175, where reference is made to "Smith's use of the economic stages" as "general categories in terms of which the experience of different peoples can be interpreted rather than as templates to which that experience must be made to conform." Cf. also Coats, Adam Smith and the Mercantile System, p. 223: "Book III . . . is specifically designed to show how . . . the 'natural' course of events has repeatedly been perverted or checked by human interference." (See also ibid., p. 232.)

20. See Skinner, Adam Smith: Economic Interpretation, pp. 161, 162, 164, and 168 for a variety of references to *political* as distinct from *economic* determinants of institutional arrangements of various kinds, which seem to belie the great emphasis placed elsewhere in his paper upon "the almost Marxian reliance which is placed [by Smith] on economic forces" (ibid., p. 155).

21. But see the discussion of various privileges granted to townspeople by the sovereign, where we see Smith attempting to avoid purely "conjectural" statements as far as possible: "Whether such privileges had before been usually granted along with the freedom of trade, to particlar burghers, individuals, I know not. I reckon it not improbable that they were, though I cannot produce any direct evidence of it. But however this may have been, the principal attributes of villanage and slavery being thus taken away from them, they now, at least, became really free in our present sense of the word Freedom" (p. 375).

22. Stewart, *Biographical Memoir*, pp. 33-34. Cf. also the remarkable assertion (ibid., p. 37): "In most cases, it is of more importance to ascertain the progress that is most simple,

than the progress that is most agreeable to fact; for, paradoxical as the proposition may appear, it is certainly true, that the real progress is not always the most natural. It may have been determined by particular accidents, which are not likely again to occur, and which cannot be considered as forming any part of that general provision which nature has made for the improvement of the race."

23. Stewart included Smith's discussions of Book 3 as falling within the category of "conjectural" history *(Biographical Memoir,* p. 36). However, some questions have been raised regarding the justice of Stewart's designation of the method of the Scottish historians in the light of their formal adherence to the principle of empirical evidence. Thus Meek, *Economics and Ideology,* p. 38, objects that the Scottish school "tried consciously to base itself on the study of concrete historical facts, in opposition to the abstract speculation and conjecture (particularly with regard to the so-called 'state of nature') which had so often been employed in the past."

In *Social Science and the Ignoble Savage,* pp. 237-38, Meek suggests that Stewart did not have "mainly in mind" the four-stages theory in his description of conjectural history, but rather what Meek refers to as "Smith's theory of 'the natural progress of opulence' — the theory that capital is 'naturally' directed first to agriculture, then to manufacture, and finally to commerce. And as applied to this theory, what Stewart says is perfectly true." This suggestion is not totally convincing. There is admittedly some ambiguity attaching to certain passages in Book 3, Chapter 1 (cf. ibid., 16n), but Book 3 as a whole entails themes falling within the range of the Scottish historical tradition, and there is evidence of a reading back of contemporary behavior patterns into the record.

24. If landed property were divided equally between the children of the owner, then upon his death much of the estate would be put on the market, and the artificial scarcity in Europe would be somewhat reduced. The problem did not exist in North America where "uncultivated land" was available "almost for nothing, or at a price much below the value of the natural produce; a thing impossible in Europe, or, indeed, in any country where all lands have long been private property" (p. 393).

25. A further contemporary distortion was the monopoly granted to British merchants in the colony trade. The effect, in the first instance, was an increase in the rate of profit on mercantile trade, which rendered investment in domestic land improvement relatively unattractive. Moreover, the increase in the average profit rate tended to keep up the interest rate to the detriment of landowners by lowering the price of land relative to the rent yielded: "The price of land in proportion to the rent which it affords, the number of years purchase which is commonly paid for it, necessarily falls as the rate of interest rises" (p. 577).

26. See note 13 for the discussion of risk differentials, which appears more appropriate for the capitalist exchange economy than for the historical context within which it appears.

27. Cf. "Every individual is continually exerting himself to find out the most advantageous employment for whatever capital he can command. It is his own advantage, indeed, and not that of the society, which he has in view. But the study of his own advantage naturally, or rather necessarily leads him to prefer that employment which is most advantageous to the society" (p. 421). "He generally, indeed, neither intends to promote the public interest, nor knows how much he is promoting it. By preferring the support of domestic to that of foreign industry, he intends only his own security; and by directing that industry in such a manner as its produce may be of the greatest value, he intends only his own gain, and he is in this, as in many other cases, led by an invisible hand to promote an end which was no part of his intention" (p. 423).

28. See Samuel Hollander, *The Economics of Adam Smith* (Toronto: Univ. Toronto Press, 1973), Ch. 10, for details of the model, including the role of international trade theory.

29. While the theory of temporal investment priorities has not perhaps been sufficiently appreciated in the secondary literature, there is a good deal of emphasis upon the "system-building" aspect of Smith's work in general terms. See in particular, William Letwin, *The Origins of Scientific Economics* (New York: Doubleday, 1964), pp. 227-28; J. H. Hollander, in *Adam Smith, 1776-1926,* (New York: Kelley, 1966), p. 19, states "But if the *Wealth of Nations* showed little trace of scientific self-consciousness, it was distinguished in a very high degree by the second and more notable characteristic of an epoch-making work — a body of principles setting forth the uniformities and sequences that obtain in the subject matter assembled. As against the detached solutions of monograph writers or the unfulfilled engagements of more ambitious projectors, Adam

Smith visualized the broad extent of economic purpose and result and ventured interpretations of that which he saw or pictured."

Jacob Viner has similarly observed, in *Adam Smith, 1776-1926*, pp. 116-17, that Smith's major contribution is his "detailed and elaborate application to the wilderness of economic phenomena of the unifying concept of a co-ordinated and mutually interdependent system of cause and effect relationships which philosophers and theologians had already applied to the world in general. Smith's doctrine that economic phenomena were manifestations of an underlying order in nature, governed by natural forces, gave to English economics for the first time a definite trend toward logically consistent synthesis of economic relationships, toward 'system-building'."

The criticism by J. A. Schumpeter, *History of Economic Analysis* (New York: Oxford Univ. Press, 1954), pp. 184-85, to the effect that Smith's "mental structure was up to mastering the unwieldy material that flowed from many sources and to subjecting it, with a strong hand to a rule of a small number of coherent principles" would doubtless have been read as high praise indeeed by Smith himself. For this is precisely a function of the scientist that he regarded to be quite essential, as is clear, for example, from the following reference in the *Edinburgh Review* of 1755: "It seems to be the peculiar talent of the French nation, to arrange every subject in that natural and simple order, which carries the attention, without any effort, along with it. The English seem to have employed themselves entirely in inventing, and to have disdained the more inglorious but not less useful labour of arranging and methodizing their discoveries, and of expressing them in the most simple and natural manner. There is not only no tolerable system of natural philosophy in the English language, but there is not even any tolerable system of any part of it." (See J. R. Lindgren, ed., *The Early Writings of Adam Smith*, (New York: Kelley, 1967), pp. 18-19.

30. Similarly, that part of the model relating to secular changes within the agricultural sector itself is used to interpret contemporary and historical patterns of land use.

31. W. R. Scott, *Adam Smith as Student and Professor* (Glasgow, 1937), p. 283. Stewart, *Biographical Memoir*, pp. 56-57, observed: "To direct the policy of nations with respect to one most important class of its laws, those which form its system of Political Economy, is the great aim of Mr. Smith's Inquiry. . . ." His object was "to ascertain the general principles of justice and of expediency, which ought to guide the institutions of legislators on these important articles."

32. In his discussion, Adam Smith and the Mercantile System, Coats sets out to reconsider Smith's "account of the mercantile system in relation to his theory of history and politics and his view of long-run socio-economic development" in Skinner and Wilson, *Essays on Adam Smith*, p. 218. The attack on mercantilism should not be viewed "simply and solely as an analysis of impediments to the smooth functioning of the competitive market economy" but rather as "an integral part of a larger system of moral, socio-philosophical, historical and political ideas" (ibid., p. 221). Yet Charles Wilson is quoted approvingly to the effect that "the arguments of *The Wealth of Nations* were the product of logic working upon material drawn from the observation of three relatively mature mercantile economies: those of England, France and Holland. They did not have the same appeal to those who were still concerned with the earlier stages of the transition from agrarian to mercantile economy . . ." (ibid., p. 235). And Coats concludes that Smith's "protest was directed against a body of restrictive regulations which had long outgrown their usefulness in Britain; and it was backed by a powerful corpus of analysis, much of which has survived to this day" (ibid., p. 236).

6

Power and Value Relationships in *The Wealth of Nations*

🍂 LAURENCE S. MOSS

THERE are fairy tales, folktales, and silent movies about cunning landlords who make it excruciatingly painful for sober working people to carry out their plans. It may be surprising to learn that this theme and its associated prejudices are part of Adam Smith's *The Wealth of Nations*. According to Smith, Europe adopted feudalism after the decline of Rome as a rational response to the political uncertainty and the ever-present danger of violent death at the hand of invading armies.

> When the German and Scythian nations over-ran the western provinces of the Roman empire, the confusions which followed so great a revolution lasted for several centuries. The rapine and violence which the barbarians exercised against the ancient inhabitants, interrupted the commerce between the towns and the country. . . . During the continuance of those confusions, the chiefs and principal leaders of those nations, acquired or usurped to themselves the greater part of the lands of those countries. A great part of them was uncultivated; but no part of them, whether cultivated or uncultivated, was left without a proprietor. All of them were engrossed, and the greater part by a few great proprietors [p. 361].

Once in control, however, the rich and powerful landlords and their descendants sustained the feudal way of life long after the threat of foreign invasion had subsided. Although the up-and-coming artisans in the towns had savings to invest in land improvements, the landlords were unwilling (and unable by feudal law) to sell any part of their land holdings; and by the eleventh century the vestiges of the old order had become a fetter on the economic development of Europe. Eventually the mercantile spirit did burst forth, capital accumulated, and the ensuing competition for workers led to a rise in their real wage and (most important in terms of Smith's commitment to the moral improvement of man) to the development of the sober habits of foresight, rationality, and independence.

Laurence S. Moss is Associate Professor of Economics, Babson College, Wellesley, Mass.

I shall argue in this essay that Smith offered significantly more than a historical account of the development of modern Europe: he offered a microeconomic theory of the transition from feudalism to the market economy. Furthermore, this theory is consistent with his statistical account of the secular behavior of commodity prices over a four-hundred-year span of European history. Smith's statistical discussion is presented at the end of Book 1 of *The Wealth of Nations*, and his account of the transition from feudal to modern times is the subject of Book 3. By pointing out the connections between the arguments of Books 1 and 3, I hope to further an appreciation of the essential unity and enduring relevance of Smith's great classic.[1]

RELATIVE PRICES AND ECONOMIC DEVELOPMENT

Reevaluation of the theoretical framework of *The Wealth of Nations* reveals that the book contains a sophisticated and remarkably advanced theory of economic development.[2] Smith used this theory (1) to determine to what extent the economic development of Western Europe had been deflected from its "natural," or "ordinary," course; (2) to determine the causes and implications of this deflection; and (3) to describe the mechanism by which these obstacles were circumvented for a return to the normal pattern of development.

Historians of economic thought generally credit the classical economists (and especially Smith) with contributing to the theory of general economic development, but at the same time they criticize them for ignoring the problem of how the market allocates scarce resources among alternative ends.[3] We now know that such an assessment of classical economics is improper, at least when it comes to Smith's work. Smith demonstrated that through the market mechanism resources are allocated for maximal economic growth. Theories of resource allocation and economic development are unified in Smith's writings.[4] Specifically, the mechanism that promotes development involves changes in relative prices. An economy starts out with a relative abundance of some resources and a relative dearth of others. As production proceeds and population grows, supplies of resources change with resultant changes in input prices and, finally, changes in relative commodity prices. Certain investments become more lucrative than others, and the investment process takes a new direction.

Let us summarize Smith's theory of development.[5] At the earliest stage of economic development, land is abundant in comparison with other productive factors. Consequently, its rental price is so low that the agricultural sector provides investors greater opportunities for profit making than either manufacturing or international commerce. Initially, forests are cleared and wastelands drained to make fields on which to grow corn. Wild game supplies whatever meat is needed by the (small) farming population. Lumber for constructing fences and building houses is readily acquired as a by-product of clearing land for tillage. Thus at the earliest stage of agricultural development there is no need for either a meat or a lumber industry; corn production is the only organized agricultural activity.

However, as population grows and tillage expands, wild game and virgin forests become less abundant, and the market begins to price meat and lumber. In time the price these products command reaches such a level that land is diverted from corn production to the organized production of cattle and timber. At this point the economy acquires both a meat and a lumber industry. The reconversion of tillage into pasture and forest parallels changes in relative commodity prices that reflect changes in the abundance of resources. The process of agricultural development described in *The Wealth of Nations* is one of balanced structural growth where the investment pattern responds to the price structure.

Relative price changes are also used to explain how an agricultural economy eventually acquires manufacturing trades. As capital accumulates and additional acreage is brought into production, land becomes increasingly scarce and its rental price rises relative to the prices of labor and capital. This alteration in the structure of input prices encourages capitalists to embark on more labor-intensive types of production such as manufacturing. Thus the pattern of investment alters in favor of manufacturing, and the development of that sector is encouraged. The capital invested in manufacturing is used to hire domestic labor to make goods for domestic markets. According to Smith, the investment of capital in foreign markets also comes about quite "naturally," but only at an advanced stage of economic development. Smith offered a rudimentary "factor proportions" theory of economic development in which alterations in relative factor prices play an important if not essential part in guiding the developmental process.[6]

In Book 3 of *The Wealth of Nations* Smith explained that, in the evolution of manufacturing trades, towns spring up alongside agriculture and thereafter each nurtures the development of the other. Smiths, carpenters, wheelwrights, ploughwrights, masons, bricklayers, tanners, shoemakers, tailors, butchers, brewers, and bakers all find their way to the towns and settle there. Their income derives from servicing the great landed estates, which trade some of their produce for the merchants' wares.

> The inhabitants of the town and those of the country are mutually the servants of one another. The town is a continual fair or market, to which the inhabitants of the country resort, in order to exchange their rude [produce] for manufactured produce [p. 358].

In Western Europe the great growth of town life occurred in the thirteenth century when the medieval traders (well-established since the eleventh century) discovered they "could get goods of better quality in towns than on the manor, because specialization made possible by the larger market resulted in more skillful workmanship."[7]

Smith goes on to say that the most successful (that is, efficient) merchants make profits, which they save to buy land for farming on a commercial basis.

> The wealth acquired by the inhabitants of cities was frequently employed in purchasing such lands as were to be sold, of which a great part would frequently be uncultivated. Merchants are commonly ambitious of becoming country gentlemen, and when they do, they are generally the best of all improvers [p. 384].

This trend favors national economic development. The merchants apply to agriculture the talents and practices that they perfected in the towns; and with the transfer of acreage from the old proprietors to the new up-and-coming merchant farmers, improved methods of land management (for example, in fencing and irrigation) replace the decaying practices of the feudal order. In the following typical passage Smith compares the managerial abilities of a merchant with those of a country gentleman:

> A merchant is accustomed to employ his money chiefly in profitable projects; whereas a mere country gentleman is accustomed to employ it chiefly in expence [to spend it on final goods and services]. The one often sees his money go from him and return to him again with a profit: the other, when once he parts with it, very seldom expects to see any more of it. Those different habits naturally affect their temper and disposition in every sort of business. A merchant is commonly a bold, a country gentleman, a timid undertaker. . . . The habits . . . of order economy and attention to which mercantile business naturally forms a merchant, render him much fitter to execute, with profit and success, any project of improvement [pp. 384-85].

Thus in the natural course of events, town and country form a symbiotic relationship permitting some of the town merchants to acquire the money capital needed to purchase land and become capitalistic farmers.

> Had human institutions, therefore, never disturbed the natural course of things, the progressive wealth and increase of the towns would, in every political society, be consequential, and in proportion to the improvement and cultivation of the territory or country [p. 359].

FEDERAL RESTRICTIONS ON PROPERTY TRANSFER

Unfortunately, the economic development of Europe did not follow this "natural," or "ordinary," course of events. When the northern invasions ended in the eleventh century, most of the land was divided among a few great landed proprietors and regulated by feudal law. The principal goal of the social order was military protection and survival; therefore the law of primogeniture, which prevented the subdivision of the estate, made good sense. Since the eldest male heir inherited the entire estate, the military power of the holding could not be weakened by subdivision of the land among several heirs. The laws of entail also made it difficult if not impossible for a prodigal heir to sell parts of his estate during his lifetime. In the feudal period these restrictions on land transfer amounted to restrictions on the dissipation of political power. And since the *raison d'être* of the feudal order was the preservation of power, these laws were an ingenious response to the uncertain political conditions of the day.[8]

> When [the] great landed estates were a sort of principalities, entails might not be unreasonable. Like what are called the fundamental laws of some monarchies, they might frequently hinder the security of thousands from being endangered by the caprice or extravagance of one man [p. 363].

By preventing the prosperous town merchants from "buying in" and applying their skills to agriculture, vestiges of the feudal order inhibited the improvement of agriculture and the development of the economy was thwarted. Smith wrote that "laws frequently continue in force long after the circumstances, which first gave occasion to them, and which could alone render them reasonable, are no more" (p. 362). The landlords entombed in their great estates had become pitiful relics of a bygone age. These descendants of the great chiefs and tribal leaders were completely incapable of business calculation and scientific management of their estates. Instead they were preoccupied with the vanities of their aristocratic position. With the substitution of standing armies under the direct supervision of the king for the feudal defense system, the landlords were not only militarily obsolete but also, as Smith explained, a fetter on the development of the national economy. At the same time that Smith criticized the relevance of feudal institutions to an emerging economy he did not hesitate to express his negative feelings about the mental and moral character of the landlords. The merchant traders not only promoted economic development but also possessed many mental habits that Smith valued highly. In addition, the merchants were self-reliant—something essential for "order and good government."[9]

> To improve land with profit, like all other commercial projects, requires an exact attention to small savings and small gains, of which a man born to a great fortune, even though naturally frugal, is very seldom capable. The situation of such a person naturally disposes him to attend rather to ornament which pleases his fancy, than to profit for which he has so little occasion. The elegance of his dress, of his equipage, of his house, and household furniture, are objects which from his infancy he has been accustomed to have some anxiety about [p. 364].

Smith credited himself and David Hume with noticing the connection between "commerce and manufactures" and the development of "order and good government, and with them, the liberty and security of individuals . . . who had before lived almost in a continual state of war with their neighbours, and of servile dependency upon their superiors" (p. 385).[10]

By the sixteenth century things had changed. A large number of merchants had gained control of the land and instituted capital-intensive methods of farming. How were the obstacles posed by feudal law overcome? What role did the marketplace play in this development? Before we summarize Smith's fascinating account of this transition process, let us state the problem in the language of *The Wealth of Nations*.

AGRICULTURAL SURPLUS AND ITS APPLICATIONS

Agricultural yield, according to Smith, is invariably in excess of what is needed to feed those who work the land. The existence of an agricultural surplus is a technological observation that few students of agricultural history would care to fault.

Of the physical productivity of land Smith wrote:

> Land, in almost any situation, produces a greater quantity of food than what is sufficient to maintain all the labour necessary for bringing it to market, in the most liberal way in which that labour is ever maintained. The surplus too is always more than sufficient to replace the stock which employed that labour, together with its profits. Something, therefore, always remains for a rent to the landlord [p. 146].

However, Smith further claimed that in a money economy the market value of corn is in excess of the wages and profits incidental to harvesting and marketing the corn. Consequently, a value surplus is produced and "originally" accrues to proprietors as feudal or contractual rents. Apparently Smith believed that this value surplus persists in an advanced economy, and that the major problem of economic development is simply how the food surplus is redistributed among the other members of society. In a competitive market economy where resources bear prices related to the value of their output, the problem is to explain why the physical surplus of the land becomes a value surplus as well. Why does not the supply of agricultural output keep increasing until the market price falls to the cost of production and no value surplus remains? The Physiocrats, for the most part, simply asserted the existence of a value surplus accruing to land without offering much by way of proof. François Quesnay, however, denied the tendency of the price of corn to fall toward the cost of production by explaining that the price of corn is determined internationally and hence a value surplus, or rent, is inherent in corn production. Apparently Smith followed Quesnay on this point.[11]

If food surplus remains with the great landed proprietors, the developmental process is inhibited. If it is transferred to the merchant traders to be used as capital for land improvements or to promote local manufacturing, the development is enhanced. In feudal times, Smith explained, the entire surplus accruing to the landlords was used to support huge bodies of soldiers, servants, and a variety of other retainers. This body of "unproductive" labor was attached to the great estates.

In a country which has neither foreign commerce, nor any of the finer manufactures, a great proprietor, having nothing for which he can exchange the greater part of the produce of his lands which is over and above the maintenance of the cultivators, consumes the whole in rustic hospitality at home. If this surplus produce is sufficient to maintain a hundred or a thousand men, he can make use of it in no other way than by maintaining a hundred or a thousand men. He is at all times, therefore, surrounded with a multitude of retainers and dependants, who having no equivalent to give in return for their maintenance, but being fed entirely by his bounty, must obey him, for the same reason that soldiers must obey the prince who pays them [p. 385; cf. p. 671].

Those who did not "buy" their livelihood by trading either labor or commodities were pitifully dependent on the lords for their daily sustenance. Smith astutely observed that individuals are likely to become psychologically emasculated by a dependency relationship of this type.

TRANSFER OF THE SURPLUS TO THE CAPITALISTS

Thus the destruction of the feudal order paralleled the transfer of agricultural surplus from the landlords to the innovating merchant class. Once in possession of the food surplus, the merchants could use it to employ the servants and retainers from the estates in "productive" pursuits (that is, manufacturing industry and capital-intensive farming) and thereby promote the economic development of the nation.[12] This transfer did occur and without the need for a revolution or some other major restructuring of property rights; for instead of becoming capitalist farmers and manufacturers (as they would have in the "natural order" of economic development), the inhabitants of the towns invested their savings in international trade. By skipping a stage of development, they "inverted" the "natural course of things" (p. 360). The luxury items they imported appealed at once to the vanity and selfishness of the great proprietors, who, in Smith's words, "eagerly purchased them with great quantities of rude produce of their own lands" (p. 380; see also pp. 388–89, 391).

This development of international trade provided the landlords with an employment for their enormous agricultural surplus. With the change in the lords' consumption pattern from the maintenance of retainers and servants to the acquisition of fancy clothing, ornate furnishings, precious metals, and gem stones, thousands were released from the great estates to seek employment with the merchants. The landlords, addicted to frivolous expenditure and eager to increase their annual land rents, agreed to extended leases with the capitalist farmers. Now with certain knowledge about their long-term rental payments, the new group of capitalist farmers turned their attention to land improvement. Still, private property in land did not exist in the modern sense; all parties remained bound by feudal property arrangements, yet the worst abuses of the old order were circumvented and the shackles on the development of the market economy were removed.

The clergy too, like the great barons, wished to get a better rent from their landed estates, in order to spend it, in the same manner, upon the gratification of their own private vanity and folly. But this increase of rent could be got only by granting [long-term] leases to their tenants, who thereby became in a great measure independent of them. The ties of interest, which bound the inferior ranks of people to the clergy, were in this manner gradually broken and dissolved [p. 755; cf. p. 369].

At another place Smith wrote:

He [the landlord] is desirous to raise his rents above what his lands, in the actual state of their improvement, could afford. His tenants could agree to this upon one condition only, that they should be secured in their possession, for such a term of years as might give them time to recover with profit whatever they should lay out in the further improvement of the land. The expensive vanity of the landlord made him willing to accept of this condition; and hence the origin of long leases [p. 390].

At other places in *The Wealth of Nations* Smith attributed the fiscal crisis of the great proprietors not only to luxury expenditure but also to the practical need of maintaining a strong (and increasingly expensive) military posture.[13] Contemporary historians North and Thomas attribute the shift to long-term leases that occurred in the fourteenth and fifteenth centuries in Western Europe to the competition among the landlords to attract suitable tenants to their estates. Faced with severe labor shortages due to plagues and frequent wars, with rents largely fixed by customary practice and falling in real terms, the lords offered tenants life leases renegotiable only on the death of the tenant. "Life leases turned out to be a last-ditch effort by lords to retain their customary rights by signing them away for one generation of tenants."[14]

After the institution of long-term leases, the next development on the road to private property in land was the establishment of the right to pass a piece of land on to an heir. At first the lord's explicit consent was needed, but later this became common practice and the manorial courts treated the lord's permission purely as a matter of form. By the late fifteenth and sixteenth centuries it became relatively simple for a life-lease tenant to convey the land to another (nonheir) tenant. As a matter of form, the customary legal status of the lord was recognized by the phrase "at the will of the lord according to the custom of the manor" implying there were circumstances under which the lord could veto such a conveyance. In practice, however, life-lease transfers became virtually automatic. The fixity of rents and other payments in an inflationary environment reduced the real burden of the tenants to the landlords, and by 1600 rental payments were purely nominal. At the same time, the expanding common law declared these lengthy lease arrangements equivalent to "copyholds"; therefore landlord-tenant disputes were placed under the jurisdiction of the king's courts.[15] North and Thomas wrote that "the manorial economy thus met its death: labor services were now irrevocably replaced by money rent payments; land was now tilled by free tenants and/or by workers receiving money wages, who were free to seek their best employment."[16]

Unlike these recent interpretations, Smith attributed the death of feudalism to the *vanity* and *selfishness* of the landlords. They needed to finance a huge importation of luxury goods and so traded off their enormous power and authority over men. Smith's ironic description of the demise of feudalism must be cited in its entirety:

> But what all the violence of the feudal institutions could never have effected, the silent and insensible operation of foreign commerce and manufactures gradually brought about. These gradually furnished the great proprietors with something for which they could exchange the whole surplus produce of their lands, and which they could consume themselves without sharing it either with tenants or retainers. All for ourselves, and nothing for other people, seems, in every age of the world, to have been the vile maxim of the masters of mankind. As soon, therefore, as they could find a method of consuming the whole value of their rents themselves, they had no disposition to share them with any other persons. For a pair of diamond buckles perhaps, or for something as frivolous and useless, they exchange the maintenance, or what is the same thing, the price of the maintenance of a thousand men for a year, and with it the whole weight and authority which it could give them. The buckles, however, were to be all their own, and no other human creature was to have any share of them; whereas in the more ancient method of expence they must have shared with at least a thousand people. With the judges that were to determine the preference, this difference was perfectly decisive; and thus, for the gratification of the most childish, the meanest and the most sordid of all vanities, they gradually bartered their whole power and authority [pp. 38-39].[17]

Interestingly enough, the "natural" pattern of economic development is restored by way of a change in tastes originating on the *demand* side of market. In the absence of political disturbances, however, we have seen that economic development proceeds by way of price changes resulting from alterations in the relative availability of resource supplies originating on the *supply* side of the market. Apparently Smith believed actual historical processes were the result of factors originating on both the supply and demand side of markets; but it was only when supply factors dominated that Smith spoke of economic development following its "natural course."

POWER VERSUS VALUE

An ambiguity in *The Wealth of Nations* requires careful attention. At the end of Book 1 Smith explains that the landlords' share of the gross national product always rises with the development of the market economy, regardless of whether that share is measured absolutely or as a proportion of the national product (pp. 247-50). Now comparing the conclusions of Book 1 with the main conclusion of Book 3, we find Smith paradoxically asserting that with the progress of the market the landlords grow richer but at the same time less powerful.

For a long time I was puzzled by this ambiguity; then upon rereading Chapter 5 of Book 1, I found a footnote containing a quotation from Thomas Hobbes's *Leviathan*. In that passage Hobbes distinguished between riches and power: Riches by themselves are not power because they must be combined with "liberality" to procure friends and servants. A man who hoards all his riches in the form of, say, gold coins will only succeed in provoking the envy of his neighbors; envy, for Hobbes, is one of the three original (and perpetual) sources of conflict among men.[18] There is also strong indirect evidence that Smith was heavily influenced by other parts of the chapter in the *Leviathan* in which this distinction appears, especially where Hobbes defined the value, or price, of a person as being determined like "all other things" by what another individual will give for the use of that individual's "power." What an object or a person is worth is what another will give to acquire it (him), and therefore value is "dependent on the need and judgment of another."[19]

It is a short step from this concept to Smith's famous labor-command theory of value, which is the subject of the section of Chapter 5 (of Book 1) in which this passage from Hobbes appears. After pointing out that a man is rich or poor according to the number of necessities and conveniences he can afford, Smith explained that in a society with a highly developed division of labor the real measure of the exchange value of any object is the "quantity of labor which it enables [the owner] to purchase or command."

> Every man is rich or poor according to the degree in which he can afford to enjoy the necessaries, conveniencies, and amusements of human life. But after the division of labour has once thoroughly taken place, it is but a very small part of these with which a man's own labour can supply him. The far greater part of them he must derive from the labour of other people, and he must be rich or poor according to the quantity of that labour which he can command, or which he can afford to purchase. The value of any commodity, therefore, to the person who possesses it, and who means not to use or consume it himself, but to exchange it for other commodities, is equal to the quantity of labour which it enables him to purchase or command. Labour, therefore, is the real measure of the exchangeable value of all commodities [p. 30].

Thus the exchange value of an object is an index of power over the labor of other men—a notion that Karl Marx and other writers in this tradition considered basic to an understanding of social processes.[20]

As far as the landlords are concerned, their share of the national product rises in nominal as well as in real terms. Smith stated that "the real value of the landlord's share, his real command over the labour of other people not only rises with the real value of his produce, but the proportion of his share to the whole produce rises with it" (p. 247). Yet although the landlords grow richer during the transition from feudalism to capitalism, they *do not become more powerful.* By *diverting* their income from supporting an "unproductive" labor force to consuming material objects supplied by merchant traders, the landlords trade off their agricultural surplus. While the landlords enjoy the option of employing increasing numbers of the nation's work force directly on the estates, they do not exercise it. The proprietors apparently ignore Hobbes's prescription of combining riches with liberality; instead they switch their expenditure from consumption of services to possession of luxury goods — silver plate, diamonds, rubies, ornate furniture, and rare birds. The labor released from the estates is "productively employed" in the manufacturing trades or on the merchant-farmer's managed farms.[21]

SECULAR PRICE MOVEMENTS

The market mechanism that breaks down the rigidities of the feudal order first involves a shift in the tastes or preferences of the landlord class.[22] In turning from the consumption of services to the consumption of material goods, the lords effect the transfer of surplus farm produce (or surplus value) to the rising merchant class. As rents rise and the demand for luxury goods expands, the prices of such goods would be expected to rise relative to the prices of other commodities. This is precisely the effect described in the last chapter of Book 1, which includes Smith's long "Digression on Silver." In analyzing the secular development of the European price structure over the 400-year period corresponding to the transition from feudal to market institutions, Smith found that when prices are correctly measured in terms of a commodity of relatively constant labor content such as corn, the prices of silver plate, precious stones, furniture, and wild fowl tend to show the largest secular rise. Inasmuch as we are told in Book 3 that these are the commodities in increasing demand by the lords and barons during the transition from feudalism to capitalism, Smith's statistical work actually supports his general theory! Smith wrote:

> As art and industry advance, the materials of cloathing and lodging, the useful fossils and minerals of the earth, the precious metals and the precious stones should gradually come to be more and more in demand, should gradually exchange for a greater and greater quantity of food, or in other words, should gradually become dearer and dearer [p. 175].

The purpose of the "Digression on Silver" is to show that in the absence of silver discoveries or political interventions such as the Bounty of 1688 the natural tendency is for the real value (that is, resource cost) of silver to rise. That rise is due to an increased transactions demand for silver money that accompanies growth and to an increased demand on the part of the landlords for silver plate and ornaments running up against diminishing returns in the extractive industries (p. 215). Smith explained that Fleetwood and others did not detect the rise in the value of silver because they measured the price of silver in units of commodities that themselves varied in real value (pp. 176–91). Elaborating on his earlier suggestion (pp. 30–46) that the commodity closest to an "invariable measure of value" (at least for long-term comparisons) is corn, Smith argued that the corn price of silver tends to rise over the long course of European history (pp. 176–242). According to Smith, there is a class of rude produce that it is not in the "power of human industry to multiply," and that class includes rare birds and wild fowl whose prices show the greatest rise (even greater than that of silver) over time (p. 218).

For many years historians of economic thought have been puzzled by Smith's long chapter on rent complete with the "Digression on Silver" and have questioned whether it is important to the main argument(s) of *The Wealth of Nations*. Some have called it "filler" or the product of an eighteenth-century dilettante reluctant to omit anything of possible importance. Others have recognized that the digression portrays the secular behavior of broad groupings of commodities over several centuries of European history and employs the supply-and-demand approach to great advantage. What has not been recognized is that the evidence presented there complements Smith's interpretation of the transition from feudal to modern market institutions.[23]

While it would be imposing too much of the twentieth-century philosophy of science on Smith to say that his statistical work attempts to test a hypothesis about the transitional process from feudal to modern institutions, it would certainly be correct to say that his statistical findings at the end of Book 1 are consistent with the transitional process described in Book 3 of *The Wealth of Nations*.[24] What I wish to emphasize is that the transition from feudal to modern times is the consequence of a market process that is spontaneous and not of human design and revealed piecemeal through alterations in market prices. Smith wrote:

> A revolution of the greatest importance to the public happiness, was in this manner brought about by two different orders of people, *who had not the least intention to serve the public.* To gratify the most childish vanity was the sole motive of the great proprietors. The merchants and artificers, much less ridiculous, acted merely from a view to their own interest, and in pursuit of their own pedlar principle of turning a penny wherever a penny was to be got. Neither of them had either knowledge or foresight of that great revolution which the folly of the one, and the industry of the other, was gradually bringing about [pp. 391–92].[25] [Emphasis added.]

Having cleared up one ambiguity, another remains. Obviously, Smith intended to demonstrate that the landlords trade off their enormous command over labor for luxury goods. But is it not true that they only delegate that command to the emerging merchant capitalists who employ these same workers in the mines and factories to satisfy the new consumption patterns of the landlords? Inasmuch as the luxury-good industries expand simultaneously with the decrease in the number of those employed on the great estates, a large proportion of the work force is still employed by the landlords, even though that employment is indirect and disguised by the market mechanism. Furthermore, if the lords grow richer with the accumulation of capital, as we are told at the conclusion of Book 1, then are not the lords commanding an ever larger portion of the nation's work force? Indirectly, the landlords remain as economically powerful as they were before in terms of the volume of labor they command (although the political relationship has been changed substantially, as explained below).

DISAPPEARANCE OF POLITICAL POWER IN THE MARKET

It is difficult to decide whether Smith was aware of this problem. At one place he regarded the switch from the production of services to the production of material goods as beneficial to the working class, since after outliving their usefulness to the rich the more durable (luxury) commodities percolate down to the workers by way of secondhand markets and the like. Thus the lower income groups eventually do benefit from the landlords' change in taste despite the swelling share of the work force originally tied up in providing for their consumption.

> The houses, the furniture, the clothing of the rich, in a little time, become useful to the inferior and middling ranks of people. They are able to purchase then when their superiors grow weary of them. . . . In countries which have long been rich, you will frequently find the inferior ranks of people in possession both of houses and furniture perfectly good and entire, but of which neither the one could have been built, nor the other have been made for their use [p. 330].[26]

However, there are grounds for believing that Smith was groping for a more comprehensive theoretical position.

What Smith might have had in mind in Book I, Chapter 11 and the "Digression on Silver" (but failed to express it adequately) is that as the landlords become richer, they transfer their expenditure to commodities of high value in relation to the quantity of labor contained in their production. Thus the residual element—that is, the difference between the selling price of a good and the labor cost of production—goes to the capitalists as profit and promotes the accumulation of capital. This interpretation suggests that the landlords command a *decreasing* portion of the work force. Smith only hinted at this possibility.

Smith explained that, while the lowest prices that can be charged for the precious metals (gold and silver) are regulated by cost of production, there is no limit to the height their prices can rise. The reason is that "the demand for those metals arises partly from their utility, and partly from their beauty." Smith went on to claim: "with the greater part of rich people, the chief enjoyment of riches consists in the parade of riches, which in their eye is never so complete as when they appear to possess those decisive marks of opulence which nobody can possess but themselves." It would seem that the precious metals could sell at prices far above their labor or resource cost, but then Smith added that "the merit of an object . . . is greatly enhanced by its scarcity, or by the great labour which it requires to collect any considerable quantity of it, a labour which nobody can afford to pay but themselves." Similarly, when speaking of the demand for precious stones, Smith claimed they are desired entirely for their beauty because "they are of no use, but as ornaments; and the merit of their beauty is greatly enhanced by their scarcity, or by the difficulty and expence of getting them from the mine." But Smith added that "wages and profit . . . make up, upon most occasions, almost the whole of their high price" (p. 172).

We can only speculate as to whether their secular rise in price corresponds to a relatively smaller or larger quantity of expended labor. When discussing the secular rise in the prices of rare birds and fish, Smith attributed this to a rise in "wealth and luxury." While he admitted there is no upper boundary on price and human effort cannot increase the available supply, it is quite possible that the "high" price is just sufficient to compensate for the time spent in hunting the wild game (p. 218).

Finally, after dealing at length with the peculiarities of mining and the failure of monetary incentives (tax rebates) to affect either the rate or location of new ore discoveries, Smith explained that the price of the metal is regulated by the price at the most fertile mine (rather than the "least" fertile mine as David Ricardo would argue later). But any suspicion that Smith was willing to let the real value of metals run ahead of their labor cost is shattered by Smith's remark that "the greater part of mines do very little more than pay the expence of working and can seldom afford a very high rent to the landlord" (p. 168). Thus there is only the barest suggestion that while the prices of luxury goods rise, that rise also represents a worsening "labor terms of trade" between agriculture and the luxury industries.

In the end, Smith's economic argument, that the landlords get richer but less powerful with the advent of the market economy, is less convincing than his political argument. In Smith's view the political power lost by the landlord class is not gained by the merchants. In fact, he held that the great virtue of modern commercial institutions is that the old demoralizing relationship between the hungry retainer and the rich lord is destroyed once and for all. When men can draw their subsistence from only a few benefactors, they must repress their ambitions and aggressions to avoid rejection. Thus concentrated power creates a society of dependent men, completely devoid of the virtues of independence of mind and love of liberty that Smith himself cherished.[27]

A competitive market economy — not without defects of its own — at least is not characterized by the severe paternalism of feudal institutions.[28] A typical merchant derives a living from satisfying a portion of the needs of hundreds if not thousands of customers but is never wholly dependent on the benevolence of any one. The same is true of an economic system making widespread use of the division of labor.[29] The spending by any one individual may indirectly contribute to the subsistence of over 10,000 people, so that the power of any one consumer over the lives of others is so minimal that it is best described as "non-existent."

When the great proprietors of land spend their rents in maintaining their tenants and retainers, each of them maintains entirely all his own tenants and all his own retainers. But when they spend them in maintaining tradesmen and artificers, they may, all of them taken together, perhaps, maintain as great, or, on account of the waste which attends rustic hospitality, a greater number of people than before. Each of them, however, taken singly, contributes often but a very small share to the maintenance of any individual of this great number. Each tradesman or artificer derives his subsistence from the employment, not of one, but of a hundred or a thousand different customers. Though in some measure obliged to them all, therefore, he is not absolutely dependent upon any one of them [pp. 389-90].

The impersonality of the market process was, in Smith's view, necessary to the moral improvement of man.

MORAL LESSON FOR OUR TIME

The application of Smith's wisdom to our own time does not offer the most promising picture. With both major political parties in the United States calling for central planning, it is questionable whether the worst aspects of the feudal order have been put to rest once and for all. It is said that the uncertainties of the market mechanism lead individuals to demand central planning.[30]

While my knowledge of psychology is not extensive enough for me to challenge the correctness of this description of individual behavior, I do question whether central planning is either a moral or effective means for achieving economic security. Consider those intellectuals who are compelled to speak out against injustice in its many forms. The adoption of central planning is likely to usher in precisely the type of dependency among men that is inconsistent with the free expression of social criticism. As Leon Trotsky pointed out after his disillusionment with the Russian Revolution: "In a country where the sole employer is the State, opposition means death by slow starvation. The old principle, who does not work shall not eat, has been replaced by a new one: who does not obey shall not eat."[31]

Let us hope that the moral message of *The Wealth of Nations* is not forgotten now that the book has passed its two-hundredth birthday. In rereading Smith's account of the transition from feudalism to the market economy, we must not forget that the ingenious economic analysis also serves a moral purpose.

NOTES

1. Parts of this essay parallel Nathan Rosenberg's excellent article, Adam Smith, Consumer Tastes, and Economic Growth, *J. Polit. Econ.* 76(June 1968):361-73. Rosenberg did not consider the relationship of Book 3 to the "Digression on Silver" at the conclusion of Book 1 nor did he dwell on the "power" aspects of the transition from feudal institutions to modern institutions as I do in the final part of this essay.
2. See G. Rosenbluth, A Note on Labour, Wages, and Rent in Smith's Theory of Value, *Can. J. Econ.* 2(May 1969):308-14; Samuel Hollander, *The Economics of Adam Smith*

(Toronto: Univ. Toronto Press, 1973); and Laurence S. Moss, The Economics of Adam Smith: Professor Hollander's Reappraisal, *Hist. Polit. Econ.* 8(Winter 1976):564-74.

3. See, for example, Hla Myint, The Classical View of the Economic Problem, *Economica* 13(May 1946):119-30.

4. See Moss, Economics of Adam Smith, pp. 566-67.

5. The following discussion is adapted from Samuel Hollander, Some Implications of Adam Smith's Analysis of Investment Priorities, *Hist. Polit. Econ.* 3(Fall 1971):238-64. Most of the analysis summarized in the text can be found in Smith, *Wealth*, pp. 218-37, 341-55. Cf. Andrew S. Skinner, Adam Smith: An Economic Interpretation of History in *Essays on Adam Smith*, A. S. Skinner and Thomas Wilson, eds. (Oxford: Clarendon Press, 1975), pp. 154-78.

6. On the claim that Smith offered a "factor proportions" theory of development, see Hollander, *Economics of Smith*, pp. 288-90.

7. Douglass C. North and Robert P. Thomas, *The Rise of the Western World: A New Economic History* (New York: Cambridge Univ. Press, 1973), p. 57.

8. For Smith's discussion of feudal property institutions and their impact, see *Wealth*, pp. 361-72. "Feudal law did not recognize ownership in land . . . the key to property was jurisdiction." See Douglass C. North and Robert P. Thomas, The Rise and Fall of the Manorial System: A Theoretical Model, *J. Econ. Hist.* 31(Dec. 1971):800.

9. An extended discussion of these points with additional references to Smith's other writings may be found in Nathan Rosenberg, Adam Smith on Profits: Paradox Lost and Regained, *J. Polit. Econ.* 86(Nov./Dec. 1974):1184-85.

10. Smith especially refers his readers to two of Hume's essays, "Of Commerce" and "Of Luxury" that appeared in the *Political Discourses.* The first essay is reprinted in Eugene Rotwein, ed., *David Hume: Writings on Economics* (Madison: Univ. Wis. Press, 1970), pp. 3-18. Smith also refers to the 1773 edition of Hume's *History of England*, vol. 3, p. 384. It is beyond the scope of this paper to compare Hume's view of modern history with that of Smith.   .

11. Smith apparently followed Quesnay when explaining why rent necessarily accrues to corn production; see Hollander, *Economics of Smith*, p. 174. At other places Smith realized that a value surplus depends on special assumptions about supply in relation to demand and in the case of woodland or mines need not exist at all; cf. ibid., p. 166.

12. This point is largely implicit in Smith's discussion in Book 3. At the beginning of *The Wealth of Nations*, Smith explains that the size of a nation's annual revenue depends on the proportion of its work force engaged in productive as opposed to unproductive pursuits (p. lvii). In Book 2 he identifies unproductive labor with the labor of menial servants and others not involved in the fabrication of material goods, that is, durable goods. Also, an important part of the stock of capital consists of wage goods needed to feed workers engaged in capitalistic (i.e., time-consuming) methods of production (pp. 314-32). From the discussion preceding Book 3, I think it is correct to interpret Smith as viewing the transfer of the food surplus from the landlords to the merchants as a necessary condition for the transfer of laborers from unproductive to productive pursuits and the development of manufacturing industry. See also note 21 below.

13. Cf. Skinner, Adam Smith, p. 161.

14. North and Thomas, Rise and Fall, p. 798.

15. See Charles Montgomery Gray, *Copyhold, Equity, and the Common Law* (Cambridge: Harvard Univ. Press, 1963), pp. 3-21.

16. North and Thomas, Rise and Fall, p. 799.

17. Cf. Rosenberg, Adam Smith, Consumer Tastes, pp. 368-70.

18. The quotation from Hobbes that appears in *The Wealth of Nations* is: "Also riches joined with liberality is Power, because it procureth friends and servants: without liberality not so, because in this case they defend not but expose men to envy as a prey" (p. 31, note 3). The Hobbes passage is from Thomas Hobbes, *Leviathan*, C. B. MacPherson, ed. (1651; repr., Baltimore: Penguin Books, 1972), p. 150. On the sources of social conflict, see ibid., pp. 183-88. Also see Laurence S. Moss, Some Public-Choice Aspects of Hobbes's Political Thought, *Hist. Polit. Econ.* 9(Summer 1977):pp. 256-72.

19. Hobbes, *Leviathan*, pp. 151-52.

20. See, for example, Oskar Lange, *Political Economy*, 2 vols. (New York: Pergamon Press, 1963), vol. 1, pp. 65-91; Maurice Dobb, *Theories of Value and Distribution Since Adam Smith: Ideology and Economic Theory* (New York: Cambridge Univ. Press, 1973), pp.

141-55; and Paul M. Sweezy, *The Theory of Capitalist Development* (New York: Monthly Rev. Press, 1956), pp. 41-55.

21. Smith discusses silver-related trades in the city of Birmingham in *Wealth*, pp. 207-9; and later describes manufactures as the "offspring of agriculture" (p. 383). On the division of labor in manufactures, cf. pp. 242-47.

22. Rosenberg discussed this concept at length in Adam Smith, Consumer Tastes, but he did not point out that tastes are important in reestablishing the natural pattern of development that is normally guided by relative factor supplies rather than by tastes.

23. Mark Blaug stated that "the 'Digression' . . . makes use of the labor standard in analyzing the history of prices. This is Adam Smith at his best as an economic historian" in *Economic Theory in Retrospect* (Homewood, Ill.: Irwin, 1968), p. 54. Blaug added that Chapter 11 is one of the most interesting in *The Wealth of Nations* and identified its "thesis" as being that in the course of economic progress agricultural goods prices rise relative to the prices of manufactured goods. Joseph Schumpeter's appraisal of Chapter 11 (which he called "swollen by a gigantic digression") also emphasized the worsening terms of trade between manufactured and agrarian goods as an essential theme of the chapter, in *History of Economic Analysis* (New York: Oxford Univ. Press, 1954), p. 190. V. W. Bladen surveyed the main price trends identified in The Neglected and Exciting Chapter XI: On the Rent of Land, in *From Adam Smith to Maynard Keynes: The Heritage of Political Economy* (Toronto: Univ. Toronto Press, 1974), pp. 47-57. See also Samuel Hollander's treatment of the main price movements in *Economics of Smith*, pp. 171-79. The tendency among these and other writers is to view Chapter 11 as revealing Smith the technical economist at his best, but no one, to my knowledge, has commented on how the conclusions of this chapter support Smith's important argument about the transition from feudalism to capitalism.

24. On Smith's method(s) of inquiry, see Henry J. Bittermann, Adam Smith's Empiricism and the Law of Nature: I, *J. Polit. Econ.* 48(Aug. 1940):487-520; and II, 48(Oct. 1940):703-34; Herbert F. Thomson, Adam Smith's Philosophy of Science, *Quart. J. Econ.* 79(May 1965):212-33; and J. Ralph Lindgren, Adam Smith's Theory of Inquiry, *J. Polit. Econ.* 77(Nov./Dec. 1969):897-915.

25. This is one of the most remarkable yet seldom mentioned examples of the working of the "invisible hand" in *The Wealth of Nations*. Cf. the more famous "invisible hand" passage (p. 423), and Friedrich A. Hayek's discussion of forms of "social order" that result from human action but not from human design, in *Law, Legislation, and Liberty: A New Statement of the Liberal Principles of Justice and Political Economy* (Chicago: Univ. Chicago Press, 1973), vol. 1, pp. 35-54.

26. Cf. Rosenberg, Adam Smith, Consumer Tastes, p. 372. See also references in note 21.

27. See Rosenberg, Adam Smith on Profits, pp. 1184-86, for discussion and references.

28. On the abuses of capitalism and the incentive the capitalists have in bringing down wages and monopolizing markets, see ibid., pp. 117-90; and Jacob Viner, Adam Smith and Laissez-Faire, *J. Polit. Econ.* 35(Apr. 1927):198-232.

29. On the interdependencies brought about by the division of labor, see ibid., pp. 11-12.

30. Erich Fromm, *Escape from Freedom* (New York: Holt, Rinehart, and Winston, 1941).

31. Leon Trotsky, *The Revolution Betrayed: What Is Soviet Union and Where Is It Going?* Max Eastman, trans. (Garden City, N.Y.: Doubleday, 1937), p. 76. For an example of how a scientist was punished for the "sin" of displaying minimal intellectual independence under Russian socialism, see To Shrink a Scientist, *Newsweek* Aug. 8, 1977, pp. 35-36.

7

Adam Smith's Heavenly City

HENRY W. SPIEGEL

THE general consensus of informed opinion makes Smith an illustrious figure of the Enlightenment, of the Age of Reason that in Kant's words marks the liberation of man from his self-caused state of minority. The Enlightenment enthroned reason, and by exalting reason disregarded or assigned a lower place to tradition and religion, to magic and mysticism, to the passions and emotions that had inspired the dreams of an earlier age. Nevertheless, as thoughtful students of the Enlightenment have made clear, the break with the past was neither absolute nor abrupt, and the cold light of reason was often refracted by the lodestars of a bygone age. Cloaked in the language of the philosophers of the Enlightenment, old ideas would reappear in new garb and occasionally assume a dominant position in the structure of their thought.

This interpretation of the Enlightenment stands out in the title of Carl Becker's *Heavenly City of the Eighteenth-Century Philosophers,* a book that created quite a storm when it was published in 1932. While there was no absence of adverse criticism, Charles A. Beard expressed the opinion that no American had ever written a better book, and Thurman Arnold could not think of any book greater than *The Heavenly City* and modeled his own *Folklore of Capitalism* upon it.[1] More recently Crane Brinton[2] stated that, in contrast with second-rate figures, the great figures of the Enlightenment, among whom he ranks Smith, were not "terrible simplifiers," that is, in the words of Goya's caption, fanatics whose dreams of reason produced monsters. To call on another witness, whose own work loudly carries the message of the Enlightenment, one may quote the famous words of Adam Smith's close friend David Hume: "Reason is, and ought only to be, the slave of the passions, and can never pretend to any other office than to serve and obey them."[3]

This writer had the great good fortune of meeting Carl Becker at Cornell in the late 1930's, and the man and his work have never lost the spell

Henry W. Spiegel is Professor Emeritus of Economics, Catholic University of America, Washington, D.C.

that they cast over him. Following the path that Becker broke, I have set myself the task of examining some thought structures of *The Wealth of Nations* that seem to me to reflect spiritual and intellectual influences stemming from configurations of the mind that antedate the Enlightenment or run counter to its central tendency, the enthronement of a reason that interprets the world without recourse to the supernatural.

The four themes selected here for discussion are presented under these headings: Smith's view of human nature, the role of secular eschatologies in his thought, the magic of numbers, and the providential function of the market. For purposes of comparison, and in order to make Smith's position stand out more clearly, references to other figures in the history of economics are included.

SMITH'S VIEW OF HUMAN NATURE

There are dozens of different definitions of man such as Plato's "biped without feathers," Aristotle's "political animal," St. Augustine's "rational animal," Ben Franklin's "tool-making animal," and so forth. If Smith were to define man, he would refer to him as a being equipped with "the propensity to truck, barter, and exchange one thing for another." This is stated forcefully in the beginning of the work in the opening paragraph of Chapter 2 of *The Wealth of Nations*. According to Smith, this propensity "is common to all men, and to be found in no other race of animals " (p. 13). Smith then goes out of his way to underline that the propensity to truck, barter, and exchange is *the* distinctive characteristic of human beings, and he remarks: "Nobody ever saw a dog make a fair and deliberate exchange of one bone for another with another dog." This observation, which in the context is linked with other references to differences in behavior between man and animals, so provoked Smith's modern editor Cannan, who was often inclined to be censorious, that he appended this footnote: "It is by no means clear what object there could be in exchanging one bone for another" (p. 13). Cannan apparently refused to take Smith's observation seriously, but Smith's insistence on a distinctive difference between man and animals calls for extended comment. He elaborated on a matter that was of deep concern to his contemporaries and the subject of a protracted debate in the eighteenth and earlier centuries.[4] In the seventeenth century, Descartes had considered animals to be machines that lack the mind characteristic of man. In the eighteenth, La Mettrie broke the line that separated man from animals by asserting that *man* is a machine— *L'Homme machine,* as the title of his book indicates. This was published in 1747, an English translation appearing two years later. La Mettrie's views scandalized many people in eighteenth-century England who were nurtured by the tradition of Aristotle and the medieval scholastics. These had accorded a unique stature to man. As doubt was cast on this stature, doubt also was cast on the immortality of the soul as a unique prerogative of man.

When four years after the publication of his book La Mettrie, still in his early forties, died from overindulgence in food, not a few considered this a well-deserved punishment. The discussion, however, went on, with some thinkers insisting on the traditional separation of man from the animal kingdom, while others followed the opposite path. A milestone on their road was the discovery that the intermaxillary bone, hitherto believed to exist only in animals, not in man, was part of the human body as well. We do not know of Smith's reaction to this multiple discovery, which Goethe shared with the French anatomist Vicq d'Azyr, but there is little doubt that Smith meant to ally himself with the older tradition that assigned a unique position to man. His remarks do not address themselves to Goethe or Vicq d'Azyr, but to someone closer to home. They may well have been provoked by the theory which Lord Monboddo, a Scottish judge and great eccentric, had launched in 1773, just a few years before the publication of *The Wealth of Nations.*

Monboddo's views were set forth in a book on the *Origin and Progress of Language,* a subject of considerable interest to Smith and one about which he himself had written an essay in 1761. That Smith was familiar with Monboddo and his theories can be taken for granted. Both Smith and Monboddo were among the fifteen founder members of the Select Society, established in Edinburgh in 1754. Many years later, in 1780, Richard Price would close a letter to Monboddo with the request that Monboddo remember him to Smith if Smith should come Monboddo's way at Edinburgh.[5]

According to Monboddo's theory, which he developed at considerable length, there was no strict line of division between man and animals. More specifically, he was convinced of the humanity of the orangutan and of the descent of apes, monkeys, and man from a common ancestor. Unfortunately, he tried to fortify his hypothesis by insisting on the existence, in various parts of the world, of men with tails. Lovejoy, a high authority on intellectual history, credits Monboddo with having anticipated Darwin and refers to him as "the first British proponent of evolutionism, or near-evolutionism, in biology."[6]

It would seem that Smith, by underlining the difference between man and animals, meant to reply to Monboddo. Monboddo would not deny that man, "by means of our arts and sciences," might acquire characteristics that made him superior to the orangutan. But Smith believed that man was born with these characteristics, specifically with the propensity to truck, barter, and exchange. He left it open whether it is "one of those original principles in human nature, of which no further account can be given; or whether, as seems more probable, it be the necessary consequence of the faculties of reason and speech" (p. 13).

To sum up: Smith underlined what in his opinion separates man from animals and was thus closer to the older theological views than to the nascent evolutionary views of his time. What about the quality of Smith's argument? It can be presumed that many would prefer to see the distinction between man and animals made on loftier grounds than on man's ostensible propensity to truck, barter, and exchange. Thoughtful people might rather adhere to the older argument based on man's ability to formulate abstract concepts. Considerations of this sort may have considerable weight, but they are in no way decisive, because Smith nowhere claims that the propensity to truck, barter, and exchange is the *only* thing that separates man from animals.

There is yet a second view of human nature that is revealed in *The Wealth of Nations,* but at a much later stage of the discussion. Beginning in Chapter 3 of Book 2 and later repeated four times, there are references to "the desire of bettering our conditions." When Smith introduces this second propensity, he declares that it "comes with us from the womb, and never leaves us till we go to the grave. In the whole interval which separates these two moments, there is scarce perhaps a single instance in which any man is so perfectly and completely satisfied with his situation, as to be without any wish of alteration or improvement of any kind" (pp. 324-25). In the next reference Smith writes of "the uniform, constant, and uninterrupted effort of every man to better his condition . . ." This effort is said to be "frequently powerful enough to maintain the natural progress of things toward improvement" (p. 326). A few pages later he reiterates his opinion of the individuals' "universal, continual, and uninterrupted effort to better their own condition" (p. 329). At a later stage of the discussion "natural progress" is linked with "the natural effort of every individual to better his own condition" (p. 528) and again, some hundred pages later, Smith writes of "the natural effort which every man is continually making to better his own condition" (p. 638).

Thus, in addition to the propensity to truck, barter, and exchange man is held to be equipped with a second propensity, which becomes an engine of progress. Man is viewed here as Faustian, never satisfied with conditions as they are and always eager for improvement. With Goethe's Faust, he will never cling to any moment's happiness but look for new worlds to conquer. It almost seems as if Smith had drafted Faust's pledge to Mephisto:

> When on an idler's bed I stretch myself in quiet
> There let, at once, my record end.
> When thus I hail the moment flying:
> "Ah, still delay — thou art so fair!"
> Then bind me in thy bonds undying,
> My final ruin then declare![7]

When the Angels vindicate Faust, they do it in words that ring like Smith's:

> Whoe'er aspires unweariedly
> Is not beyond redeeming.[8]

Smith's man shares with Faust a quality that Santayana, an unfriendly critic, designated as romanticism's "mystical faith in will and action."[9] The

Faustian romanticism that underlies Smith's notion will be brought into still sharper relief when one traces what may have served as the source or stimulus of Smith's idea of "the desire of bettering our conditions." It is not far-fetched to look for this source in the writings of another thinker who has often been characterized as a romantic; that is, Rousseau, who in his *Discourse on the Origin of Inequality* extols the faculty of self-improvement, which is said to distinguish man from animals, about which there can be no dispute, and which gradually develops all the rest of our faculties. As is often the case in such circumstances, the adapter is carried away by his model and exaggerates certain of its features, as does Smith when he characterizes the faculty for self-improvement in the passages that have been cited.

It seems on the whole that the influence of Rousseau on Smith is more noticeable in the later sections of *The Wealth of Nations* than in earlier ones. As Viner has pointed out, it comes to the fore in the discussion of the adverse effects of the division of labor in Book 5, which contrasts so sharply with the far more favorable view of the division of labor expressed in Book 1.[10] The strong words which Smith uses at the end of his work when characterizing the ill effects of specialization have their parallel in certain passages of Rousseau's *Discourse on the Origin of Inequality.* They depict man as dehumanized, that is, alienated, in consequence of the division of labor. Thus alienation, in the modern sense of the word, may be traced to Smith as well as to Rousseau. Alienation, however, long before it acquired its modern usage, was a theological concern and considered part of the human condition resulting from the fall of man. While religion would dispel the gloom of alienation with the hope of redemption, reconciliation, or salvation, Smith offers education as a means of relief. It is indeed in order to support state aid for education, an exception from the laissez-faire principle, that Smith introduces his statement about the ill effects of the division of labor in that part of his work that treats of the expenses for education which require the attention of the state.

Yet, however much education may accomplish to undo the harm caused by specialization, Smith's man remains tainted in a pervasive way. Landowners "like to reap where they never sowed," a disposition which, according to Smith, they share with all other men. Employers and businessmen are apt to practice collusion and conspire against the public. Corporate directors neglect "other people's money." Lawyers who are paid by the length of their brief are inclined "to multiply words beyond all necessity." Great wealth frequently is "an apology for great folly." Smith writes of the "mean rapacity" of businessmen and observes that "all for ourselves, and nothing for other people, seems, in every age of the world, to have been the vile maxim of the masters of mankind" (pp. 49, 66-67, 128, 700, 680, 460, 387). Hence, no class in society has escaped the fall from grace. This gloomy view of the human condition recalls the ancient theological concern with original sin. It is not in tune with the optimistic views of the prophets of progress who were Smith's contemporaries, nor is it relieved, as in the writings of Mill and Marx, by glimpses of future earthly bliss in the stationary state or the society to come.

THE ROLE OF SECULAR ESCHATOLOGIES IN SMITH'S THOUGHT

Alienated man is liable to be especially susceptible to the idea of a millennium. That there are secular eschatologies, that is, doctrines of last things or goals in which human history will find fulfillment, has been recognized in the literature. The principal reference is to Marx, who is said to have replaced divine providence by materialistic determinism, the chosen people by the proletariat, and the Kingdom of God by the classless society. Other references are to Condorcet's belief in the unlimited perfectibility of the human race, Hegel's view of the progressive unfolding of freedom culminating in the Prussian monarchy, Comte's irreversible movement from the theological stage to the metaphysical and positive stages, and Spencer's universal view of evolution through a process of successive differentiations.

It is not so well recognized that the history of economics is studded with secular eschatologies that purport to predict the end of an economic order and the coming of a new one. These eschatologies are conventionally referred to as the stationary state, of which there are a number of variants depending upon whether the golden age is placed in the past or in the future. The pessimistic eschatologies, which place the golden age in the past, begin with Boisguilbert (1646–1714), according to whose vision economic development will come to a halt when agricultural production reaches a maximum and is no longer capable of expansion.[11] They continue with Ricardo's well-known views about the stationary state, the coming of which he anticipated with considerable alarm, and the subsequent modification of the idea by John Stuart Mill, who in 1848, after the repeal of the Corn Laws, believed he could afford a more complacent attitude. The zero-economic-growth projections that are currently in vogue present the eschatology of the stationary state in still another garb.

Although Adam Smith introduced the expression "stationary state" into the terminology of economics, the concept does not play in his system so crucial a role as in Ricardo's or Mill's. This is, first of all, due to the fact that the term is not singled out for exclusive attention but appears coordinated with parallel terms. Smith distinguishes between the progressive, the stationary, and the declining state, and relates the distinction to the conditions of the wages fund, which might be rising, constant, or falling, and the resulting conditions of the laboring class.

Smith's stationary state is described as one that has "acquired that full complement of riches which the nature of its laws and institutions permits it to acquire" (p. 17). This would place the onus for the stationary situation on the government and on inadequate, restrictive, and faulty laws that hamper economic progress. At first glance the stationary situation appears to reflect not an inexorable law of nature but human weakness. Since the latter is capable of giving way to strength, the sting does perhaps not hurt as deeply as it would if it could not be removed. There is, however, another reference to the stationary state. There a country's "full complement of riches which is consistent with the nature of its laws and institutions" is brought into a relationship with "the nature of its soil, climate, and situation" (p. 95). In this context, the latter—the nature of the soil, climate, and situation—is viewed as a remote but absolute limit to progressiveness. Whether the limit will be reached will depend on the factor mentioned before, that is, on laws and institutions. Thus a country's "complement of riches" "may be much inferior to what, with other laws and institutions, the nature of its soil, climate and situation might admit of." Considerable leeway is thus given to fend off the stationary state by means of suitable institutional arrangements.

Besides low wages, Smith's stationary state has a second characteristic, that is, low profits. As ever more capital becomes accumulated, competition among the capitalists would tend to drive profits down. This is stated more as a hypothetical than a real case, because, according to Smith, perhaps no country has as yet grown that wealthy. Faulty laws and institutions have established effective limits to accumulation that become operative long before the absolute limit that is set by the nature of soil and climate is reached.

Smith, of course, was not alone in postulating a declining tendency of profits. He shared this view with a number of great figures in the history of economics, including Marx, Ricardo, and Keynes, who all postulated such a tendency. Their reasons differ; those of Keynes being perhaps more reminiscent of Smith than the others. Economists proverbially are supposed to disagree. It surely is a curious fact that so many great economists would agree, although for different reasons, on a declining tendency of profits. Perhaps for Marx the wish was the father of the thought. None of the others was hostile to profits on grounds of ideology; rather the opposite was the case. Maybe below the level of consciousness they wished to make profits more palatable to those hostile to them by ascribing to them a declining tendency. This does not sound unreasonable if one considers that the profession grasped at such straws as the word "abstinence" in order to buttress the position of the capitalist and make his productive service appear coordinate with that of labor.

Smith's views about the stationary state do not sound unreasonable in themselves and sound even less so if one compares them with the millennial hopes of the exponents of an optimistic eschatology, who place the golden age in the future. Gossen's thought (1854) represents a utilitarian variant of this attitude. He claimed, on the penultimate page of his book and in enlarged print, that the adoption of his system of all-pervasive utilitarianism would turn the earth into a paradise. It is difficult to deny that there is an affinity between the eschatologies of Marx and Gossen and the peculiar institution of primitive peoples known as cargo cult. The cargo cultists look for salvation in the form of huge cargoes of desirable manufactures hitherto held up by greedy European traders. The arrival of the cargo will mark the beginning of a new social order. Substitute capitalists or enemies of utilitarianism for the European traders, and an underlying structure of messianic utopianism reveals itself that links Marx, Gossen, and the prophets of the cargo cult.[12] Smith was no vatic seer, and he is not to be found in this company.

SMITH AND THE MAGIC OF NUMBERS

Nowhere are the magical implications more pronounced, and nowhere are opportunities for mystification greater, than in the employment of numbers. Smith did not succumb to the magic of numbers. He kept aloof from the two variants of mathematical economics, the pure one and the one concerned with measurement, both of which had some following already at his time. Smith was not a Platonist, one who considers reality as something that cannot be grasped through the senses but only through contemplation of eternal mathematical forms. He did not follow the precepts of French rationalism, which make the mind give birth to comprehensive structures of thought that appear to follow from a few "self-evident" premises. Smith gave an account of the constructions of the Physiocrats, which constituted an early exercise in pure mathematical economics, but he did not make them his own. He did not live up to his early intention of dedicating *The Wealth of Nations* to Dr. Quesnay, either because Quesnay had died before the work was published or because he wanted to preserve his detachment from Quesnay's views or for both reasons. He was not concerned with optimization problems, which offer an irresistible invitation to mathematical treatment. Smith may have romanticized man when he gave him Faustian features, but he did not anticipate the never-ending search for optimum positions with which later generations of economists occupied themselves. Smith did not look for maxima or minima and made no use of the word "equilibrium," which the Physiocrats had introduced earlier into the language of economics.

Smith's Aristotelianism[13] reflected the pattern of a British tradition of empiricism for which Bacon had set the precedent. Bacon had written: "Empiricists are like ants, they collect and put to use; but rationalists, like spiders, spin threads out of themselves."[14] Like Bacon, Smith was more impressed with the ants than with the spiders. Bacon had little use for a mathematics that at his time still was permeated with magic. This might be exemplified by the career of Bacon's contemporary, Dr. Dee, who was equally famous as the country's foremost mathematician and as a magician. While Dee had enjoyed the favor of Queen Elizabeth, her successor had no use for him and he died poor and discredited.

There is a dim echo of the connection between magic and numbers in the career of the versatile Petty, the founder of political arithmetic. Besides being a gadgeteer who invented a ship with a double bottom that promptly sank when put to use, Petty was a wonder-worker of sorts, whose medical career culminated in the revival of a person apparently dead.[15] In regard to Smith's reaction to Petty, he had a working habit of not drawing attention to authors whose views he rejected. Thus he never cited Sir James Steuart, whose *Principles of Political Economy* had been published only nine years ahead of *The Wealth of Nations*. In *The Wealth of Nations* there are a few references to political arithmetic, but Petty is not mentioned. Other exponents of political arithmetic are cited very sparingly, Gregory King twice and Davenant once. When Smith mentions them, he employs considerable subtlety to keep them at a distance. He cites an estimate of Gregory King but endorses it with the lukewarm and reserved observation that King's skill in political arithmetic is much extolled by Dr.Davenant. At another place King is introduced with much condescension as "a man famous for his knowledge in matters of this kind" (pp. 77, 196).

That Petty and his works found no favor with Smith is not surprising because many of Petty's quantitative estimates are the result of dubious shortcuts. Davenant, Petty's principal apostle, who was more inclined to stress his merits than his faults, accused him in at least one instance of having doctored his figures to please their user.[16] Smith stated loudly and clearly: "I have no great faith in political arithmetic" (p. 501).

PROVIDENTIAL FUNCTION OF THE MARKET

Smith did not avail himself of the magic of numbers, but many will attribute an element of mystery to a magical process that transforms actions motivated by self-interest into actions beneficial to society. Those who are familiar with the history of economic ideas will be aware of the fact that Smith's invisible hand and the related concept of the self-regulating market and of nonpurposive social formations in general (which are not the result of design but of the interplay of the actions of individuals who pursue purposes of their own) are secularizations of thoughts that originally and earlier appeared in theological contexts, in which the unintended consequences of individual actions were attributed to divine providence. John R. Commons, for one, recognized this connection more than once in his writings,[17] but no one, as far as I know, has given a detailed account of it.

Let me mark off a few milestones along the road that leads to the signpost labeled invisible hand. In the fourth century John Chrysostom, one of the Greek Fathers of the Church, made the observation that economic activities pursued for the sake of private gain may turn out to the benefit of society. Work for one's own advantage and work for the benefit of others are so closely linked that no worker can earn his pay without producing something that satisfies the wants of others. The exchange economy thus conforms to the divine plan in which men are linked with one another by their needs.[18]

More than a thousand years later the reader would find in Tommaso Campanella's *City of the Sun* (1623) a reference to the Spanish conquest of the Indies that is of relevance in our context. The Spaniards, Campanella holds, were motivated by the desire for treasure, but providence directed them to spread the gospel. "We do not know what we are doing but are the instruments of God," Campanella concludes.[19] Some fifty years later, in Milton's *Paradise Lost* (1667), the idea reappears in modified form in these words of Mammon:

> Our greatness will appear
> Then most conspicuous, when great things of small,
> Useful of hurtful, prosperous of adverse,
> We can create, and in what place soe'er
> Thrive under evil, and work ease out of pain
> Through labor and endurance.[20]

Eight years later, in 1675, the French Jansenist Pierre Nicole in his *Essais de morale* came still closer to Smith's idea when he related the pursuit of enlightened self-interest *(amour-propre éclairé)* to beneficial effects identical with those that love for one's fellowmen *(charité)* would produce if it were practiced, that is, effects beneficial to society. Nicole's *Essais* were widely read at the time. John Locke translated a few of them that apparently were not published then, but a full English translation appeared soon. Nicole's discussion of the matter may be found in an essay "Of Grandeur" in the second volume of the work, and in one "Of Charity and Self-love" in the third volume.[21] Gilbert Chinard has called attention to these passages, which may well constitute the earliest close approximation to the invisible hand.[22] In the essay "Of Charity and Self-love" it is argued that by means of trade, that is, by exchanging goods and services, all necessities of life are in some way supplied without the intervention of charity. So that in states in which charity is not practiced because the true religion is banished there, men nevertheless enjoy as much peace, safety, and accommodation as if they were living in a community of saints. In the essay "Of Grandeur" the same idea is restated; the context there is the public order under which exchange occurs and which facilitates it. Here we find a paragraph enthusiastically depicting the blessings of the great society, in which the life of the individual is enriched by his ability to draw on the resources of the world to make his life comfortable, a portrayal of the exchange economy that has much in common with the concluding paragraph of the opening chapter of *The Wealth of Nations*. At both places the reader encounters remarks comparing the position of an individual in the exchange economy with that of a king. Nicole says that a million of men work for him;[23] Smith, not carried away as easily, writes of "many thousands" (p. 11ff.).

Nicole's life spans the seventeenth century; Smith was a figure of the eighteenth. In that century a man of learning would realize his highest ambition if he succeeded in detecting the pattern of the "natural order." This applies to the Physiocrats as well as to earlier writers who were more closely attached to the ties of the religious tradition. Such writers would be inclined to identify the natural order with providence, and if the free market reflected the natural order, it also reflected the workings of providence. No one expressed this linkage of ideas more forcefully than Boisguilbert. "Nature," he wrote, "which is nothing but providence," has arranged things in such a manner that if it is left alone—"on laisse faire la nature"—there will be an equilibrium in which sellers will be adequately recompensed and sufficient supplies secured.[24] Here is one of the origins of the ostensibly mundane and this-worldly laissez-faire doctrine, which later in the eighteenth century was to shed its theological implications.

The writings of Mandeville, who early in the century published his celebrated Fable of the Bees, play a more equivocal role in the doctrinal history of nonpurposive social formations. Mandeville scandalized the reading public of his time by making private vices such as greed and luxury the source of public benefits. He is best interpreted as mischief maker and satirist, who posed as the strictest of moralists and as such judged mankind enmeshed in total depravity. Since he was a man of considerable talent and wit and rather widely read, every moral philosopher of the period had to face up to him. Smith's reaction to his views can be gleaned from a communication to the old Edinburgh Review at midcentury, in which the sedate and restrained philosopher referred to him as "the profligate Mandeville."

Smith did indeed not need Mandeville's paradoxes to assist him in the formulation of the laissez-faire doctrine. Moreover, Mandeville was not an exponent of "the obvious and simple system of natural liberty" to which Smith was attached. He may have been a libertine but was no libertarian. To Smith it was competition that made the pursuit of private interest beneficial to society, whereas Mandeville considered "the dexterous management of a skillful politician" indispensable to turn private vices into public benefits.[25]

The later history of the doctrine of Smith that is embodied in the invisible hand is of no concern in the present context. Suffice it to say that there is an echo of it in Goethe's Faust, where Mephisto refers to himself as "part of that power, not understood,/Which always wills the bad, and always works the good."[26]

There is an affinity also with the "cunning of reason," which according to Hegel, who was a casual student of economics, equips man with unreasonable passions to realize ends that are not of his intentions, and even with an occasional thought of Marx, who in a passage brought to light by Thomas Sowell has this to say: "For what each individual wills is obstructed by everyone else, and what emerges is something that no one willed."[27] No reference to providence here!

CONCLUSION

We may reiterate that Smith's view of human nature, with its emphasis on the uniqueness of man, conforms to a theological tradition of long standing, even though the basis of his argument, man's alleged propensity to truck, barter, and exchange, is alien to this tradition. Again, the

Faustian character of man's persistent striving for betterment, which Smith makes all-pervasive, smacks of romanticism rather than of classic restraint. Smith, however, refused to be a prophet, who would exalt his audience by promising the millennium or chastise it with the threat of catastrophe. Nevertheless he provided ammunition to later seers with his legacy of the words "stationary state." In a soft science, words have a special power of their own.

Moving on to the invisible hand and all that this figure of speech implies, there is little doubt about its derivation from earlier theological views about a providential ordering of the universe. Lastly, as far as the magic of numbers is concerned, Smith refused to submit to its spell.

To the question of whether Smith built a heavenly city some may reply in the affirmative, making the most of his vision of free men and the free market, a vision in which the works of Mammon and Mephisto are transformed into public benefits. Others may conclude that Smith built no heavenly city, but that, master builder that he was, he used for the construction of the city of man a number of durable building blocks purveyed from the heavenly city. If one gazes at the mighty edifice of *The Wealth of Nations*, parts of it are in ruins, witnesses to the relentless demolition brought about by scientific progress. Other parts still stand, and what has best been preserved is a magnificent facade with a portal inscribed The Market.

No part of Smith's message has proved more durable and influential than his doctrine of nonpurposive social formations. As we have noted, it is a doctrine that has a miraculous or mystical flavor. Could it be that it is this feature of it that accounts for the doctrine's amazing strength and durability? Applying a suggestion of Bettelheim, one might surmise that the strong appeal with which this doctrine of Smith is equipped reflects the fact that it accommodates certain basic psychological needs of the reader, an accommodation perhaps characteristic of every great piece of writing. As Bettelheim puts it in Freudian terms, interest in all "cognitive intellectual endeavors, however much the content may be selected realistically and intelligently with regard to ego needs, gains its emotional fervor only from id and superego."[28]

The study of economics, like all serious study, provides by itself a cognitive ego achievement. In the case of *The Wealth of Nations* the superior purposes embodied in individual liberty and society's well-being further satisfy the superego, while the workings of the invisible hand, a mysterious term that refers to a somewhat miraculous process, cannot fail to gratify the id. It was by hitting the three chords of the human mind that Smith gave his message a resonance that has not been stilled for two hundred years.

NOTES

1. B. T. Wilkins, *Carl Becker* (Cambridge: Harvard Univ. Press, 1961), p. 184.
2. Enlightenment, *Encyclopedia of Philosophy* (New York: Collier-Macmillan, 1967), vol. 2, p. 525.

3. *A Treatise of Human Nature*, L. A. Selby-Bigge, ed. (Oxford: Oxford Univ. Press, 1896), p. 415.
4. For a survey of the controversy see Morus (Richard Lewinsohn), *Animals, Men and Myths* (London: 1954), Ch. 15.
5. William Knight, *Lord Monboddo and Some of His Contemporaries* (New York and London: J. Murray, 1900), pp. 11, 123; J. F. Bell, Adam Smith, Clubman, *Scot. J. Polit. Econ.* 7(1960):111-12.
6. Arthur O. Lovejoy, *Essays in the History of Ideas* (Baltimore: Johns Hopkins Univ. Press, 1948), p. 53.
7. J. W. von Goethe, *Faust*, Bayard Taylor, trans. (Boston: 1879), vol. 1, p. 94.
8. Ibid., vol. 2, p. 24.
9. George Santayana, *Three Philosophical Poets* (Cambridge: Harvard Univ. Press, 1910), p. 8.
10. John Rae, *Life of Adam Smith*, with a new Introduction, Guide to John Rae's Life of Adam Smith, by Jacob Viner (New York: Kelley, 1965), p. 36.
11. See Michel Lutfalla, *L'Etat stationnaire* (Paris: 1964), Ch. 7.
12. A leading anthropologist has confirmed this observation: "This vision [the phantom cargo] differs from Western descriptions of the millennium only because of the bizarre prominence of industrial products." Marvin Harris, *Cows, Pigs, Wars and Witches: The Riddle of Culture* (New York: Random House, 1975), p. 134ff.
13. For an application and further elaboration of the distinction between Platonism and Aristotelianism in the history of economics see H. W. Spiegel, A Note on the Equilibrium Concept in the History of Economics, *Economie Appliquée* 28(1975):609-17.
14. *The Works of Francis Bacon*, J. Spedding et al., ed. (London: Longman, 1859), vol. 3, p. 616 (from *Cogitata et Visa*, 1607).
15. Lord Edmond Fitzmaurice, *The Life of Sir William Petty* (London: J. Murray, 1895), p. 18ff., esp. p. 113.
16. "He rather made his court, than spoke his mind." Charles Davenant, *Discourses on the Public Revenue and on the Trade of England* (1698), repr. in his *Works* (London: 1771), vol. 1, p. 130.
17. John R. Commons, *Legal Foundations of Capitalism* (New York: Kelley, 1924), pp. 137, 204.
18. Ignaz Seipel, *Die wirtschaftsethischen Lehren der Kirchenväter* (Vienna: 1907), p. 108ff.
19. The most readily accessible reference is *Ideal Empires and Republics*, with an Introduction by Charles M. Andrews (Washington and London: 1901), p. 317.
20. Book 2, p. 257ff. Cited by Max Weber, *Gesammelte Aufsätze zur Wissenschaftslehre*, 2nd ed. (Tübingen: H. Laupp'schen Buchhandlung, 1951), p. 33.
21. Pierre Nicole, *Moral Essays*, 3rd ed. (London: 1696), vol. 2, p. 83ff.; vol. 3, p. 78ff.
22. Gilbert Chinard, *En lisant Pascal* (Lille: 1948), p. 112ff. Henri Bremond *Histoire littéraire du sentiment religieux en France* (Paris: 1920), vol. 4, Ch. 10, 11, are devoted to Nicole, but Bremond has nothing to say about the aspect of Nicole's work discussed in this essay. This makes doubly relevant Bremond's observation: "It is sad, almost scandalous, that no one has ever written a study in depth of Nicole. The young scholars who would assume this task could be generously rewarded for their effort," p. 419.
23. Nicole, *Essays*, vol. 2, p. 99ff.
24. Pierre Boisguilbert, *Détail de la France sous le règne présent*, 2nd ed. (Brussels: 1712), vol. 1, p. 230. Cited by August Oncken, *Geschichte der Nationaloekonomie*, Pt. 1 (Leipzig: Duncker and Humblot, 1902), p. 251.
25. See Jacob Viner, Introduction to Bernard Mandeville, *A Letter to Dion* (1732), originally published in 1953 and reprinted in *The Long View and the Short* (New York: Macmillan, 1958), p. 341ff.
26. Goethe, *Faust*, vol. 1, p. 74.
27. Cited by Thomas Sowell, *Say's Law: An Historical Analysis* (Princeton: Princeton Univ. Press, 1972), p. 231.
28. Bruno Bettelheim, Janet and Mark and the New Illiteracy, *Encounter* 43(Nov. 1974):18.

III   Politics in the Eighteenth and Twentieth Centuries

8

The Justice of Natural Liberty

🍂 JAMES M. BUCHANAN

THE 1976 bicentennial of the publication of Adam Smith's *The Wealth of Nations* occurs amid a still accelerating discussion of the principles of justice, stimulated in large part by John Rawls. His catalytic book, *A Theory of Justice,* published in 1971,[1] has caused economists and other social scientists and philosophers to devote more attention to "justice" in the first half of the 1970s than in perhaps all the preceding decades of this century combined. This discussion has been hailed as the return of political and social philosophy to its former status of intellectual interest and respectability. My purpose in this essay is to reexamine Adam Smith's norms for social order, notably for justice, especially as these may be related to the modern post-Rawlsian discussion. I want, in particular, to evaluate Smith's "system of natural liberty" in terms of criteria for justice akin to those employed by Rawls.

To do this, it will first be necessary to define, as fully as possible, Smith's underlying model or paradigm for social interaction, a paradigm influenced by the historical setting of Scotland in the 1770s. In addition, it will be useful to discuss briefly Smith's methodology. Once these steps are taken, we can outline Smith's ordering of the priorities for reform. From this we should then be able to suggest how a returned Adam Smith might view our society in 1976, and how his modern ordering of reform priorities might differ from those two centuries removed. This imagined Smithian stance may then be compared and/or contrasted with that of John Rawls. In what may be surprising results (especially to those only casually familiar with the works of each man) I shall demonstrate that the similarities outweigh the differences. A returned Adam Smith would be a long distance from the modern libertarian anarchists, and even from the espousal

James M. Buchanan is University Distinguished Professor and General Director of the Center for Study of Public Choice, Virginia Polytechnic Institute and State University, Blacksburg.

I am indebted to my colleagues, Victor Goldberg, Nicolaus Tideman, Gordon Tullock, and Richard Wagner for helpful comments on earlier drafts.

of the minimal state described by Robert Nozick.[2] But Rawls is also a long distance from the position attributed to him, that of being a "defender of the liberal welfare state, somewhat modified in the direction of greater egalitarianism."[3] These philosophers would surely be closer to each other than either would be to the image that intellectual fashion has imposed upon him.

THE REAL AND CONCEPTUAL WORLDS OF ADAM SMITH

Adam Smith was one of the leading figures of the Scottish Enlightenment, which suggests that his interests were in no way provincial. His intent in *The Wealth of Nations* was to offer a readily generalizable criticism of what he labeled the "policy of Europe." But he lived and worked, nonetheless, in eighteenth-century Scotland. Because his writings (notably *The Wealth of Nations*) retain so many elements of direct and current relevance, it is easy for the modern reader to neglect the necessary influences of time and place on his analysis as well as on his normative priorities.

What were the essential structural characteristics of the society Smith observed? Almost two centuries would elapse before a popular tract could condemn an "affluent society." The Industrial Revolution, with its technological counterpart, was in its very early and formative stages. Indeed, its full achievements might never have become reality save for the impact of some of Smith's ideas. The modern corporation was foreshadowed only in the government-sponsored international trading companies. Still largely agricultural, Britain was only beginning to become "a nation of shopkeepers."

The society Smith observed was highly stable relative to that of our own century. This society was also very poor by twentieth-century standards; Smith's analysis was applied directly to what we would now call a "developing" or an "underdeveloped" society. The expansion in material goods generated by the technological revolution of the post-Enlightenment era was not predictable in 1776. Most men were born to live, work, and die in the same local community.

Some appreciation of this historical setting is helpful in any attempt to define Smith's working model for social interaction. Two central elements of this model or paradigm may be isolated here, elements that are important in understanding his conceptions of justice. The first of these involves what we should now call the utility of income to the individual. Smith did not use this terminology, and he was not intellectually hidebound by the now dominant orthodoxy that largely neglects basic questions about the meaning of utility itself and then proceeds to impose a particular form on the utility function. Instead, Smith carefully distinguished between that which drives men to action—the promised or anticipated utility from an increasing stream of real goods and services or from a growing stock of assets—and that which measures the actual satisfactions secured subsequent to the receipt of such incremental flows and stocks. Beyond a certain level of real income (a level that was nonetheless presumably out of reach for the average or representative member of the working class) the anticipated marginal utility of income to an individual exceeds the realized marginal utility. This divergence constituted, for Smith, the great deception that was essential in driving the whole system and acted to insure that self-interest would generate increasing prosperity and economic growth.[4]

In some sense, therefore, differentials in measured or received incomes among individuals and among social classes or groups were, to Smith, considerably less important than to his counterpart who inhabited the modern welfare state. Smith was not nearly so ready to translate these into differences in achieved satisfaction, happiness, or well-being. And who is to attribute the naivete to Adam Smith in this respect? The balance is not on one side alone.

Smith expressed little or no normative concern with income differences among persons; he was primarily concerned with the absolute levels of income generated and with the differences in these levels among time periods, that is, with growth. He did infer a direct relationship between the aggregate income generated for the whole society and the well-being of the laboring classes.

A second element of Smith's model for social interaction is helpful in evaluating his conceptions of justice. He did not assume or postulate significant differentials in capacities among human beings. The differences between the "philosopher and the street porter" were explained largely in terms of upbringing, training, and education. In the current debates Smith would find himself arrayed squarely on the side of those who stress environmental factors and who play down the relevance of genetic endowments. Smith was also writing before Cairnes and Mill had developed the economic theory of noncompeting groups. In his conceptual model, individual income differences (at least in regard to wage or salary incomes) were explained largely in "equalizing" terms. That is to say, in an operative "system of natural liberty" the observed differences would be those that would be predicted to emerge when all persons freely exercised their choices among occupations and employments. By implication, at least for the members of the laboring class, in such a system all persons would be equally advantaged at the onset of making career and occupational choices.

THE SCOTTISH METHOD

A. L. Macfie makes the distinction between what he calls the Scottish method, characteristic of Smith's approach to problems of social policy, and the scientific or analytical method, which is more familiar to modern social scientists.[5] In the former the center of attention lay in the society as observed rather than in the idealized version of that society in abstraction. As suggested above, Smith had an underlying model or paradigm for social interaction; he could scarcely have discussed reforms without one. But his interest was in making the existing social structure "work better," in terms of the norms he laid down, rather than evaluating the possible limitations of the structure as it might work ideally if organized on specific principles. Frank Knight suggested that critics of the enterprise system are seldom clear as to whether they object to market order because it does not work in accordance with its idealized principles or because it does work in some approximation to these principles. Applied to Smith, his position was straightforward. He was critical of the existing economic order of his time because it did not work in accordance with the principles of natural liberty. He was not, and need not have been, overly concerned with some ultimate evaluation of an idealized structure.

Smith's methodology has been turned on its head by many modern scientists. The post-Pigovian theory of welfare economics has largely if not entirely consisted in a search for conceptual flaws in the workings of an idealized competitive economic order, conceived independently of the flawed and imperfect order that may be observed to exist. Partial correctives are offered in both the theory of the second best and in the still emerging theory of public choice, but the perfect-competition paradigm continues to dominate applied economic policy discussions.

This methodological distinction is important in our examination of Smith's conception of justice. In one sense John Rawls's efforts in defining and delineating "a theory of justice" are akin to those of the neoclassical economists who first described the idealized competitive economy. (This is not to suggest that Rawls's attempt has had or will have comparable success or even that the basic subject matter is amenable to comparable analytical treatment.) By contrast Adam Smith saw no need of defining in great detail the idealized operation of a market system and of evaluating this system in terms of strict efficiency criteria. Similarly, he would have seen no need of elaborating in detail a complete theory of justice, of defining the principles that must be operative in a society that would be adjudged to be "just." In comparing Smith with Rawls, therefore, we must somehow bridge the contrasting methodologies. We can proceed in either one of two ways. We can make an attempt to infer from Smith's applied discussion of real problems what his idealized principles of justice might have embodied. Or we can infer from Rawls's treatment of idealized principles what his particular applications of these might be in an institutional context. Both these routes will be followed in the discussion below.

JUSTICE AS SECURITY

Adam Smith did not publish the book on jurisprudence that he had projected, although a student's notes from his lectures apparently include most of the material that might have been incorporated.[6] In these lectures "justice" was listed as only one of the four great objects of law. In the section specifically on justice, Smith referred almost exclusively to the relatively narrow conception of security. "The end of justice is to secure from injury."[7] In this context the treatment seems quite different from that of Rawls, for whom "justice is the first virtue of social institutions."[8] But even here the difference can be exaggerated. Smith explicitly calls attention to security as a necessary attribute of any well-functioning society, and he reflects commonsense usage of the term "justice" in his discussion. Two centuries later Rawls takes this aspect of justice more or less for granted and shifts his discussion to another level. He would presumably agree fully with Smith that any just society would also require security of person and property. Rawls's primary interest is "beyond justice" in the more restricted definition employed by Adam Smith.[9]

Their difference lies in the fact that Smith did not make a comparable extension. Distributive justice, in the modern meaning of this term, is largely neglected by Smith, at least in terms of explicit treatment. This is explained in part by Smith's underlying presuppositions about utility differences and in part by the relatively greater importance appropriately assigned to economic development in the eighteenth-century setting. As I shall demonstrate, however, Smith's suggestions for policy reforms generate distributive results that may be reconciled readily with Rawlsian criteria. We need not accept Jacob Viner's interpretation that writers in the Scottish tradition were minimally interested in reform in the modern meaning of this term.[10]

NATURAL LIBERTY

Adam Smith explicitly rejected a contractarian explanation for the emergence of government and for the obligation of persons to abide by law, preferring instead to ground both on the principles of authority and utility.[11] Furthermore, he did not recognize the possible value of using a conceptualized contract as a benchmark or criterion with which to evaluate alternative political structures. However, his device of the "impartial spectator" serves this function and is in many respects akin to the conceptualized contract. Smith's norms for social order were not strictly utilitarian in the Benthamite sense, and justice was an important attribute — justice that embodied the security to person and property previously noted but extending beyond this when his whole structure is considered.[12] Beyond security, Adam Smith would have surely ranked "natural liberty" as his first principle of justice.

> To hurt in any degree the interest of any one order of citizens, for no other purpose but to promote that of some other, is evidently contrary to that justice and equality of treatment which the sovereign owes to all the different orders of his subjects [p. 618].[13]

In several applied cases he makes clear that violations of natural liberty are unjust — e.g., apprenticeship requirements (pp. 121-22), restrictions on migration (p. 141), entry restrictions (p. 497).

Smith's great work, *The Wealth of Nations*, has been widely interpreted as being informed normatively by efficiency criteria. This emphasis is broadly correct, provided that the efficiency norm is not given exclusive place. Smith's purpose was that of demonstrating how the removal of restrictions on free market forces and how the operation of his "system of natural liberty" would greatly increase the total product of the economy; and more importantly, how this would generate rapid economic growth, thereby improving the lot of the laboring classes. What is often missing from this standard interpretation is Smith's corollary argument, sometimes implicit, to the effect that this system of natural liberty would also promote his ideal of justice. Failure to allow individuals to employ "their stock and industry in the way that they judge most advantageous to themselves, is a *manifest violation of the most sacred rights of mankind*" (p. 549). (Emphasis added.) There was, to Smith, no trade-off between "efficiency" and "equity" in the more familiar modern sense. As a general principle of social order, the freedom of individual choice would produce efficiency; but it would also be a central attribute of any social order that was just.

Emphasis here is on this aspect of Smith's argument, so that we can compare his first principle of "natural liberty" with Rawls's first principle of "equal liberty." Smith's method forces us to look at his examples rather than expecting to find any elaborate discussion of the concept per se. These examples suggest that Adam Smith was by no means an eighteenth-century Robert Nozick, who conceived natural moral boundaries to individuals' rights and claimed that any invasion of these rights was unjust. The Smithian system of natural liberty is not anarchy—either the Hobbesian war of each against all or the more confined Rothbard-Nozick setting where individuals mutually respect the boundaries of each other. "Boundary crossings," to employ Nozick's helpful terminology here, violate Smith's natural liberty in some cases; but such violations must be assessed in essentially pragmatic terms. Smith's sanctioned violations of natural liberty did not seem invariant to the environmental setting in which individuals might find themselves.

Almost by necessity we look at Smith's treatment from the vantage point of modern welfare economics. When we do so, his limits to the exercise of natural liberty seem to coincide surprisingly with the extensions of potentially warranted collective action that might be laid down by a careful and sophisticated application of externality analysis. In Smith's view there is clearly an unwarranted invasion of natural liberty if an individual's freedom of choice is restricted when there are no demonstrable spillover damages on others in the community. On the other hand, Smith sanctioned interferences with individual freedom of choices when the exercise of such choices (for example, the building of walls that were not fireproof) "might endanger the security of the whole society." Smith explicitly stated that such latter restrictions on individual choices might be "considered as in some respect a violation of natural liberty," but that such choices ought to be "restrained by the laws of all governments" (p. 308).

Adam Smith distinguished between what we would now call pecuniary and technological externalities. His approved interferences with natural liberty extended only to cases where genuine technological externality could be demonstrated, and he quite explicitly stated that possible pecuniary spillovers gave no cause for restrictions on trade. See, in particular, his discussion rejecting imposition of restrictions on entry into retailing trades even "though they [shopkeepers] may so as to hurt one another" (p. 342). It would be absurd to suggest here that Smith's final array of potentially justifiable interferences with the freedom of individual choices corresponds fully with that which might be produced by the modern welfare economist. Furthermore, his own array of examples of potentially warranted interferences with natural liberty would surely be different in 1976 from that in 1776.

On balance, however, there seems no question but that Smith's implied analysis of potential restrictions on the freedom of individual market choices can be made reasonably consistent with modern efficiency analysis, utilizing Pareto criteria for meaningful improvement. That is to say, even if Pareto optimality or efficiency is held up as the only relevant norm, many of Smith's particular examples would qualify. What is important for the purpose here, however, is that Smith sanctioned interferences only when efficiency criteria overweighed those of justice, conceived here not in distributional terms at all, but in terms of the value of natural liberty. If we leave aside considerations of administration and enforcement, modern economic analysis would suggest the introduction of restrictions when overall efficiency is enhanced, with no explicit recognition of the necessary trade-off with individual freedom of choice. With Smith, by contrast, any restriction on the freedom of individuals "may be said . . . [to be] a manifest violation of that natural liberty which it is the proper business of law, not to infringe, but to support" (p. 308). Possible efficiency gains must therefore be reckoned against the costs in liberty — in "justice" in the broader sense here considered.

In evaluating his own work, there is some evidence that Smith considered *The Wealth of Nations* to be a demonstration that the "system of natural liberty," which emerged more fundamentally from normative criteria of justice, could also meet efficiency criteria.

In Rae's citations from the notes of John Millar, one of Smith's best students, there is the following passage:

> In the last of his lectures he examined those political regulations which are founded, not upon the principle of *justice* but that of *expediency,* and which are calculated to increase the riches, power, and prosperity of a state. Under this view he considered the political institutions relating to commerce, to finances, to ecclesiastical and military establishments. What he delivered on these subjects contained the substance of the work he afterwards published under the title of *An Inquiry into the Nature and Causes of the Wealth of Nations.*[14]

It is perhaps our relative overconcentration on Smith's major treatise that causes modern interpreters to overlook the noneconomic or, more generally, the nonutilitarian foundations for the "natural system of perfect liberty and justice" (p. 572).

RAWLS'S PRINCIPLE OF EQUAL LIBERTY

Smith's principle may be compared with John Rawls's first principle of justice, that of "equal liberty," to which he assigns lexicographical priority over his second principle. These two principles or conceptions of liberty are, in practice, substantially equivalent, although, strictly speaking and perhaps surprisingly, Rawls must be classified as a more ardent laissez-faire theorist than Smith. This is due to Rawls's lexical ordering of the principle of equal liberty as prior to his distributive precept. Smith, by comparison, inserts a threshold before marginal trade-offs can be considered, a threshold beyond which invasions of apparent natural liberty might presumably be sanctioned. But their positions are similar in that neither Smith nor Rawls is utilitarian in the sense that final evaluation is reduced to a single standard. To Smith, the "impartial spectator" would not condone piecemeal interferences with natural liberty, even if aggregate social production was thereby maximized. To Rawls, the maximization of expected utility is rejected as the objective, even behind a genuine veil of ignorance.

The principle of equal liberty, as presented by Rawls, is stated as follows: "Each person is to have an equal right to the most extensive total system of equal basic liberties compatible with a similar system of liberty for all."[15] In his discussion Rawls emphasizes the implications of this principle for political institutions (for example, for equality of franchise, for freedom of speech and press), but he tends to neglect the comparable implications for economic institutions, which were central to Adam Smith's concern. In several places Rawls states that the principle of equal liberty suggests a market system, saying, "I assume in all interpretations that the first principle of equal liberty is satisfied and that the economy is roughly a free market system. . . ."[16] But he does not go on to particular examples or cases. Nonetheless, any attempt to apply the Rawlsian principle must lead to a condemnation of many overt restrictions on individual choices that have been and may be observed in the real world. Particular interferences that would in this way be classified as "unjust" by Rawlsian criteria would correspond very closely to those Smith classified in the same way.

Consider only two of the most flagrant modern-day examples. The uniform minimum wage regulations imposed by the Congress under the Fair Labor Standards Act, as amended, would clearly be "unjust" under either Rawlsian or Smithian criteria. Mutually agreeable contractual terms between unemployed persons (notably teenagers) and potential employers are prohibited, with an absence of comparable restrictions on others in society. Minimum wage legislation would also be unjust by Rawls's second principle, since the primary groups harmed are those who are least advantaged, that is, those with relatively low economic productivity. Or consider the regulations of the Interstate Commerce Commission in restricting entry into trucking—clearly an invasion of the natural liberty of those who might want to enter this business freely, as well as a violation of the principle of equal liberty. The listing could be readily extended to such institutions as tenure in universities, restrictive licensing of business and professions, prohibition or sumptuary taxation of imports, subsidization of exports, union shop restrictions in labor contracts, and many others.

It is unfortunate that Rawls did not see fit to discuss more fully the application of his first principle to such institutions, especially since his treatise and general argument have attracted such widespread attention from social scientists generally. Economists have continued to call attention to the inefficiency of these institutions, but since Smith they have rarely called attention to their fundamental injustice.[17] Had they or Rawls done so, these institutions might have proved more vulnerable to criticism than they have appeared to be.

Difficulties arise when we attempt to apply the Rawlsian principle of equal liberty to restrictions on individual choices that might be plausibly defended on familiar externality grounds. As noted above, Smith's less constraining norm allows natural liberty to be violated under some circumstances, provided that the costs are properly reckoned. But Rawls's lexical ordering prevents this sort of trade-off, even with the insertion of an appropriate threshold. Consider for a real-world example the closing of the Saltville, Va., plant of the Olin Corporation in the early 1970s as a result of government-imposed water-quality standards. Local residents were left unemployed; long-term contractual agreements between these persons and Olin were terminated, clearly a restriction on liberties. Presumably, defense of this government action was based on the alleged benefits of improved water quality to the general population of the whole country. It does not seem possible to stretch Rawls's principle of equal liberty to cover such instances. The liberties of some persons were restricted for the alleged benefits of others and without appropriate compensation. There was no trade-off with other liberties, as Rawls might have required; the defense could only have been advanced on utilitarian-efficiency grounds. To Rawls, this government action could only be classified as "unjust."

This is not to suggest that the idealized Rawlsian constitution could not allow for escapes from the genuine externality–public goods dilemmas that fully independent private adjustments might produce. Such a constitution would require that such escapes be accomplished through more inclusive contractual agreements, that would embody compensations to those who might be harmed by change. The point here is to indicate that the Rawlsian principle of equal liberty would not allow for government-imposed changes without compensation, regardless of the benefit-cost ratios.

Working from the principle of equal liberty alone, therefore, and keeping in mind the lexical priority assigned to this in his whole construction, we must conclude that John Rawls is far from the "defender of the liberal welfare state" that he has been made out to be, and, indeed, that his implied institutional structure for the economy closely resembles that first described by Adam Smith. Only a "system of natural liberty," a regime of effectively operating free markets, could meet Rawlsian requirements for "equal liberty," and, through these, for "justice."

DISTRIBUTION AND JUSTICE

Rawls has been misinterpreted because of his relative neglect in elaborating the implications of his first principle for economic institutions and, more important, because of his relative concentration on the second principle he adduces, that which addresses the distribution of the social product. It is here that Adam Smith and John Rawls seem most apart; Rawls explicitly discusses the system of natural liberty only to reject it in favor of what he terms the system of democratic equality.[18] But we need to see precisely wherein these two philosophers diverge. I shall try to demonstrate that, once their methodological differences are acknowledged and their empirical presuppositions are fully exposed, there need be little variance in their assessments of reform priorities in a 1976 setting.

Let us first examine the distributional consequences of Adam Smith's system of natural liberty under the empirical presuppositions that Smith himself adopted. In 1776 a very large part of the total population was made up of members of the laboring classes, and Smith did not think that inherent differences in capacities were significant. The economic position of an average or representative member of this group could best be improved by allowing markets to emerge freely and to operate by removing all or substantially all restrictions on trade and by eliminating all constraints on the flow of resources, human and nonhuman, among alternative uses. Such a system would predictably generate differences in incomes among separate members of the laboring classes, but these would tend to equalize the relative advantages of separate employments. Those who were not members of these classes — employers who accumulate capital and utilize it productively in hiring labor — would secure differentially higher incomes from profits. But Smith makes it clear that it is precisely the attraction of such incomes that drives the whole process and insures that the economy grows and prospers. Even here, however, Smith raises some questions about the efficacy of exceptionally high incomes from profits, and he warns against the tendency toward profligacy that such excesses create.[19] Smith is not clear on the possible allocative role played by rental incomes secured by landowners. Given his pre-Ricardian but quasi-Ricardian model of the economy, he probably would not have been opposed to taxes on land rent.

There are distributional consequences of Smith's system, but, strictly speaking, the distribution of products among social classes or among members of any one class is clearly secondary to production, to securing maximal national income. This was to be accomplished by the removal of disincentives throughout the economy. The overriding objective was to increase the economic well-being of the members of the laboring classes, while adhering to the precept of justice the system of natural liberty represented.

At first glance Smith's system seems a world apart from the Rawlsian setting, where the emphasis is on distribution, with production being largely neglected. The difference principle of distribution, appended lexically to that of equal liberty, states that inequalities in access to primary goods are acceptable in the just society only insofar as they are shown to be advantageous to the least-advantaged members of the community. But in the empirical setting postulated for Smith, what would an application of this Rawlsian difference principle have implied? An argument for a tax on land value might have been produced, along with an argument for taxation of excessively high incomes from profits, with a redistribution of proceeds generally to members of the laboring classes. Perhaps more important, from his discussion of the favorable effects of less restrictive laws of land ownership and transfer in the English as opposed to the Spanish and Portuguese colonies, we may infer that Smith would have supported legal reforms designed to open up prospects for greater mobility of persons between the landowning and nonlandowning groups (pp. 538-39). Such reform implications of his system could have been readily accepted by Smith, who might, however, have treated such reforms as being of minor importance relative to the more fundamental steps that involved the removal of government constraints on individual liberty.

Rawls projects the distributional issue to center stage perhaps because he presumes empirically that only a relatively remote relationship exists between the pattern of income receipts and of asset holdings in society and the aggregate size of the total product. Furthermore, he seems to assume that a distribution of natural or inherent capacities exists among persons, a distribution tending to generate nonequalizing income-wealth differentials that carry with them neither economic nor moral justification. In the Rawlsian paradigm the philosopher is not merely an educated porter.

The "system of natural liberty" that Rawls explicitly discusses and rejects is not that of Smith.[20] Rawls uses this designation to refer to a system that embodies economic efficiency (Pareto optimality) as its only objective, and his critical remarks suggest that he does not impose the constraints made quite explicit in Smith. Rawls does not examine Smith's system in itself, but from his more general discussion we may infer that his central objection would be focused on the dependence of distributional outcomes on initial asset holdings or initial endowments. Before treating this point in some detail, I reemphasize that Rawls does not criticize the market-determined distribution of product, given the set of initial endowments—a source of much confusion in the continuing critique of social institutions.[21]

His attention is properly concentrated, on the premarket distribution of endowments to which, contrary to Nozick, Rawls attributes no moral qualities.

Adam Smith did not discuss the distribution of initial endowments; but for his system of natural liberty to meet the Rawlsian precepts for justice in the postulated Rawlsian setting, two conditions would have to be met. First, any deliberately imposed change in the basic institutions of society designed to bring about greater equality in initial endowments must be shown to worsen the position of the least advantaged. It does not seem likely that this condition could be fulfilled.[22] Even here, however, it should be recognized that the most glaring inequalities in initial endowments could scarcely arise in a genuine system of natural liberty. How many great family fortunes would exist had not the government employed its power to enforce and to police monopoly privileges? Second, there would have to be a direct relationship between the economic position of the least-advantaged members of society and the total income generated in the economy. This condition seems more likely to be met, regardless of how the least-advantaged members are to be defined, provided that the difference principle is applied in a dynamic setting.

Critics of Rawls have pointed to the ambiguities that arise in defining "least advantaged," and Rawls has acknowledged the difficulties involved when dynamic or intergenerational issues are introduced. Even if the least advantaged are defined to be members of society who are wholly non-productive, growth-retarding policies will violate the difference principle if the intergenerational discount rate is sufficiently low. The indigent of the 1970s are in a better position than they would have been had a Rawlsian difference principle of justice been applied in the 1870s without consideration of the intergenerational impact.

Institutional changes that tend to retard or stifle economic growth seem likely to harm the position of the least advantaged rather than to improve it, almost regardless of the motivation for such changes.

The "quality of life" or environmental regulations that have now become widespread seem to offer the best examples. These institutional changes are acknowledged to have differentially harmed those who are in differentially disadvantaged economic positions. Quite apart from possible violations of the principles of equal liberty, these changes would have to be classified as unjust by the difference principle.

I do not want to make Adam Smith and John Rawls seem to be more similar in their basic philosophical positions than a careful interpretation of their published works might warrant. Even when we take into account the historical and methodological distance between them and try to apply their criteria for justice in the converse empirical settings, we cannot legitimately infer a Smithian distributional interest comparable to Rawls. In 1976 a returned Adam Smith might or might not be an egalitarian of Rawlsian stripe. Because of his relative underemphasis on the relationship between material goods and human happiness, the most judicious evalua-

tion suggests that Smith would not have been motivated to stress distributional inequities to the extent of Rawls. It also seems clear that even in the
affluence of 1976 Smith would have paid considerably more attention to
the net benefits measured in terms of both efficiency and justice, to be
secured by a dismantling of restrictions on freedom of individual choices.

Finally, we should note a possible difference in the implications of a
commonly shared philosophical rather than empirical presupposition for
normative discourse. Even if he should have recognized empirically that
persons differ substantially in basic capacities, Adam Smith might well
have argued that such inequalities have no place (in fact, must be presumed away) in the process of designing a just and viable social order. The
basic institutions of society must be based on the presumption that men are
"equals" in some fundamental generic sense.[23] This is the attitude that
clearly forms the U.S. Declaration of Independence, and the coincidence
of dates between this and the publication of *The Wealth of Nations* is not
merely historical accident. From this presumption or presupposition un-
due concern with distributional outcomes might be considered to be, at
base, aberrant. In this light the onus would be on John Rawls to defend his
concentration on the distributional principle as appended to the principle
of equal liberty rather than on Adam Smith to defend his failure to make a
comparable extension.

CONCLUSIONS

I have had several objectives in this essay. First, I have tried to show
that Adam Smith's system of natural liberty, interpreted as his idealized
paradigm for social order, embodies justice as well as economic efficiency.
Indeed, Smith may well have conceived his masterpiece to be an argument
to the effect that the system acknowledged to embody justice could also be
efficient. Second, I have attempted to compare Smith's first principle of
natural liberty with John Rawls's first principle of equal liberty. Although
I have not examined an exhaustive list of examples here, a straightforward
application of either of these principles implies significant restrictions on
the propriety of governmental-political interference with the freedom of
individuals to make their own economic decisions. The ultimate, and
perhaps most important purpose has been to use the timely discussion of
Adam Smith's precepts for justice as a vehicle for correcting what has
seemed a grossly neglected aspect of John Rawls's much-acclaimed and
much-discussed book. Both Smith and Rawls are libertarians in that principles of liberty hold positions of priority in their orderings of objectives.
Neither is utilitarian in the Benthamite or even in the more constrained
Paretian sense of this term.

The differences between Smith and Rawls lie in the fact that Smith's
discourse is concentrated on the efficiency-producing results of natural
liberty; the corollary attributes of justice are not stressed. And, for the
several reasons noted, the distributional results are not explicitly evaluated
against criteria of justice. On the other hand, Rawls treats liberty sketchily

despite the lexical priority assigned to it, and he concentrates on the distributional qualities of an idealized social order. Translated into practical reform proposals, however, both philosophers accept an effectively operative market economy as a basic institution in any society that could be classified as just.

The differences in distributional emphasis are important, but these are at least partially explained by differences in empirical and possibly philosophical presuppositions. One implication of the comparison should be that a libertarian position is not inconsistent with an egalitarian one, despite attempts to make these seem contradictory by both the libertarian-antiegalitarians and the collectivist-egalitarians. A strong defense of the liberties of individuals, which can only be secured in an operating market economy, may be joined with an equally strong advocacy for the reform of basic social institutions designed to produce greater equality among individuals in their initial endowments and capacities. This is how I interpret Rawls's position, which comes close to that associated with Henry Simons,[24] whose explicit emphasis on free markets is clearly akin to that of Smith. If my interpretation is accepted, the normative distance between Adam Smith and John Rawls is surely less than the sometimes careless comparisons of images would suggest.

NOTES

1. John Rawls, *A Theory of Justice* (Cambridge: Harvard Univ. Press, 1971).
2. Robert Nozick, *Anarchy, State and Utopia* (New York: Basic Books, 1974).
3. Marc F. Plattner, The New Political Theory, *Public Interest* 40(Summer 1975): 120.
4. For the most direct statement on this see Adam Smith, *The Theory of Moral Sentiments*, Introduction by E. G. West (New Rochelle: Arlington House, 1969), pp. 263-65.
5. A. L. Macfie, *The Individual in Society: Papers on Adam Smith* (London: Allen and Unwin, 1967), p. 19.
6. Adam Smith, *Lectures on Justice, Police, Revenue, and Arms*, E. Cannan, ed. (Oxford: Clarendon Press, 1896).
7. Ibid., p. 5.
8. Rawls, *Theory of Justice*, p. 3.
9. Cf. ibid., p. 7.
10. See Jacob Viner, Guide to John Rae's *Life of Adam Smith*, in John Rae, *Life of Adam Smith* (New York: Kelley, 1965), p. 112.
11. Smith, *Lectures*, pp. 11-13.
12. For a good discussion on this, see Macfie, *Individual in Society*, pp. 68-71.
13. Note the similarity of this statement of Smith to Rawls's definition of the principle of equal liberty (see note 15).
14. See, Rae, *Life of Adam Smith*, p. 55.
15. Rawls, *Theory of Justice*, p. 250.
16. Ibid., p. 66.
17. In his treatise on liberty, F. A. Hayek does not represent liberty or freedom as an attribute of "justice" but rather as an independent "source and condition of most moral values" (p. 6). At one point (p. 99), however, he suggests that justice requires something akin to the Rawlsian principle of equal liberty. Cf. F. A. Hayek, *The Constitution of Liberty* (Chicago: Univ. Chicago Press, 1960).
18. Rawls, *Theory of Justice*, pp. 65-75.
19. This aspect of Smith's argument is stressed by Nathan Rosenberg, Some Institutional Aspects of *The Wealth of Nations*, *J. Polit. Econ.* 68(Dec. 1960):557-70.
20. Rawls, *Theory of Justice*, pp. 65-75.

21. For explicit discussion of this point see James Buchanan, Political Equality and Private Property: The Distributional Paradox, in *Markets and Morals*, G. Dworkin, G. Bermans, and P. Brown, eds. (Washington, D.C.: Hemisphere, 1977), pp. 63-84.
22. An argument to this effect could be plausibly advanced with respect to certain of the more obvious proposals. One such argument that might possibly be extended in this way relates to the confiscatory taxation of inheritances. See Gordon Tullock, Inheritance Justified, *J. Law Econ.* 14(Oct. 1971):465-74.
23. For a discussion of this presumption of fundamental equality, even in the context of empirical inequalities, see James Buchanan, *The Limits of Liberty* (Chicago: Univ. Chicago Press, 1975), esp. pp. 11-12.

 Rawls accepts this presumption in his basic contractarian derivation of the principles of justice. The presumption is not at issue here. The possible difference lies in the implications of this presumption for distributional norms.

 Care must be taken to distinguish a presumption of equality in some "original position" and/or in some basic philosophical sense, and the elevation of distributional equality as an ideal attribute of the just society. Rawls is somewhat vulnerable on this count, especially because he derives his principles of justice from "fairness" notions. Insofar as "fairness" applies to the rules of games, by extension to ordinary games it becomes questionable to speak of achieved or final equality as an ideal. This would amount to "condemning a footrace as unfair because someone has come out ahead." On this point see Frank H. Knight, *The Ethics of Competition* (London: Allen and Unwin, 1935), p. 61.
24. See Henry Simons, *Economic Policy for a Free Society* (Chicago: Univ. Chicago Press, 1948) and *Personal Income Taxation* (Chicago: Univ. Chicago Press, 1938).

 There are some ambiguities in Rawls that make my interpretation less persuasive than might appear. He does not seem to recognize the necessary relationship between an operative market economy and the dispersion of property ownership. For this reason, particular sections of his treatise may be interpreted as collectivist in flavor. (See especially Rawls, *Theory of Justice*, pp. 271-72.) On balance, these seem to represent failures to follow through carefully the full implications of the first principle of equal liberty.

9

Adam Smith's Economics of Politics

E. G. WES'

IN this essay the newer and broader use of the term "politics" will be adopted. It is now fashionable to divide this into three dimensions: the economics of the preconstitutional stage of society, the economics of constitution making, and the economics of postconstitutional politics.[1] The preconstitutional dimension, or the state of anarchy, has reemerged in the 1970s as a topic for considerable reexamination and discussion. New interest in the second dimension, constitution making, has been stimulated by philosopher John Rawls and economists James Buchanan and Gordon Tullock, among others. The third, or postconstitutional dimension, which up to the early 1970s has been the one typically assumed in twentieth-century economics, is concerned with legislative tactics within given majority rules, given property rights, and given electorates. The leading pioneering work here has been that of Anthony Downs in *An Economic Theory of Democracy,* published in 1957.

The main proposition in this essay is that Adam Smith's economics of politics is concerned primarily with the second of the above dimensions, constitution making, and that modern critics have lost perspective because they have concentrated on the third level. I shall not argue that Smith's writings contain an explicitly coherent analysis of political behavior. The Smithian works to be quoted were indeed predominantly occupied with other matters. Nevertheless, Smith did inform us that he had conceived a book on law and government, and it is not an idle task to piece together the numerous insights on this subject that lie scattered through his published works. While arguing that there is a definite theme in Smith, I concede at the outset that much of what follows is conjecture. However, the exercise seems worthwhile for two reasons. First, it yields a better understanding of Smith's strengths and weaknesses. Second, it brings other writers, new and

E. G. West is Professor of Economics, Carleton University, Ottawa, Canada.
Without implicating them, I wish to acknowledge the benefit of comments on an earlier version of this paper from George Stigler, F. A. Hayek, James Buchanan, Gordon Tullock, Mark Blaug, Michael Sydenham, Gilles Paquet, and Tom Rymes.

132

old, into sharper relief. Among "new" writers, for instance, this study will make a brief comparison with Rawls, and will bring further to the surface the emerging difference between the modern Virginia School associated with James Buchanan and the Chicago School of George Stigler, the former focusing on the first two dimensions of politics and the latter upon the third dimension. Among "old" writers, this investigation will bring some new significance especially to Joseph Schumpeter's fear that capitalism and democracy are incompatible. Among classical authors Smith will be compared with Hume and Rousseau. The sequence of this examination of Smith will be arranged according to the three dimensions of politics already outlined.

ANARCHY

The foremost classical views here are those of Proudhon, Godwin, and Hobbes.[2] Proudhon pictures anarchy as a natural harmony wherein each person freely pursues happiness and develops his own talents. His view, however, is not supported by any systematic evidence. Its most serious deficiency is that it does not face up to the need for reconciliation of tastes among heterogeneous individuals in social interaction. Godwin believed there would be so much abundance that conflict would not be provoked. The Hobbesian view of anarchy is opposite and nonromantic. It recognizes heterogeneity and assumes there will always be some individuals in the state of nature who would take by force the goods produced by others.

It is from the Hobbesian view that most economists, from Adam Smith on, have begun. What has impressed them most is the sheer waste involved in a state of anarchy by those who undertake the effort of stealing and by others who use more resources for their defense. In modern terms a Pareto-superior redistribution can be reached where collective enforcement of property rights is cheaper than individual enforcement. A system of collective protection of private property rights is created, which then becomes a public good from which "free riders" are excluded.[3] Three corollaries should be stressed. First the establishment of the legal framework can be predicted on the simple assumption of self-interest; second, the larger the potential wealth, the larger the incentives to establish the framework; third, once established, succeeding economic prosperity, provided it is not too unequally or unjustly distributed, will for all members dramatically increase the opportunity costs of abandoning it and reverting to anarchy.

In *The Wealth of Nations* Smith argues that among nations of hunters there is no incentive to establish "an established magistrate" or any regular administration of justice because there is very little in the way of potential property, or at least "none that exceeds the value of two or three days labour" (p. 669). In these circumstances conflict between propertyless individuals is a negative-sum game. In Smith's words: "Though he to whom the injury is done suffers, he who does it receives no benefit." Personal violence in this setting is prompted by malice and resentment; but most men, Smith observes "are not very frequently under those passions." Other passions that are "much more steady in their operation" are brought into play where, in contrast, there is much property. These passions are "avarice and ambition in the rich" and, in the poor, "hatred of labour and the love of present ease and enjoyment." It is these that "prompt to invade property." Extensive property accumulation can therefore succeed only under "the powerful arm of the civil magistrate" (p. 670). But while the law is needed to protect the rich against the poor, prior to its establishment the latter were poorer still. In *The Wealth of Nations* capital accumulation is a necessary condition for economic growth; but since Smith explicitly argues that growth benefits all ranks of society, so must the property-rights system.

These initial quotations might suggest very sweeping judgments by Adam Smith about his fellowmen. He believed, however, that there was a high probability in most men of developing refined moral sensibilities and respect for others, but only after a system of law had been established. In the first instance this system would, or could, emerge from the narrowest self-interest. In Smith's words:

> Society may subsist among different men as among different merchants, from a sense of its utility, without any mutual love or affection; and though no man in it should owe any obligation, or be bound in gratitude to any other, it may still be upheld by a mercenary exchange of good offices according to an agreed valuation. . . . . If there is any society among robbers and murderers, they must at least, according to the trite observations abstain from robbing and murdering one another.[4]

Smith's friend David Hume was even more vigorous in maintaining that self-interest was the basis of the constitution. He argued that a convention or contract was inevitable. "By this means every one knows what he may safely possess; and the passions are restrained in their partial and contradictory motions."[5] By abstaining from the possessions of others, we promote not only their interests but ours as well. By such means "we maintain society, which is so necessary to their well-being and subsistence, as well as to our own."[6] The characteristics of the human mind, according to Hume, were selfishness and limited generosity: "It is only from the selfishness and confined generosity of men, along with the scanty provision nature has made for his wants, that justice derives its origin."[7]

With such reasoning, Hume and Smith were able to meet a problem associated with the Lockean and Hobbesian theories. Their historical social contract could not easily be the foundation of political obligation for new generations who were not a party to it. To Hume and Smith the self-interest of succeeding generations usually dictated a tacit consent to conventional rules in existence. Each generation would thus behave as if it had signed the social contract anew. In his Glasgow lectures of 1762 Smith explicitly acknowledged some of these points. There were no grounds, he asserted, for believing in any social contract (in the historical sense): "Ask a common porter or day-labourer why he obeys the civil magistrate, he will tell you that it is right to do so, that he sees others do it, that he would be punished if he refused to do it. . . ." Men are induced, Smith argued, to enter into and remain in civil society by the two principles, "authority and utility or obedience and the instinct of self-preservation."[8]

It is not so well known, and to many it will come as a surprise, that Smith had considerable respect for Jean Jacques Rousseau's work *The Social Contract*. It is reported that in his later life Smith spoke of Rousseau "with a kind of religious respect" and expressed the belief that his *Social Contract* "will one day avenge all the persecutions he suffered."[9] Interestingly enough, in the developing theories of public choice Rousseau is being rediscovered.[10] The new focus of interest is Rousseau's treatment of the obstacle of egoism in the constitution. The problem is that each individual may place his private interest before that of the public and so become a free-riding consumer of a public good, each to the detriment of himself in the long run. Rousseau had only one public good in mind—that of the constitution or system of law itself.

Adam Smith and Rousseau shared a characteristic that distinguished them from Hume. Hume was mainly concerned with predicting a long-run system that suited individuals who were characterized by selfishness and limited generosity. Smith and Rousseau, in contrast, emphasized that the balance of these characteristics or passions is changed by the very experience of living in a stable society. Men cannot be virtuous in a state of nature; only in a society based upon law do they become virtuous, and the nonselfish virtues can increase with time. In Rousseau's proposals such virtue should be helped by the development of what he calls a "civil religion"[11] that could be inculcated by the sovereign. The religion would consist of a few simple dogmas expressed as categorical imperatives. They would include tolerance, sanctity of the social contract, and respect for law.

The civil religion, by inculcating social morals, was one way of resolving what we now call the free-rider problem.[12] If successful it could indeed be a more efficient method than conventional policing since fewer resources would be needed. Such a solution is recognized to some degree in the modern economics of trust and altruism. And it certainly offers a partial answer to the major question concerning the Hobbesian model: if formal rules exist, these must be enforced, and how is the enforcer himself to be controlled?

In Adam Smith's writings the word "civilization" is used interchangeably with "commerce," and this implies a system of property rights. But for Smith, like Rousseau, a constitution drawn up by merchants as a mercenary exchange of goods was only a beginning. Eventually people can become more conscious of their long-term self-interest and be readier to adopt civilizing virtues. This development is associated by Smith with wisdom, temperance, prudence, and fellow feeling, qualities that he especially champions in *The Theory of Moral Sentiments*. Moral improvement is aided in Smith, however, not by Rousseau's civil religion, but by each individual's consultation with the impartial spectator. This agency can be an imagined or real person who has sympathy with each "actor" and with others. Continual consultation or checking with the spectator by each individual in turn acts as a social mirror for his own individual action. Since each party seeks the sympathy of the spectator, there is ultimately a moderation of passions and a development of fellow feeling. The shaping of the constitution requires the most sensitive understanding of men and presents the impartial spectator with the most difficult task of all.

Implicitly for Smith, as for Rousseau, the development of morals reduces the policing problems of the state. Yet whereas Rousseau desired a complete "transformation of human identity, not merely a transformation of values"[13] wherein self-interest finally disappeared, Smith certainly did not go this far. The individual should indeed maintain his identity, but at the same time he should be developing a proper regard for others. And it was not from civil religion but from Christian religion that Smith reached this judgment. In his words: "As to love our neighbour as we love ourselves is the great law of Christianity, so it is the great precept of nature to love ourselves only as we love our neighbour, or, what comes to the same thing, as our neighbour is capable of loving us.[14] Clearly, some form of constitution was imperative for Smith, and he did not spend too long in establishing such a fairly obvious point. What was more complex was the remaining technical question of selecting the appropriate constitutional model for each set of historical circumstances. The predominant choices available were from aristocracies, monarchies, democracies, and republics. It is this second dimension of politics with which Smith was most occupied and upon which he offered his most considered judgments.

THE CONSTITUTION-MAKING DIMENSION

Rousseau had distinguished carefully between the legislative sovereign body and the executive or government in any constitution. He believed it was an empirical fact that all governments had a tendency to encroach upon the territory of the sovereign rights of the people; there was, in other words, a tendency to overgovernment whereby the particular private interests usurped those of the general interest. The checks and balances of a republican system based on the separation of powers were, Rousseau argued, the best delay to this eventual corruption of the law. The word "law" in Rousseau had a very special meaning. It was the expression of the general will, that is, the will of the body of the people. "A people, since it is subject to laws ought to be the author of them." Not only individuals but the government, too, is subordinate to the law. Government is a body charged with the execution of the laws and the maintenance of freedom. But there is a necessary division of labor; while the people are fitted to be the source of legislation, they will fail if they try simultaneously to act as the executive.[15]

While the democratic form of government of the small city-state came nearest to perfection, Rousseau believed it to be the most likely to change to another form largely because of the growth of population. Where vast multitudes had to be governed, he preferred what he called "elective aristocracy." Unlike monarchy, which was the other alternative, this had the advantage of distinguishing more clearly between the sovereign and the government. Provided the law carefully regulated the procedure of elections, wise government could be fairly guaranteed and a strong republican constitution would emerge.

Adam Smith seems to have reached a very similar position after an extensive, if not too systematic, survey of historical evidence. This survey, illustrated in Table 9.1, suggests that Smith's pronouncements were not uninformed conjectures. While he was more pragmatic than Rousseau, he placed the same importance upon the general need for checks and balances. One of the most important tasks of the constitution in Smith, as in Rousseau, was to secure individual liberty. In the Glasgow *Lectures* Smith wanted what he called "a happy mixture of all the different forms of government properly restrained, and a perfect security to liberty and property." One had to proceed by trial and error and to retain what experience showed to be valuable. For instance, the element of some separation of powers that had developed in the British constitution Smith thought to be a welcome feature. Monetary affairs had to take place in the Commons; the judges were independent of the king; the Habeas Corpus Act was further security to individual freedom. The jury system was also a "friend of liberty." It is well known of course that Smith speaks of an "obvious and simple system of natural liberty" that in the private market often leads to the reconciling of private with social interests. However, when he examines the "political market," he shows the same apprehension as Rousseau. For here liberty seemed to be in danger of being in unstable equilibrium. Smith reveals himself repeatedly as an arch-opponent of established oligarchies, entrenched aristocracies, oppressive religious establishments, and cunning political lobbies.

It is interesting to contrast Smith's theory of justice with that of John Rawls, the leader of the contractarian revival in the 1970s. Advancing the notion of "justice as fairness," and that just principles would emerge from the unanimous agreement of men, each of whom was behind a veil of ignorance concerning his own position in the postcontractual world, Rawls, like Smith, established individual liberty as the supreme principle. The conspicuous difference is that Rawls produced a second principle of justice, the "difference principle," wherein economic inequalities were to be arrayed to the advantage of the poorest in society. No such principle is to be found anywhere in Smith. His system of natural liberty was sufficient and directed to the release of men's energies. Smith was more interested in the pursuit of income than its size and in the process of contracting rather than its actual outcome. One can find no social welfare functions in Smith calculated to guide some "distributive branch" of government. Indeed

Table 9.1.   Comparative Systems and Constitutions in Smithian Literature

Hobbes' social contract	Smith, *Lectures,* p. 12
Nations of savages, shepherds, clans, aristocrats, "little republics"	Smith, *Lectures,* pp. 14–28
Shepherd nations: Arab and Tartar nations, North American Indians	WN, p. 653ff.*
Greek republics, agrarian states, European monarchies	WN, p. 657ff.
Federal governments	WN, p. 669ff.
Standing armies and the constitution — best security to peace when the sovereign is the general	WN, p. 667
China — opulent but stationary because of constitutional laws and institutions unfavorable to commerce	WN, p. 95
Governments and constitutions of mercantile companies in the East Indies compared with "the genius of the British constitution," which protects and governs North America	WN, p. 73
Constitutional distinction between Greek and Roman colonies	WN, pp. 523–25
Circumstances leading to the constitutions of European colonies in the West Indies and America	WN, p. 525
Political institutions of the English colonies more favorable to land cultivation than the French, Spanish, and Portuguese	WN, pp. 538–39
The constitution of North American establishments "an ever-memorable example at how small an expense three millions of people may not only be governed, but well governed"	WN, p. 541
British control over American colonies compared with the king of France's authority over French provinces	WN, p. 585
Roman republic's decline due to refusal of citizenship rights to its allies	WN, p. 587
The need for taxation and parliamentary representation of the American colonies	WN, pp. 586–87
British constitution would be successfully completed by union with the colonies	WN, p. 589
The church's relationship to the state — religious persecution politically unwise for the sovereign. Fear is a "wretched instrument of government."	WN, p. 750
The constitution of the Church of Rome in the tenth to the thirteenth centuries — the "most formidable combination that ever was formed against the authority and security of civil government"	WN, p. 754
Inverse relationship between the size of beneficies and the influence of the church upon the common people — only in presbyterian countries are the people successfully converted to the established church	WN, p. 762
Economic invention and commercial development destroyed the temporal constitutional power of the clergy. It destroyed that of the great barons also.	WN, p. 755

* Adam Smith, *The Wealth of Nations* (New York: Random House, Mod. Lib. Ed., 1937) (here and after WN).

there is no such branch. Smith's impartial spectator is emphatically not (as Rawls seems to believe) ultimately some supreme planner.[16] "Every man," Smith argues, "is, no doubt by nature first and principally recommended to his own care; and as he is fitter to take care of himself, than of any other person, it is fit and right that it should be." No quotation could better endorse Smith's concern for liberty.

From Smith's point of view Rawls's scheme indeed seriously compromises liberty. For in it liberty is a luxury good. In Rawls's words:

> As the conditions of civilization improve, the marginal significance for our good of further economic and social advantages diminishes relative to the interests of liberty, which become stronger as the conditions for the exercise of the equal freedoms are more fully realized.[17]

To Smith, liberty was a means as well as an end; the liberties of the person, trade, and contract were essential to the very economic progress that Rawls believed to be a prior condition for liberty. Smithian liberty is best secured when protected in the highest degree from the coercion of government. Coercion was to be confined to the substantive general rule of law. Such a rule, with the aid of the principle of separation of powers, keeps all parties including governments and legislatures under the law.

Rawls's second principle suffers in the Smithian scheme of things because all economic changes have to be monitored in an attempt to maximize the total income of the least advantaged, and the chief monitor is government. Modern democratic governments are based on simple majority voting. Rousseau and Smith were enamored neither of government nor of such voting rules. Rawls's attempt at redistribution would not, in their eyes, have much chance of success anyway; for in such systems self-interest groups will use their votes to foster their interests and not those of the poor. Similarly, it is too much for an increasing number of people today to believe that a sense of justice will even marginally restrain the caprice of the majority. As Hayek argues, "In any group it is soon believed that what is desired by the group is just."[18] Some economists maintain that simple majority voting in practice tends to result in social expenditures that hurt both the rich and the poor for the benefit of the middle class.[19]

In Smith's theory of justice most weight is placed on general laws. And the basic function of these was to protect property. This was not, moreover, the reflection of an upper-class interest; for, to Smith, the "most sacred and inviolable" property was "the property which every man has in his own labour" (pp. 121–22). It was for this reason that he condemned the statutes requiring long apprenticeship laws; such laws were a violation of property. In my interpretation, Smith saw them as the main source of inequality. If government could enact such obstacles, presumably it would be all the more dubious an agent to be entrusted with general redistribution of income. And while many writers argue as if Smith had quite an extensive agenda for government, a careful examination will show this to be incorrect. Smith's discussion of the need for public works and institutions is largely an inquiry about the desirability of the sovereign altering the constitution to allow new legal instruments such as joint stock enterprise and limited liability into certain areas. Smith's use of the word "public" is predominantly in the context of the desirability of "public companies," that is, private, not "nationalized," concerns. The public institutions include private joint stock—canals, water, insurance, banking, and foreign trading companies. Smith's partial exceptions provided that roads and education were to be dealt with by general enabling provisions, and preferably the user was to finance them.[20]

Democratic governments are usually based on simple majority voting. In Smith's view, the use of this whole apparatus was more conducive to monopoly than any other—the key to statutory protectionism. Implicitly, the vote was a property right that violated other more legitimate property rights. The evidence for this view is Smith's reference to statutory regulations that enable members of the same trade to tax themselves to provide sickness and welfare funds. By giving them a common interest to manage, Smith observed, the regulation "renders such assemblies necessary." After that a simple majority vote is given statutory respect, and this in turn is followed by a severe setback to the Smithian system. In his words:

> An incorporation not only renders them [the assemblies] necessary, but makes the act of the majority binding upon the whole. In a free trade an effectual combination cannot . . . last longer than every single trader continues of the same mind. The majority of a corporation can enact a bye-law with proper penalties, which will limit the competition more effectually and more durably than any voluntary combination whatever [p. 129].

Notice that the statute itself need not be based on democratic majority voting; Smith's system was aristocratic, and he was complaining here about an unwise area in its legislation. Nevertheless, the implication is that in a full democracy, with active governments operating on simple majority rules, one can predict group-interest legislation such as tariffs, bounties, and price-fixing laws. Organized pressure for legislation will become a commercial undertaking itself.[21]

As Jacob Viner once detected, Smith believed in some degree of representation in the law-making authority, but his criteria of representation were not fully democratic.[22] In my judgment Smith was not disturbed by this because, as Schumpeter was later to argue, capitalism and full democracy are not compatible. Not that Smith was opposed to constitutional democracy altogether. He was more concerned with the establishment of general laws of procedures that laid down permanent limits to the coercive powers of government than with the precise voting rules within it. He was convinced that arbitrary monarchial despotism had to be ruled out; for this was not a satisfactory answer to the petty domination of small coalitions in democracies, since the despot is only a smaller coalition still.

Smith seems to have had much in common with the founding fathers of the American Constitution, which was a blend of republicanism and democracy. In a full democracy the will of the people (or "popular passion" as eighteenth-century writers like Smith were likely to call it) reigns supreme. In a republic it is not the will of the people that predominates but a rational consensus, which is implicit in the term "consent." Such a republic, if ruled by wise men, can enjoy a liberty that is not threatened by tyrannical majorities. As Smith's politician friend, Edmund Burke, told his constituents, he owed them only his judgment; he was not going to sacrifice this universally to their opinion. We confront here the most vulnerable part of the political philosophy of Smith and Rousseau. Both writers ultimately leaned heavily upon the guidance of the wise lawgiver, that is, upon "good" natural leaders.

Although it is still arguable that the chances of receiving laws that originate behind some Rawlsian "veil of ignorance" are greater when a legislator is qualified more by wisdom and "other-regarding" virtues than by simple lobby support, in any real world we must "start from here" with imperfection, unequal endowment, and inadequate communication and knowledge. As recently argued, "Rules for social order . . . will [always] reflect the struggle among interests, and will rarely if ever qualify as just in accordance with any idealized criteria."[23] Adam Smith expresses the same realism in the following words from *The Theory of Moral Sentiments:*

> The man whose public spirit is prompted altogether by humanity and benevolence, will respect the established powers and privileges even of individuals, and still more those of the great orders and societies into which the state is divided. Though he should consider some of them as in some measure abusive, he will content himself with moderating what he cannot annihilate without great violence. When he cannot conquer the rooted prejudices of the people by reason and persuasion, he will not attempt to subdue them by force. . . . He will accommodate, as well as he can, his public arrangements to the confirmed habits and prejudices of the people, and will remedy, as well as he can, the inconveniences which may flow from the want of those regulations which the people are adverse to submit to. When he cannot establish the best system of laws, he will endeavour to establish the best that the people can bear.[24]

This judgment is repeated in *The Wealth of Nations.* Referring to some welcome modification of the corn export bounty, Smith observes: "With all its imperfections, however, we may perhaps say of it what was said of the laws of Solon, that, though not the best in itself, it is the best which the interests, prejudices, and temper of the times would admit of" (p. 510).[25]

Thus it was the especially complex and arduous task of the legislator of constitutions that was the central focus of the economics of politics scattered through *The Wealth of Nations.* Smith was more occupied with finding workable improvements in the rules of the game than with the tactics of the games played within the existing imperfect rules by "that insidious and crafty animal, vulgarly called a statesman or politician, whose councils are directed by the momentary fluctuations of affairs" (p. 435). If Smith was not optimistic about the chances of free trade ever being adopted, he was even less so concerning the supply of wise statesmen. Indeed, their useful influence on affairs was usually fortuitous; but when it did occur, it was at the constitutional level.

The leader of the successful party, however, if he has authority enough to prevail upon his own friends to act with proper temper and moderation (which he frequently does not), may sometimes render to his country a service much more essential and important than the greatest victories and the most extensive conquests. *He may re-establish and improve the constitution,* and from the very doubtful and ambiguous character of the leader of a party, he may assume the noblest of all characters, that of the reformer and legislator of a great state; and, by the wisdom of his institutions, secure the internal tranquility and happiness of his fellow-citizens for many succeeding generations.[26] [Emphasis added.]

It should be reemphasized that Smith's wise legislator was not directly appointed by a majority of citizens, for they did not yet have the franchise. The noble object of his efforts was not the expedient, incremental legislation that satisfies some particular lobby demanding specific reform proposals, but the nonincremental shift in or development of the fundamental and general laws that underpin the basic structure of the constitution. Such a change is the outcome of a systematic, philosophic, and long-term consideration of the fabric of the social order itself. Similarly Adam Smith's economics of politics were typically concerned, not with pragmatic legislation dealing with particular programs, but with a shift in basic paradigms that shape and inform all serious legislation. He sought to dislodge the whole system of mercantilist thought that had been modifying if not weakening the basic constitution for centuries. Smith's general principle was that the removal of effective government restrictions on trade would produce long-term results that would be preferred by all concerned. It was a principle of ordered anarchy, and it was based on well-defined individual rights and respect for voluntary contracts relating to them.

THE POSTCONSTITUTIONAL STATE

In the third category of this essay political activity is set in the postconstitutional state. Typically, pragmatic or incremental legislative activity takes place therein within some form of constitution, however perfectly or imperfectly constructed. Modern progress in the economics of parliamentary politics based on such fixed rules has stemmed largely from the work of Arrow, Black, and Downs in the 1940s and 1950s.[27] It brought to light what is believed to be a curious dichotomy in economic analysis. Economists had hitherto spent considerable energy in making sophisticated demonstrations of market failure in private exchange processes, processes that were analyzed upon the hypothesis of individual self-interest. However, when turning to the government sector, often implicitly or explicitly looked to for improvement, reference to such profit-maximizing behavior had been replaced by more obscure goals such as "the public interest" or to the attainment of theoretical "optimality conditions." The new analyses of the 1940s and 1950s, in basing themselves on the hypothesis of individual self-interest in all spheres, paved the way for the emergence of theories of government failure. Many of these were implicit in *The Wealth of Nations* two centuries earlier. This is especially so of Downs's work, which analyzed political parties analogously to the theory of profit-maximizing firms.[28]

Numerous empirical studies have indeed produced systematic evidence to support the proposition that in a weakening political constitution self-interest rather than public interest is a more explanatory behavioral rule in politics. Individuals attempt to maximize their wealth through political activity, especially through allegiance groups who purchase from the sellers of "political power for wealth" — the political parties. It has been shown, for example, that in America employees, managers, or shareholders of a given private industry are well aware that they will all profit if they can share the major resource of the state. And as George Stigler has reminded us, the essence of the resource of the state is coercion.[29] Such power of compulsion can be used, for instance, in the form of statutorily encouraged industry regulation. This, as Adam Smith recognized, is in the interests of a majority of existing operators and against those of potential new entrants and the customers of industry. It is, in other words, in the same mercantilist world that Smith was challenging. Meanwhile the industry purchases legislation with the two things needed most by the party — votes and resources.[30]

In the political process the rewards of individual political effort are usually only indirect. Stigler suggests, for instance, that legislative leaders probably enjoy extra political payments by way of unusual customer loyalty to a congressman's legal firm, bank, or insurance company.[31] Economists, he seems to argue, must adjust themselves to the fact that a government agency that operates openly to foster special interest is not a passing imperfection but is characteristic of the system and predictable in it. To advise a representative merely that it is the public interest that requires his support for policy is quixotic. In Stigler's words:

> A representative cannot win or keep office with the support of the sum of those who are opposed to: oil import quotas, farm subsidies, airport subsidies, hospital subsidies, unnecessary navy shipyards, an inequitable public housing program, and rural electrification subsidies. . . . And the frequent complaint of economists that the I.C.C. conducts pro-railroad policies is as appropriate as a criticism of the Great Atlantic and Pacific Tea Company for selling groceries.[32]

After such trenchant criticism of modern economic analysis it is only to be expected that similar scrutiny will now be made of the works of the classical economists. Criticizing with hindsight is easy, and the history of thought is especially conducive to it. It is surprising, however, to discover that the classical writer to be chosen by Stigler for especial reappraisal and criticism is Adam Smith.[33] More surprising still is his conclusion that because Smith "failed to see the self-interest written upon the faces of politicians and constituencies" his "ship of state" was almost a ghost ship, or certainly one that suffered from such serious leaks as to make it pretty well unseaworthy. Stigler's basic question appears to be Downsian and is certainly rooted in our third dimension of the economics of politics.

Why did Smith not ask, "If self-interest dominates the majority of men in all commercial undertakings, why not also in all their political undertakings?"[34] My answer is that Smith did not have to ask; he knew better than anybody. But his economics of politics were not predominantly couched in terms of the third dimension — the postconstitutional stage. Only 2 percent of the population yet had the vote. Smith's concern was to stop Stigler's nightmare world from developing. To do this required that errors in the emerging constitution should be anticipated and checked by those in a position to do so. This is a normative position no doubt, but an unavoidable one nevertheless.

Stigler's criticism is prefaced with the following quotation from *The Wealth of Nations:*

> The natural effort of every individual to better his own condition, when suffered to exert itself with freedom and security, is so powerful a principle, that it is alone, and without any assistance, not only capable of carrying on the society to wealth and prosperity, but of surmounting a hundred impertinent obstructions with which the folly of human laws too often incumbers its operations; though the effect of these obstructions is always more or less either to encroach upon its freedom, or to diminish its security [p. 508].

Stigler's point is that Smith should have been more consistent and should have shown, without surprise and presumably with resignation, that the "hundred impertinent obstructions" erected by legislators were the product of the same self-interest that led men to seek and achieve prosperity. Stigler amply demonstrates that Smith was indeed aware that self-interest groups were behind much legislation.[35] Smith recognized, for instance, that the beneficiaries of the Statute of Apprenticeship were the owners of corporations; the beneficiaries of wage-fixing laws were the employers; and the beneficiaries of laws restricting tobacco planting were the tobacco farmers. Stigler's major criticism is that when Adam Smith came to prescribe policy he apparently forgot these lobbies and addressed himself to some ideal government. He failed to remember that party governments need votes and the spoils of office. Consider for example Smith's famous canons of taxation. These recommended convenience (to each subject), certainty, minimum exaction, and ability to pay. Such canons, Stigler argues, are straight from the armchair of a professor of moral philosophy. According to George Stigler's Chicago School approach, only two canons are appropriate to the self-interest of real-world governments; and neither is mentioned by Smith. These are that taxes should not unduly lose votes and that they should produce revenue.

In defense of Smith it can be argued that he was operating predominantly at the constitutional level (the second dimension of the economics of politics); he was not addressing himself to some ideal government; and there was something in Smith that could best lead to the public interest, and that was a wise constitution and a firm rule of law.

First, let us reexamine Stigler's quotation of Smith that individual self-interest will enable people to surmount "a hundred impertinent obstructions with which the folly of human laws too often encumbers its operations." A more balanced view is given when we include the sentence that precedes the passage quoted above:

> That security which the *laws* in Great Britain give to every man that he shall enjoy the fruits of his own labour, is alone sufficient to make any country flourish, *notwithstanding these and twenty other absurd regulations of commerce* . . . [p. 508; emphasis added].

This quotation more than any other shows that Smith had the vision of law that was common in the eighteenth century but is today almost forgotten. The law meant general rules of just conduct; it did not mean "every expression of the will of the duly authorized representative body,"[36] and it was the latter that was responsible for the absurdities.

It is this emphasis upon the basic laws that leads to the view that it is the constitutional dimension that dominates the work of Smith. For those recognizing this in *The Wealth of Nations* it is easier to answer Stigler's question of why Smith should tell the sovereign that free trade was desirable if he had no method of disarming the merchants and manufacturers who had obtained the protectionist measures.[37] It seems fair to interpret Smith as believing that he had some method of disarming the merchants; he was addressing (or thought he was addressing) himself to a change in the rules, that is, in the constitution. His clients were the custodians, the draftsmen, and the innovators of the constitution, not a passing government intimidated by the mob.

Smith's proposals with respect to existing monopolies were expressed with extreme caution. Changes should be very gradual. The sovereign had unwisely granted (sold) the monopoly in the first place in pursuit of a short-term gain. The sovereign should at least learn one lesson: existing monopolies were already potential cancers in the constitution; the development of others, monopoly escalation, should be prevented by every means. In this advice Smith largely escapes Stigler's criticism.

As Smith puts it:

> This [the manufacturer's] monopoly has so much increased the number of some particular tribes of them, that, like an overgrown standing army, they have become formidable to the government, and upon many occasions intimidate the legislature. . . . The legislature, were it possible that its deliberations could be always directed, not by the clamorous importunity of partial interests, but by an extensive view of the general good, ought upon this very account, perhaps, to be particularly careful neither to establish any new monopolies of this kind, nor to extend further those which are already

established. *Every such regulation introduces some degree of real disorder into the constitution of the state, which it will be difficult afterwards to cure without occasioning another disorder* [pp. 438-39; emphasis added].

The above advice is clearly conditional upon the possibility of a lawgiver being directed to an extensive view of the general good rather than to partial interests. It is difficult to believe that Smith would have gone to such trouble in formulating his advice if he thought there was no possibility at all of implementing it. While there may have been romantic elements in his thinking, it would be difficult to describe Smith's advice to avoid new monopolies as entirely unworkable or academic, even though he was not very explicit; for legislation since his time has demonstrated its practicality. Antitrust laws, at least since Senator Sherman, have been grafted onto the American constitution; for all its imperfections it is still arguable that one day they can be removed. Moreover, experience under monopoly legislation shows that merger control of potential monopolies is normally easier than dismemberment of mature ones.[38] Furthermore the Chicago School's habit of classifying behavior as either self-interested or romantic can easily mislead. The "self" in Smith's idea of self-interest can extend to an identification with one's country. Smith and Rousseau drew from history to show crucial acts of patriotism by individuals who gave their country wise laws.

Rousseau observed that "a people does not become famous until its constitution begins to decline. We do not know for how many centuries the constitution of Lycurgus gave happiness to the Spartans before there was talk about them in the rest of Greece."[39] After exactly two centuries the relevant question in America today is whether its constitution is in disarray. In my opinion, Smith would be the first to ask this question rather than the one Stigler poses. Smith, like Rousseau, concluded from the study of history that an efficient constitution called for the most judicious balance and diffusion of power. This should accommodate the sovereign's interests at one end and those of his subjects at the other. The bulk of the revenue of the sovereign (Smith is insistent on reminding his readers) must be drawn from the masses of the people. It is always in the sovereign's interest, therefore, to increase as much as possible "the annual produce." This is especially so if his revenue comes chiefly from land rent. Consequently, there was need for the most extensive market and "the most perfect freedom of commerce, in order to increase as much as possible the number and the competition of buyers; and upon this account to abolish, not only all monopolies, but all restraints upon the transportation of the home produce . . ." [p. 602].

Smith, therefore, certainly appealed to self-interest. In the first instance it was the self-interest of the sovereign. The sovereign could and should preserve the constitution and prevent it from being rewritten by and in the interests of special groups. At a time well before universal franchise, Smith's advice could be more easily followed than today. Nevertheless, he appealed to the self-interest of the rest of the population; but in all cases it was long-term not short-term self-interest. In the long run rich and poor alike would prosper under order and liberty protected by law.

Stigler's several illustrations of Smith's naivete take on a different light when examined in my perspective. I shall concentrate here on one particularly striking example. It relates to Smith's fiscal advice to the French government. "Why tell the French sovereign," Stigler demands of Smith, "to abandon the *taille* and capitations and increase the *vingtièmes,* when only a revolution can dislodge the tax-favoured classes?"[40] The first thing to notice is that Smith did warn that the interest and opposition of the favored subjects would be an "obstacle."[41] Next and more important, we should remember that a few years after Smith's advice a revolution did dislodge the tax-favored classes. And in retrospect, considering what happened to the sovereign, it is arguable that Smith was not such a bad adviser after all! This argument does not necessarily lean on the benefit of hindsight or a special coincidence of events. Smith's advice was probably based on much more profound reasons than the dictates of short-term parliamentary politics.

In the France that Smith visited in 1764 there were, according to modern estimates, about 22 million peasants out of a total population of 30 million. The peasant class was thus a significant political constituency by any definition of a constitution. It was a time when peasant revolts were endemic throughout Europe. The central concern of the French economy at all times was the price of bread. After poor harvests many individuals retrogressed to that very lawless "state of nature" about which Smith was so apprehensive but which he predicted in societies where the mass of the people enjoy very little property. The unemployed and the starving formed marauding bands of "half beggars." In the words of the historian Alfred Cobban: "Illiterate and brutalized by misery . . . they were always a potential menace to law, and property. . . ."[42]

Adam Smith saw glaring official errors that aggravated the problem. These included price-fixing that produced entirely the wrong incentives and aggravated the shortage. Price fixing itself could sometimes *generate* a famine. Smith believed that where there was free trade "the most unfavourable seasons can never . . . produce a famine" (p. 493). Also, the average output of corn per year was too low because there was insufficient investment in agriculture. This insufficiency in turn was due to the mercantilist policy that favored manufacturers, commerce, and the colonial trade. The supreme error to Smith, however, was the French system of taxes that was crippling the poor peasants. The severity of these taxes was the last straw. The *taille* to which they were subject (and the taxes levied in conjunction with it) yielded the bulk of the revenue. In origin it was a servile obligation; indeed, it was hated for this reason alone. It involved high transaction costs and serious excess burden; it was arbitrary and varying; it made the country people hostile to the towns (wherein its severity was escaped); it forced the privileged (tax exempt) to defend themselves against the unprivileged. The total sums to be collected were never adjusted to the capacity of the taxpayers, and the militarily ambitious monarchies were failing to relate their projects to their resources. The total burden was distributed arbitrarily between the *généralités* wherein each intendant divided it, again arbitrarily, between the parishes. The responsibility for paying the *taille* in each parish was a collective one. Even peasants of substance had an incentive to move to the town, an event that increased the per capita burden in the country. The jails became full of collectors who had been caught absconding with money or who had failed to raise their quotas.[43]

In this historical context more than any other, the constitutional adoption of Smith's famous canons of taxation appears as good political advice in all senses. Similarly his immediate counsel to switch the tax burden from the *taille* onto the *vingtièmes* was by no means the advice of an uninformed political amateur. It was possible in some degree to attack the nobles' tax privileges. The successful establishment of the *vingtièmes* (a tax of 5 percent on properties) in 1750, was testimony in itself. Turgot emphasized this point in 1775: "It is therefore a fact that the pretension of the nobility not to be subject to any tax is actually in vain."[44]

It was quite impossible politically to spread the tax burden by imposing the *taille* on the nobles. The social stigma of this tax would have been insufferable to them. The government, moreover, was becoming increasingly persuaded of the superiority of the *vingtième* over the *taille*. The former was a tax on the individual not on the community. It was therefore more compatible with the ideas of distributive justice "to which the French Government became increasingly addicted."[45] Again, it was easier administratively because in practice it came to fall mainly on landholdings, and these could be more accurately and less arbitrarily assessed.

While it is true that the nobility usually resisted attempts to increase the *vingtième*, it had been successfully doubled in 1756; in 1760 it had been tripled.[46] When Adam Smith was writing the notes for *The Wealth of Nations* in France four year later, it is understandable if he considered further increases in the *vingtième* to be politically wise — especially considering the possible alternative costs of a total uprising. I argued earlier that a return to the first dimension of politics (anarchy) would be unlikely where the constitution was based on laws that encouraged stable expectations, and the distribution of gains was not unjust. Because these circumstances did not exist in France, the relapse into anarchy was clearly threatened.

Smith's advice was directed to the interest of everybody concerned and not least to that of Stigler's "tax-favoured classes." As Buchanan argues, where the relative position of persons cannot by any stretch of the imagination reflect the relative positions that might be attainable after a detour into anarchy and out again into a new constitutional contract, "it should be rational for those who seem differentially favoured in the status quo to accept reductions in the measured value of their assigned rights."[47] In the Glasgow *Lectures,* Smith had concluded:

Exorbitant taxes no doubt justify resistance, for *no people will allow the half of their property to be taken from them;* but though the highest propriety be not observed, if they have any degree of moderation people will not complain.[48] [Emphasis added.]

Adam Smith was still in France in 1766 when his friend Turgot, the intendant in the Limousin, found that in his district the proportion of the net income of the peasant proprietors taken by the government was about 80 percent![49] In Smith's view, therefore, the time for uprising was more than ripe.

Smith argued that if his advice was taken and the *taille* was abolished, while an increase was made in the *vingtième*, "the superior ranks might not be more burdened than the greater part of them are at present" (p. 855). One implicit reason was that more stability and justice would lead to an increase in the national income. Another explicit reason was that the expense of average tax collection would be diminished. In this Smith is supported by subsequent historians. Under the prevailing unjust tax system large sums had to be spent on maintaining garrisons to catch the defaulters and rebels, "and the sums expended on lawsuits over the taxes were sometimes even larger than the taxes themselves."[50] When Louis XVI came to the throne, there was unusual pressure for reform of these grossly inefficient institutions. Turgot, who had been appointed controller-general in 1774, was indeed by 1776 beginning to implement some Smithian changes. He had just introduced reforms into the collection of the *taille* and had reestablished a free internal market in corn when *The Wealth of Nations* was published. Turgot certainly aroused the antagonism of vested interests (Stigler's "tax-favored classes") and was ousted from office in May 1776. The antagonism was one reason; but another was that the characters of the king's chief advisor Maurepas and of the king himself were weak.[51]

What else should Turgot have done? What else should Smith have advised? Stigler's argument is that "unless the basic logic of political life is developed, reformers will be ill-equipped to use the state for their reforms, and victims of the pervasive use of the state's support of special groups will be helpless to protect themselves."[52] One must agree. But Smith and Turgot were fully aware of the basic logic of current French political life. Short of revolution there was no other way of attempting to protect the long-suffering peasant victims of the entrenched political interests; and a revolution that throws people back to the state of nature is supremely costly to all. As long as his influence lasted, Turgot continually urged the king to stand firm and register the necessary constitutional edicts. Like his business counterpart, the political entrepreneur operates under all the pressures of uncertainty and the threat of bankruptcy. Turgot made a calculated risk. But it was his misfortune that he had to work with a constitution that was already too decayed and with a king who had lost his nerve.

Stigler questions several Smithian references to what he calls "the failure of self-interest" in *The Wealth of Nations*. He suspects that in each case Smith had misconstrued the situations because of people (in ways un-noticed by Smith) who were indeed doing their job of pursuing self-in-terest. "The high priest of self-interest," Stigler observes "like all other high priests, has a strong demand for sinners."[53] But if, as Adam Smith be-lieved, each successful constitution is sustained by a large base of self-interest, the failure of constitutions to survive is a real, not an imagined, sin. Is the Chicago high priest's heaven lacking in this (constitutional) dimension?

CONCLUSION

Of the three dimensions of politics—preconstitutional, constitution making, and postconstitutional—Smith was predominantly concerned with the second. The wealth of nations to Smith is substantially correlated with the wealth of wisdom in their political constitutions. It is also depend-ent on the degree of civilized behavior that true law protects and en-courages. Smith was evidently one of those sages of the eighteenth century who received a rare vision of constitutional democracy, a vision that has since been almost lost.

The Downsian economics of politics, concerning itself with my third dimension and first enthroned in the 1950s does not address itself to these higher questions. And while providing new insights and explanatory power, the Downsian system is often chilling in its implications. Smith, on the other hand, was not so much occupied with the internal efficiency of Stigler's "ships of state" as with their external or constitutional control. He wrote at a time when the second dimension of politics was more obviously relevant, when constitution making was a conscious activity and an impor-tant strategic variable. The colonies, the mercantile companies, the American problem, the Irish question, were all constitutional questions of his day. Concern with such questions has begun to reassert itself in the twentieth century.

The granting of independence to the territories of the old British em-pire has been a constitutional change; and whether too late or not, propor-tional representation that has been common in the Republic of Ireland for fifty years is now being tried as a constructive constitutional change in Northern Ireland. An attempt at what can be called "constructive con-stitutionalism" also features the enthusiasts of the new European common market; upheavals in American domestic politics are centered, as ever, on the constitution and, some would say, on its departure from the intended eighteenth-century model. Adam Smith's priorities, it seems, have not ceased to be our priorities. And many would agree that it is a Solon we still need most, not a Machiavelli.

NOTES

1. See especially James M. Buchanan, *The Limits of Liberty: Between Anarchy and Leviathan* (Chicago: Univ. Chicago Press, 1975).

2. Ibid.; Winston C. Bush, Individual Welfare in Anarchy, in *Explorations in the Theory of Anarchy*, G. Tullock, ed. (Blacksburg: Va. Polytech. Inst., 1972); Winston C. Bush and Robert J. Staaf, Property Rights and Insurance (privately circulated ms.).

3. Buchanan, *Limits of Liberty*, Ch. 7.

4. Adam Smith, *The Theory of Moral Sentiments*, Henry G. Bohn, ed. (1853; repr. New Rochelle, N.Y.: Arlington House, 1969), p. 124. Similarly, in John Rawls *A Theory of Justice* (Cambridge: Harvard Univ. Press, 1971), p. 126. Rawls emphasizes that the theory must begin by assuming that a system of justice is based on rational choice; and to be robust, it must provide for the contingency that people take no interest in the interests of one another. In these circumstances there must be gains for every individual if he is to subscribe to the constitution. In Rawls's words: "Social co-operation makes possible a better life for all than any would have if each were to try to live solely by his own efforts."

5. David Hume, *Treatise of Human Nature*, Book 3, Part 2, repr. in Frederick Watkins, *Hume: Theory of Politics* (New York: Oxford Univ. Press, 1951), p. 39.

6. Ibid., p. 39.

7. Ibid., p. 45.

8. Adam Smith, *Lectures on Justice, Police, Revenue, and Arms*, Edwin Cannan, ed. (Oxford: Clarendon Press, 1896), pp. 11-12.

9. E. G. West, *Adam Smith* (New York: Arlington House, 1969).

10. W. G. Runciman and A. K. Sen, Games, Justice and the General Will, *Mind* 11(July 1965):32-77; Elliot M. Zashin, The Logic of Collective Action: Rousseau's *Social Contract* Revisited; and James A. Roumasset, Institutions, Social Contracts and Second-Best Pareto Optimality. Zashin and Roumasset presented their papers at the Public Choice Society Meetings, Mar. 21, 1974.

11. J. J. Rousseau, *The Social Contract*, Maurice Cranston, trans. (Baltimore: Penguin, 1968), Ch. 8.

12. Roumasset, in Institutions, argues that "Rousseau's Social Contract, an implicit agreement to abide by government authority, can be thought of as a social more[s] similar to trust." He quotes Kenneth Arrow: "Citizens obey the law to a much greater extent than can be explained on the basis of control mechanisms."

13. Zashin, Collective Action.

14. Smith, *Sentiments*, p. 28.

15. Rousseau, *Social Contract*, p. 83.

16. Rawls, *Justice*, p. 22, note 9.

17. Ibid., p. 542.

18. F. A. Hayek, Economic Freedom and Representative Government, I. E. A. Occ. Paper 39, London, 1973, p. 12.

19. George Stigler, Director's Law of Public Income Redistribution, *J. Law Econ.* 13(1969):1-10. Among the classical contractarians Rousseau was the most explicit on the disadvantages of simple majority voting. In *The Social Contract* he recommended varying the majority rule to require a ratio much nearer unanimity (say 80 percent) "the more important and serious the matter be" (p. 154). Wicksell later advocated the near-unanimity rule in public finance. It was advocated along with simultaneous tax and expenditure budgets as an efficient expression of the benefit principle. Today, J. M. Buchanan and G. Tullock similarly eschew simple majority voting as a general rule. In *The Calculus of Consent: Logical Foundations of Constitutional Democracy* (Ann Arbor: Univ. Mich. Press, 1962) they argue that the optimal majority rule ratio would be chosen by an individual (in something like Rawls's original position) after he had determined the minimum costs to be expected. Decision-making costs will increase with the size of the majority demanded because costly strategic bargaining is required to persuade the last few voters whose interest may be to hold out. Those "external costs to the individual" will decrease with the increase of the number required to take collective action. The summed decision-making and external costs produce a U-shaped average cost function, and the optimum majority rule is determined from its lowest point. In many decisions the rule is likely to be well above 50 percent. Two other writers who have argued for much bigger majority rules are William A. Niskanen, *Bureaucracy and Representative Government* (Chicago: Aldine, 1971), Ch. 20, and Hayek, Economic Freedom.

20. The detailed examination of these points is in E. G. West, Adam Smith's Public Economics, *Can. J. Econ.* 10(Feb 1977).

21. Rawls himself acknowledges that the majority rule may violate liberty. Rawls, *Justice*, p. 356, note 15.
22. Jacob Viner, *Guide to John Rae's Life of Adam Smith* (New York: Kelley, 1965), p. 85.
23. James Buchanan's review of Rawls in *Public Choice*, 13(Fall 1972):123.
24. Smith, *Sentiments*, p. 340.
25. This sentence did not appear in the first edition and its addition has been attributed (by Viner, *Guide*, p. 26) to the influence of Edmund Burke. Burke was certainly rather critical of Smith's free-trade prescriptions in the light of various factions. However, the quotation from *Sentiments* (note 26) suggests that the new sentence did not represent a significant change in Smith's attitude. Recent work also shows them to be consistent with other (earlier) arguments in *The Wealth of Nations*. See S. Hollander, *The Economics of Adam Smith* (Toronto: Univ. Toronto Press, 1973) p. 270.
26. Smith, *Sentiments*, p. 340.
27. Kenneth Arrow, *Social Choice and Individual Values* (New York: Wiley, 1951); Duncan Black, *Theory of Committees and Elections* (New York: Cambridge Univ. Press, 1958); Anthony Downs, *An Economic Theory of Democracy* (New York: Harper and Row, 1957).
28. Black, *Committees and Elections*, threw attention to the strategic position of the median (middle) voter, a person whose preferences do not at all necessarily call for the best "public" good solution. Arrow showed that majoritarian institutions produced actions that were not necessarily internally consistent.
29. George Stigler, The Theory of Economic Regulation, *Bell J. Econ. Manage. Sci.* 2(Spring 1971). Most of the present paragraph draws on this article, which contains fascinating empirical findings on the economics of politics — particularly with respect to transport and occupational licensing.
30. Ibid., p. 12.
31. Ibid.
32. Ibid., pp. 11, 17.
33. George Stigler, Smith's Travels on the Ship of State, *Hist. Polit. Econ.* 8(1971):pp. 269-85.
34. Ibid., p. 265.
35. See especially ibid., Table I.
36. Hayek, Economic Freedom, p. 12.
37. Stiger, Smith's Travels, p. 273.
38. In the United States this takes eight years on the average. Richard A. Posner, A Statistical Study of Antitrust Enforcement, *J. Law Econ.* 13(1970):365-419.
39. Rousseau, *Social Contract*, p. 84.
40. Stigler, Smith's Travels, p. 273.
41. Stigler recognizes this. Ibid., note 8.
42. Alfred Cobban, *History of Modern France* (New York: Braziller, 1965), p. 140.
43. C. B. Behrens, *The Ancien Régime* (New York: Harcourt, Brace, Jovanovitch, 1967), p. 26; C. B. Behrens, Nobles, Privileges and Taxes in France at the End of the *Ancien Régime*, *Econ. Hist. Rev.* 2nd ser., 15(1965):p. 460.
44. Turgot, *Oeuvres*, Schelle, ed. (Paris: 1913-1923), vol. 5, p. 172.
45. Behrens, Nobles, p. 462.
46. Ibid.
47. Buchanan, *Limits of Liberty*, p. 85.
48. Smith, *Lectures*, p. 69.
49. Behrens, Nobles, p. 465.
50. Ibid., p. 474.
51. Cobban, *History*, p. 109.
52. Stigler, Economic Regulation, p. 18.
53. Ibid., p. 20.

10

The Division of Labor in the Economy, the Polity, and Society

KENNETH J. ARROW

DIVISION OF LABOR IN ECONOMIC THEORY

The division of labor plays a special role in *The Wealth of Nations.* The concept appears in a place of greatest prominence, in the beginning of the text after the introductory material, in a bold sentence: "The greatest improvement in the productive powers of labour, and the greater part of the skill, dexterity, and judgment with which it is any where directed, or applied, seems to have been the effect of the division of labour" (p. 3). Adam Smith goes on to explain how the division of labor may increase output. By division of labor he means that each task in the productive process, most generally conceived, is divided so that different individuals are doing different parts. He gives his famous example of a pin factory, where the making of a single pin is divided into some twenty-two distinct operations, each performed by different workers, three or four concentrating on the head, and so forth. The description is apparently taken, with no credit, from the French *Encyclopèdie.*

Smith gives three reasons why dividing and subdividing the tasks and assigning each person a specialty would improve the output, so that the division of labor is beneficial to the improvement of productivity. One is the effect of practice; the repetition of a simple task improves the performance. If you do a great many tasks, each is being repeated a lot less often and there is less gain from practice. A second reason is that changing from one job to another involves a cost in terms of time. When switching from one job to another, you may have to lay down one set of tools and pick up another. There is also a psychological investment in attention. If the task is changed, time is spent shifting attention from one job to another. This time expenditure is reduced by concentrating on a single task. Modern operations research defines this as minimization of set-up costs. These costs include preparation, the picking up of tools, and so

Kenneth J. Arrow is James Bryant Conant University Professor and Director, Project on Efficiency of Decision Making in Economic Systems, Harvard University, Cambridge, Mass.

forth. A given set-up cost can accommodate a greater or smaller run of a single process and, obviously, the greater the run, the more economical it is. If two different people are doing two tasks, then each is switching back and forth. It would save time and yield more output per unit of time if each undertook one task only.

A third reason, one stressed by Smith but which does not apply so much today, is that a worker concentrating on a limited set of tasks may see a way of developing machines for handling them. This was indeed an interesting remark in 1776 when machines were far less common than today; in this, as in so many other places, Smith took a relatively minor tendency from his time and projected it quite correctly (as the future was to show) into a general phenomenon.

However, we depend today for our new machines on the "speculators and philosophers" of whom Smith thought little. I would place the greatest stress in the concept of the division of labor on the first aspect, that of practice, properly understood. I think of specialization or division of labor (which I take to be the same thing) as primarily specialization in knowing how to do things. To do something, you must learn how, in fact, to perform as many tasks as are needed. In other words, there is an analogy between the first and second efficiency effects of the division of labor. Specialization in information can be considered as representing an analogy to (in fact a special case of) minimizing a set-up cost. When specializing, the individual is learning only what is necessary to accomplish a task and can, so to speak, spread the overhead of learning over a much longer run. A professional, such as a physician, is rather an extreme exemplification of this. A physician essentially serves you with knowledge about diseases; some dexterity and some special skills are needed but these are relatively minor. It would be possible for a person who was willing to spend five years or more at the task to acquire this knowledge. But obviously no individual can justify five years of training devoted solely to the prospect of self-medication. It is socially worthwhile for some individuals to specialize in health care when that education can be used to handle many thousands of cases. So in our economy and others it has been found expedient for individuals to specialize in some branch of knowledge that is acquired partly through education but also through the performance of the task itself. The very act of engaging in medical practice or tending machines will be a source of knowledge, as an increase in experience is gained from the particular task.

Smith goes on to develop the hypothesis that the division of labor in turn leads to and is sustained by the growth of an economy, of a market system. Two people performing different tasks ultimately trade with one another, they sell their services to a common employer, or something similar, so that these tasks can be performed for each other. Smith concentrates almost exclusively on the market as the method by which diverse abilities and performance of diverse tasks are made to complement each other, to fit together to produce more activity. Indeed, the famous title of

Chapter 3 in *The Wealth of Nations* proclaims "that the division of labour is limited by the extent of the market" (p. 17). A remarkable doctrine is developed: the more the selling of goods and services takes place, the greater can be the division of labor; at least in the early parts of Smith's book, this is all in terms of praise. The subdivision of labor can be made finer and finer as the market extends. There is a mutually reinforcing relationship between specialization, and therefore greater efficiency, on the one hand and the growth of the market economy in which people are buying and selling on the other. The resulting differentiation in tasks performed gives rise to the profitability of trade; because people are doing different things, they can gain by exchanging these services in effect.

This last proposition has been the basis of the most significant strand in the development of economics in the ensuing two hundred years. But it has taken a form that departs somewhat from Smith's formulation. Economic theory received a certain degree of systematization at the hands of David Ricardo some forty years after Smith.[1] Consider particularly Ricardo's theory of foreign trade. Of relevance to England's trade with Portugal are the different abilities of the two countries to produce. In his example Portugal is better at producing wine and England at producing linen. This difference leads to trade because both countries can gain by having each specialize in the task that it can perform best. (Strictly speaking, the advantages need only be relative; that is, Portugal can produce more additional wine than England per unit of linen foregone.)

But the Ricardian view of specialization lacks some characteristics of the Smithian; in Ricardo's system the abilities to produce are given. In Smith's view specialization is more a matter of deliberate choice. People are very much alike, but they have chosen to specialize in different ways because they can do better by being a specialist. A person could equally well have been a physician or a businessman, but some will become physicians and some will become businessmen because both will benefit by specialization and subsequent trade. Ricardo described the same phenomenon by saying there are physicians and there are lawyers without going into why they exist.[2]

The Ricardo viewpoint, extended from foreign trade to the domestic market, has been predominant in subsequent economic theory. It has been the view of the founders of modern economic theory—Alfred Marshall, Léon Walras, and Stanley Jevons in the latter part of the nineteenth century—and is largely the basis of most current theory. Like differences in natural resources, the differences in individual talents are the basis of trade.

Consider as a conjecture that Marshall's willingness to believe that people are intrinsically different and therefore find it profitable to trade may have been reinforced by the development of biology, particularly of Darwinism in the nineteenth century. Social Darwinism, a somewhat illegitimate offspring of Darwin's theories, was a predominant social attitude. The argument that biological evolution proceeds by competition, with success going to the fittest, gave rise to the analogy that economic competition was an example of a kind of competition related to evolutionary success. At any rate it is true that the biological emphasis and the accumulation of real evidence in the latter part of the nineteenth century certainly placed greater weight on the genetic factors than had been believed previously. The eighteenth-century thinkers were much more environmentalist in their views of human nature. Smith, for example, had very little belief in natural differences. "The difference of natural talents in different men is, in reality, much less than we are aware of; and the very different genius which appears to distinguish men in different professions, when grown up to maturity, is not upon many occasions so much the cause, as the effect of the division of labour" (p. 15).

The evidence is not available for complete evaluation of the relative importance of genetic factors and deliberate choice in specialization, but certainly the Smithian component of specialization is real. Smith never realized that there is something of a contradiction between this proposition and his basic economic theory of competition. The contradiction has been recognized in economic theory for fifty years or more, certainly since Piero Sraffa's paper of 1926,[3] but it has not yet been well captured in a consistent model. The argument is that if a firm can increase its relative profitability by increasing its scale, then one firm should drive all others out of a given business; if there are two firms in existence, one should be able to undersell the other and still make a profit because of the decreased costs. This is in fact the advice given by a leading management consulting firm in the United States to its clients; growth is the basic secret of success. Indeed, the proposition that division of labor is limited by the extent of the market would imply that one firm grows to the point where it dominates the entire market. But if that happens, there is monopoly and not competition. This dilemma has been thoroughly discussed; it has not been thoroughly resolved.

DIVISION OF LABOR IN SOCIETY

Let us broaden our horizons beyond the economic world. We follow Smith, for his work contains many observations on society as a whole. We should take the concept of the division of labor to be a basic structural aspect, not merely of the economic world, but of all other social worlds. The differentiation between the political and nonpolitical worlds is an example. Politics is a full-time occupation. Even though the politician is in some sense a representative of the entire country and everybody is one to some extent, the average person confines participation to following the news, periodic voting, and occasional intervention on specific issues. But efficiency by division of labor dictates the existence of a small class of people who spend the major part of their time in politics.

Values are enhanced by specialization, not only in politics, but in all aspects of society. This has been touched on by the current philosophers, for example, John Rawls, in an eloquent section toward the end of his famous book, *A Theory of Justice*.[4] He distinguishes between what he calls a private society, which is essentially a society like that of businessmen or economists where each individual sees himself as seeking only his own interests, and a society in which individuals have perceived common ends and regard themselves as social beings. He notes in this regard, "One basic characteristic of human beings is that no one person can do everything he might do; nor *a fortiori* can he do everything that any other person can do."[5] The two clauses of that sentence express Smithian and Ricardian specialization respectively. The first implies that to do anything well you have to leave some of your potential unused. An investment of time is needed to master an activity, and that fact prevents you from developing some other talent that must remain latent; time is finite, and resources are scarce. The second half of Rawl's sentence—that he is not capable of doing all that other people can—is perhaps more nearly Ricardian specialization as I have used the term. Each individual, as Rawls puts it so well, is more fully realized in society because some of his potential has been realized in other people, that is, in the activities in which they engage. An individual is completed because something he could have done but did not do was in fact done by someone else who made a different choice of activities.

COOPERATION, ALTRUISM, AND THE SENSE OF JUSTICE

As something of a side remark, it is curious to note that both Smith and Rawls regard the division of labor or the complementarity of skills of different individuals as a peculiarly human trait. Smith explains this supposed confinement of division of labor to humans by the fact that animals never engage in exchange. This is a deficiency of analysis; Smith apparently is not aware of the possibility that the interaction and cooperation of human beings or animals can be achieved by means other than the market. The market is a very important coordinating mechanism but it is by no means the only one; in the social sphere as a whole it is simply one among many. We engage in many social activities where we work jointly with division of labor but do not exchange goods for goods or goods for services. "In almost every other race of animals," Smith said, "each individual, when it is grown up to maturity, is entirely independent" (p. 14). Rawls makes a rather obscure comment that seems to say something similar. "By contrast with human kind, every individual animal can and does what for the most part it might do, or what any other of its kind might or can do."[6] The blindness common to Smith and Rawls is quite remarkable. In fact, in many though not all species, cooperation among the members is the rule. The study of cooperation in animals has been highly developed by biologists in terms of theory and observation. It is perhaps best displayed by Edward O. Wilson,[7] though it can also be found in the work of many other biologists. But surely anybody who knows anything about insect society could scarcely neglect the idea that cooperative specialized behavior is a major aspect of the bees, the ants, or the wasps. Perhaps this was not widely known at the time of Adam Smith, though it probably was a matter of common observation for many centuries. But certainly the concept became well known through the work of nineteenth-century entomologists, particularly Fabre.

It is well established today that not only in social insects but also in many mammals, such as African wild dogs or primates of different kinds, there is considerable cooperation and division of labor in such activities as hunting. This is to ignore completely the very obvious and universal characteristic among the higher animals of division of labor according to sex.

Around the turn of the century the idea appears that animal cooperation is an evolutionary factor because it is to the benefit of the group; therefore, a particular species that engages in this behavior is likely to have evolutionary value. This proposition was advanced by Peter Kropotkin in a brilliant but unfortunately neglected book.[8] Kropotkin, an anarchist, attacked social Darwinism by arguing that thorough understanding of evolutionary theory eliminated the identification of individual success with some kind of evolutionary value. The recognition of a biology of altruism leads to a new twist to the much discussed question of influence of genetic action in the economic system and indeed in society as a whole.

But whatever the biological work on altruism has been and what it ultimately leads to; we can take it for granted that for society to operate at all, to function successfully in any sense, we must have an ethical code, that is, some sense of justice. Conduct of an economy of even the most self-interested type requires a degree of recognition of others, or it will not function on its own terms.

LIMITS OF SOCIETY AND THE DIVISION OF LABOR

One of the difficulties of any theory of justice is to define the limits of society to which it is relevant. Consider a number of individuals on separate islands. They are aware of each other, but that is all. Each is cultivating an island, totally alone, and deriving whatever benefit it will yield from crops, nuts, berries, and the like. Do these people have any obligation to help one another? Is there a sense of justice or something similar that suggests an obligation to help redistribute income toward the less well off in this context? This argument has been raised against Rawls by Robert Nozick,[9] a somewhat modified anarchist though much more laissez-faire economically than Kropotkin would have been. Actually, the utilitarian theory of justice or modern welfare economics would be subject to the same objection.

However one might answer this question in the abstract, it seems clear that the concept of a social union, a society in which individuals are mutually dependent, becomes relevant. In this society the obligation to redistribute arises. In any real society the idea that the individual works alone is simply not true. The contribution an individual makes depends on those of all others. Sometimes it is argued that an individual is entitled to the marginal product, that is, to the difference in the output of society due to his participation, holding all other things constant. But this is a very unsatisfactory concept of justice, because what one contributes to society depends on what else is around. If there is a vast supply of machines, each of which requires a minimum of attention, then by one's presence a whole array of machines may be placed into motion and therefore contribute a great product to society. With the same work and the same talent, if one had to plow the ground with a pointed stick, the contribution to society would be much less. One would be doing the same work, and perhaps working a lot harder in fact, but the contribution in the marginal-product sense would be much less.

One can argue that when there is division of labor the total output is much greater than can be attributed to individuals in the sense that each is entitled, say, to what can be produced working alone outside society. In the modern world, or even in an economy no more complex than in ancient Egypt, this is a very small part of what an individual receives. Hence there is a large surplus, so to speak, that would be available for redistribution if we could agree on the appropriate principles.

The language of economic allocation of goods and services and their redistribution has been used here, but the same issues arise in other social questions. In general the complementarity of different individuals creates a margin over what one could achieve alone; and within this margin, redistribution is possible without infringing on what might be thought of as a legitimate reserved area.

NEGATIVE ASPECTS OF DIVISION OF LABOR

The division of labor, especially in its Smithian sense where individuals choose to specialize—to narrow their activities compared with their potential breadth to achieve greater depth in some direction—has its drawbacks as well as its virtues. Smith is above all a realist and he praises very few things without at the same time pointing to their defects. Rawls in this sense seems much more sentimental when one compares the two in reading them together. It is well known that Smith had a lively appreciation of the role of self-interest, but it is far from mere praise. For example, although the basic text he is preaching is the freedom of business to make profits as the best possible way to improve things, he has a very low opinion of profit makers. He explains in one place that they "seldom meet together, even for merriment or diversion, but the conversation ends in a conspiracy against the public . . ." (p. 128); there is very little that escapes Smith's eyes. Even when he sees something that is extremely important from the point of view of efficiency, he is not blind to its defects; and indeed in a later passage the division of labor appears in a different light: "In the progress of the division of labour, the employment . . . comes to be confined to a very few simple operations. . . . The man whose whole life is spent in performing a few simple operations . . . has no occasion to exert his understanding. . . . He . . . generally becomes as stupid and ignorant as it is possible for a human creature to become" (p. 734).

Admittedly, this remark follows some seven hundred pages after the passage explaining how all the improvements of mankind are due to the division of labor, but there is not necessarily a contradiction. Smith is primarily concerned in arguing that the limitation of the individual by excessive specialization is bad in itself in the first place; in addition, it prevents individuals from possessing what he calls "tender sentiments and good judgments" about public life or even about their own. The context is the need for universal primary education. In a society like the shepherd's, as contrasted with industrial society, there is no need for education because the shepherd performs a great variety of tasks and therefore maintains an all-around knowledge. But the efficiency due to the division of labor has its price in restriction of the range of the individual, and Smith feels that this lack should be overcome.

DIVISION OF LABOR AND THE COSTS OF COMMUNICATION

Smith is touching upon a very deep point. There is more to the story than he has stated, and there are more problems that the division of labor creates than he has indicated for the working of the economy and society. Division of labor increases the value of cooperation, but it also increases the costs of cooperation and can give rise to conflicts. Specialization consists above all in specialization of knowledge, both acquired and through experience. Each individual thus has a different outlook on the world, a different assessment of the way things are—his experiences have been unique.

One's empirical view of the world is contingent on what one knows. Let us assume the world is one in which we never know everything. There is a great deal of uncertainty—a fairly obvious fact, though we sometimes refuse to recognize it. Your perception, your best conception of the world, and your judgment of the relative possibilities of different outcomes are ordered by your experiences. You have observed that certain things happen and have established certain regularities. In fields that you have not observed and have not learned about, you do not recognize regularities. So different individuals with different learning processes and experiences, even different kinds of education, can develop different perceptions of the laws that govern the world.

This has been exemplified by DeWitt Dearborn and Herbert Simon.[10] They considered a number of business executives who had different specialties, for example, sales, accounting, or production management. They set forth a case, the way that business schools do, explaining in a structured way a variety of facts about a firm and pointing out that it was not doing very well. Then they asked each of the individuals to analyze the cause of the firm's difficulties. The facts presented were exactly the same for all. The sales executives saw that the sales efforts needed to be expanded, the accounting executive pointed out that the accounting was not very good, the chief executive was not in control of the figures, the production manager insisted that production methods should be improved, and so forth.

This represents a deep universal truth about human beings. In other words, start with the assumption that different individuals have different judgments about the world. To cooperate and to take advantage of the division of labor, there must be an exchange of information in one way or another. Let us draw upon communications engineering and its derivative, information theory. Individuals must communicate with each other. Smith has chosen the market as the method of communication, but that is only one possibility, although a very important one. The communications engineer argues, and we must recognize this as a central fact, that communication among human beings is costly in terms of effort, time, and difficulty in understanding. We can think in terms of mechanical use of telephones and telegraphs. There are restrictions to the rate at which communications can be put in at one end, on the signals the line can carry per unit of time, and on the rate at which the signals can be read at the receiving end. It is of course much more important that the human beings at the two ends have limited capacities for understanding and manipulating and have other things to do with their time. So communication is a costly operation.

Information theorists have studied the following problem. If you want to convey a given amount of information, how do you do it most economically? To speak of conveying information implies that it is not known in advance what is to be conveyed; if it were known, the receiving party could know the message in advance, and it would not be information. The concept of information means precisely that there is something uncertain about which one wants to receive news. If you have an idea of the kind of information you are going to transmit, you can design your system so as to be as economical as possible in communication costs and information terms. Roughly speaking, you want to phrase the messages that occur most frequently in as short a way as possible, whereas the things or concepts that you think are less likely a priori can require longer messages. We know that in any branch of scholarship we develop technical vocabularies. Concepts used repeatedly are given short technical names, so that a couple of words convey a whole thought. The concept may have been quite expensive to teach the first time but does not have to be repeated every time you communicate it. This is an illustration of a process that is sometimes called "encoding."

In society we transmit messages among individuals who have had different life experiences. These people have different judgments about what messages are likely to pass. It is fairly clear that communication among those with different life experiences is likely to be much less efficient than communication among those with very similar experiences. It is also true, however, that communication among those with differing experiences has greater benefits. You are more interested in hearing from people who know something you do not than from those who cannot increase your knowledge. But it is easier to talk to people you know.

We see everywhere an idea of this differential ease of communication. The reality of class consciousness, which seems a very real phenomenon in modern life, is an example of this. People in similar economic circumstances understand each other in ways that transcend simple economic self-interest. Employers understand each other's problems, and workers understand each other's problems. It is harder for employers and workers to understand each other. The Tower of Babel comes to mind, but the biblical story is a little different. You will recall in the Bible, God (the boss) feared the power of the united people; therefore, he created differences of language among them. The Marxists use a similar argument to explain why there are differences among the working classes, and it is called a conspiracy of the bosses. But the explanation may be somewhat different than these simple conspiracy theories. While working on the Tower of Babel, the masons and bricklayers found greater and greater difficulty in communicating with each other after years of specialization.

DIVISION OF LABOR AND A COMMON IDEA OF JUSTICE

There is a still more serious problem arising from the difficulties of communication among individuals with diverse experiences arising out of the division of labor. I have mentioned the existence of communication problems on the implicit assumption that individuals really want to communicate and cooperate, that they desire to convey the truth to each other as they know it. But why should they? In the world that Adam Smith and the economists following him set forth, individuals acted out of self-interest. "It is not from the benevolence of the butcher, the brewer, and the baker that we expect our dinner . . ." (p. 14). In a world of pure self-interest if one person is dealing with another and knows something that the second does not, the first person, instead of conveying that information, may take advantage of it, not for cooperative purposes, but for what might be called exploitation.

What may be even more serious to the economic system in the long run than this exploitation is the creation of distrust. If you know that somebody knows more than you do, you may not pay any attention to messages from that source, even though they would be helpful to you, because you may fear being manipulated.

Some of the worst possible effects of these differences of knowledge do not occur. They are avoided by some principle of ethics. Ethical codes have mutual value because on the one hand they avoid exploitation and on the other they avoid distrust. The best examples of these are the ethical codes of the professions. Without trying in any way to glorify them beyond their value, it is true that you can count on the physician to worry to some degree about your health problems and try with some degree of diligence to find out what is wrong with you. The difference between a physician and a patient is an extreme case of difference in knowledge in the division of labor. Because of the physician's superior knowledge, he has the potential of exploiting you either by prescribing medical services you do not need, or, perhaps more frequently, by neglecting to be diligent in following up diagnoses. However, the ethical codes that govern doctors tend to prevent these consequences. If exploitation occurred constantly, physicians would disappear altogether because people would distrust them; there are societies in which this has happened in the past. But the code of professional ethics is a survival mechanism, a natural social arrangement for improving somewhat the benefits of the division of labor by preventing them from getting lost in a welter of exploitation and distrust.

The fact that we need ethical codes brings us back to the problem of how to establish a system of justice in a society, in a social union. Inherent in a system of justice is the possibility for individuals to engage in meaningful moral discourse and argumentation. Philosophers have for millenia discussed what justice is, and the question probably never will be fully resolved. There are, however, some accepted ideas. A moral discourse should in some sense be impersonal, or universalizable as some philosophers say. To say that it is good for the society to do something because it is good for me is not an acceptable argument. The argument must be symmetric. It should be possible to replace you by me and me by you in the argument and still lead to the same conclusion. There are various technical devices that philosophers have used to try to make this argument clear, but that is the essential thing.

It may be that on the basis of this criterion, you may discuss the more abstract aspects of justice. But as soon as we try to apply any concept of justice to a particular concrete situation, we come against the differences among different individuals in empirical understanding, that is, in understanding what the world is like when seen by different individuals. If you and I have different ideas of what people are like and what nature is like, we may come to different judgments as to what is a just distribution of goods, even though each of us has argued in a truly impersonal way. The argument can be impersonal in that, given our knowledge, no one is putting oneself first. But we enter the argument with our personal knowledge; it is inherent in our life experiences. Therefore two different people, even though each is trying to be objective and impersonal in order to conduct a legitimate moral argument, can nevertheless disagree and disagree permanently. No amount of argument will be able to sway us because we come with different judgments about what is possible and what is empirically likely in the world, and we arrive at these different empirical judgements because we specialized and therefore had different experiences.

CONCLUSION

The pressure for efficiency in the broadest sense and the pressure to get the most out of ourselves and our resources (not merely economic but also political and social) lead to the division of labor and, in particular, specialization of knowledge. But the very act of specialization produces a world in which individuals have different experiences and therefore differing perceptions of the world, that is, different judgments of what is possible. These differences are themselves a source of gain in increasing the realization of the human potential; but when taken in conjunction with the limited capacity of human beings to exchange information, the divison of labor leads to a division of society into smaller social groups among which communciation is limited and both economic and social intercourse is restricted. Ultimately, different moral views on the nature of society can never be completely reconciled.

NOTES

1. David Ricardo, *Principles of Political Economy and Taxation*, vol. 1, *The Works and Correspondence of David Ricardo*, Piero Sraffa, ed. (Cambridge, England: Cambridge Univ. Press, 1953).
2. I learned this distinction between Smith's and Ricardo's concepts from H. Houthakker, Economics and Biology: Specialization and Speciation, *Kyklos* 9(1956): 181-87.
3. Piero Sraffa, The Laws of Return under Competitive Conditions, *Econ. J.* 36(1926): 535-50.
4. John Rawls, *A Theory of Justice* (Cambridge: Harvard Univ. Press, 1971), pp. 520-29.
5. Ibid., p. 523.
6. Ibid., p. 525.
7. Edward O. Wilson, *Sociobiology: The New Synthesis* (Cambridge: Harvard Univ. Press, 1975).
8. Peter Kropotkin, *Mutual Aid* (New York: New York Univ. Press, 1972).
9. Robert Nozick, *Anarchy, State and Utopia* (New York: Basic Books, 1974).
10. DeWitt Dearborn and Herbert Simon, Selective Perception: A Note on Departmental Identification of Executives, *Sociometry* 21(1958):140-44.

11

The Invisible Hand:
Moral and Political Considerations

JOSEPH CROPSEY

THE bicentenary of *The Wealth of Nations* tends to be overshadowed by that of the United States. But the celebration of the country's past inevitably evokes reflections on its future, and to reflect on our future is to think of our institutions—of their stability and their prospects, thus the threats to them, and in turn the basis for those threats in the complaints so often voiced against commercial liberalism. The weightiest among those complaints, or the ones perhaps most often taken seriously, are moral: What are the rights and wrongs of commercial liberalism, what conception of justice does it elevate to authority, into what ways of life does it lead its participants? Evidently, speculation about our future draws heavily on thought about what we are, and thus about whence we are sprung. But our "whence" is in some immeasurable degree a past age's thoughts that have become our own conceptions and have become incarnate in our national ways and institutions. We are led from our political past through our actual present to our political prospect and thence once more to the past, but this time to a past that lives in the pages of books. We find ourselves turning to *The Wealth of Nations* with a sense that reflection on the literary bicentenary is important not only in its own right but as the necessary preparation for investigating the issues evoked by the more splendid political anniversary.

It would be at the very least inconvenient to discuss *The Wealth of Nations* without reaching an early understanding about the name by which to call the social system the book is famous for advocating. Inattention could encourage falling in with the common practice of referring to it as capitalism; but what that name presupposes differs materially from Smith's conception of the system's essence, and the term should therefore not be used freely in this context. The name "capitalism" suggests, and was employed by Marx to affirm, that the essence of this social and economic system is the generation of profit ("surplus value"). Everything important for the manner of life in this society follows from the employment of labor

Joseph Cropsey is Professor of Political Science, University of Chicago, Chicago, Ill.

through the purchase of labor-power by possessors of "capital." To call the system of free commerce "capitalism" is thus to imply that the essential characteristic of the social order is the existence of the conditions that generate or enhance profit as such.

These conditions are conceived to include preeminently the division of the people into what are loosely called classes, especially the classes of those who do own and those who do not own the means of production. But classes in this sense have no legal status; they have only a speculative or dialectical definition. In this respect they do not differ from the "classes" of people who live on opposite sides of a street, or of the even numbers between zero and eleven. Referring to such groupings as classes rather than sets obscures the fact that they are arbitrary or convenient—designated for the purpose of pursuing a certain line of argument or speculation. On the other hand, a legal definition goes beyond a speculative one in that it carries a positive imputation of right. Thus there was an imputation of right, however misguided is not now relevant, in the legal definition of the class of slaves, while there is no imputation of right in the ratiocinative definition of dwellers on one side of a street or of a set of numbers. Evidently a large problem is opened up by attributing to "classes" a decisive political importance in a society that ignores them legally and that officially imputes no right to their existence or to membership in them.

However worthy of being pursued to a conclusion, this theme was introduced, not for itself, but to strengthen the argument for finding a name for Smith's system that is harmonious with his conception of that system. Fortunately, he in fact gave it a name, one with as heavy a freight of meaning as borne by "capitalism": the "system of natural liberty" (p. 651). As the name suggests and as *The Wealth of Nations* maintains, the essence of Smith's system is consistency with the dictate or tendency of nature—neither the generation of an invidious distributive share nor the friction of interests present in a society composed of functioning parts. Marx insists on presenting free commerce as though its essence were conflict; Smith presents it as though its essence is a kind of sociality or collaboration. Our immediate task is, not to judge between Smith and Marx, but to improve our understanding of Smith's doctrine, which we can begin to do by thinking about his phrase, "natural liberty."

Natural liberty is either a tautology or a paradox. Suppose for a moment that in his primary state (primary either in time or in principle) man is unrestrained by anything external to himself that hinders his moving or acting. Then the restraints that now hinder him must have been imposed, as laws, conventions, and practices all have been imposed by men on themselves. If the primary state is correctly called natural, then "natural" and "liberty" agree so well that the phrase resembles a tautology. Nature, or the primary, is the basis of freedom; artifice and convention are the grounds of constraint, and if freedom is accepted as the aim of society, then the effectual goal of society is to restore itself to nature, or to recapture nature through social institutions, or something to the same effect.

Simple or obvious as these notions might appear, they are full of difficulties. To begin with, the modification of society in the direction of nature — meaning the progressive weakening of the conventions and artifices that constrain — is tantamount to the weakening or even the dissolution of civil life. But the dissolution of civil life may well be equivalent to the dissolution of society itself, in which case the "naturalization" of society would be a misnomer for the dissolution of society. Then what began as a tautology would reveal itself as a contradiction: the attainment of society's essential goal, its naturalization and liberalization, would entail the dissolution of society.

There is a way to avoid this outcome. Suppose that the modification of society in the direction of nature need not mean the weakening or discarding of conventions and artifices but rather the installation of "natural" conventions and artifices — human constructions that follow the indications of nature while still restraining men's movements. This suggestion will be intelligible if nature and artifice are mutually reconcilable — if man's making can be sufficiently guided by what man does not make. But why should not the products of two makers serve a single end, the end dictated by the one maker that comprehends the other? More concretely, suppose that the whole import of the artificial social construction is the recovery of natural liberty in the form of self-legislation. After all, the liberty of natural man consisted in a freedom to do whatever he desired to do, which appears to be the condition of a being that legislates for itself. Then the conventions of self-legislation would be those natural artifacts whose possibility we were questioning.

Perhaps we could be satisifed with this if we were not conscious of a discord between doing what one desires and legislating for oneself. Doing what one desires means doing *whatever* one desires — now this, and perhaps at another time something else; while self-legislation means to lay down laws that one obeys, and presumably always and steadily obeys, with the understanding that "obeys" carries with it not only constancy but the implication of an impulse that is to be overcome by obedience. But it is precisely the conquered impulse that comprises the "desire" in the expression, "to do as one desires." Self-legislation contradicts doing what one desires and exists exactly in order to replace the rule of desire with the rule of something else, presumably something worthier, perhaps even something freer. It now appears that in progressing to the artifices that concur rather than conflict with nature, one reaches the point at which natural liberty again becomes confused: the institutions that follow those indications of nature that point to self-legislation clash with those indications of nature that consist in desire and in the impulse to act according to desire. Yet both sorts of institution or artifice can claim to give effect to freedom, indeed to natural freedom.

Perhaps we have reached confusion because we were not sufficiently precise in speaking of nature's indications and of the sense in which man the artificer might be the agent of, or a fragment of nature of, the more comprehensive maker. More exactly, we have not faced the issue of whether it is on the one hand responsiveness to desire or on the other hand self-legislation that nature sets forth as true "natural liberty." It is clear that nature cannot well teach both if self-legislation is the expression of man's freedom in a voluntary act to confine his desires.

If self-legislation is natural freedom, then obedience to the desires or instincts is natural bondage. Moreover, if self-legislation is natural freedom, then man's primary condition or natural state is bondage and not freedom, for subjection to (self-legislated) law presupposes a prior condition that calls for law. But in any case, why speak of obedience to desires or instincts as bondage? Because the desires and instincts move us as if, or perhaps literally, mechanically. Acting under mechanical impulsion or necessity is acting without intention or volition, thus acting without being the prime cause of one's acts. It is acting for causes that cannot be traced to one's own will. But as long as it remains unclear that a being existing in the order of nature, as man does, *can* separate itself from the chain of natural causes sufficiently to act under the causation of its "will" alone, so long will the suspicion linger that the will is simply a construction or hypothesis, something hypostasised to underlie "freedom," as the soul might be called something hypostasised to underlie the motion and thought of an otherwise inert body. On the assumption that every act (indeed every event) must have a cause but that "freedom" requires that there be acts not caused in the usual sense, one posits a Will that is capable of causing acts in such a way that the odium of necessity does not cling to the acts and thereby deprive them, as mere responses to externality, of their possible morality.

One could imagine that a settled determination to purge action of the moral contamination of simple causation might lead a thinker to conceive a weakening of the authority of the ordinary process of causation rather than to superimpose on that process an extraordinary higher cause unlike any that operates wholly within the order of nature. In other words, one might expect a Hume to arise who would argue that causation is mysterious rather than absolute and unshakable, instead of expecting a Kant to arise who would introduce freedom of the will and the immortality of the soul as correctives outside the causal chain of natural necessity. Reflections on Hume and Kant at this point are not a luxury but rather are indicated because of the degree to which Hume's thought impinged on Smith's and some of Smith's understandings recommended themselves to Kant. To avoid leaving the impression that the questions of natural liberty, desire, and the action of the will need to be discussed only in terms of the simple alternatives already presented, we should notice that Nietzsche, not an advocate for liberal commerce, rehabilitates instinct by *uniting it with the will* and ascends to a freedom so intimately affiliated with creativity as to be within the reach of humanity on a plane beyond the grasp of society or of politics.

In this conspectus of possibilities we must recognize one more before we turn thematically to Adam Smith, his system of natural liberty, and the invisible hand. It might be crucial to distinguish among the desires and passions when ascribing to nature certain unwilled causes of human action. According to a famous notion of Smith's contemporary, Rousseau, most of what we now possess as passion has been generated within society and does not belong to our pristine nature. Consequently, to gain ascendancy over hatred, envy, greed, or pride is not simply to master nature or to acquire control over a process of natural causation in an unqualified sense but it is rather to find a means within the order of natural causes whereby to bring the powers of nature to bear upon or against one another for a moral human end. But precisely if the present ensemble of human motivations that we think of as our natural apparatus had a genesis or history, the system of rewards, penalties, and incentives we devise to govern our impulses is partly "natural" and partly only historical: "human nature" — what now is — is emphatically not coeval with either nature or man. As far as Rousseau contemplates the adjustment of human nature as it now is to some more authoritative — more primitive, more free — natural norm, he looks for a norm "outside nature," outside what we now know to be, and what is for every practical purpose, our nature. But the prospect for finding a standpoint unequivocally and consciously outside nature, to enable mankind to master nature in the interest of freedom and morality, began with Kant, who elaborated for the purpose a metaphysics and a moral philosophy that stand or fall with the possibility that a realm of freedom, outside the realm of natural necessity, exists and is the scene of the action of the human will.

These remarks are prompted by the occurrence of the term "natural liberty" in the name that Smith applied to his sytem. They are intended to suggest that Smith's system should be regarded in its relation to a great structure of modern reflection on man's moral condition. That reflection had been brought on by the apprehension that a perfectly mechanized nature, of which humanity forms an integral part, will be graspable by man's mind exactly in proportion to the rule of regularity, predictability, or necessity in that nature. But the more necessary and knowable the natural world is, the less free are the human ingredients of it, and the more painful the predicament of modern men, who see their science and freedom as so grounded that each is a mortal threat to the other.

It is understandable that modern man should be especially afflicted with these apprehensions, for the modern age is emphatically the time of the flowering of natural science, which is a human consciousness of nature as a mechanism; and that consciousness has proved capable of becoming the consciousness not only of the whole chain of natural causes but of man's place in that chain. Does consciousness of his place in the overwhelming chain of necessity enslave man; or does his higher self-consciousness, his consciousness of *his* consciousness of nature, emancipate him by elevating him above his condition? It is very hard to be sure whether a perfectly clear view of one's entanglement seals one's bondage or rather dissolves it; but it is easier to see that a slave who does not know himself to be one is not simply enslaved. The human being for whom natural science does not exist as the intimation of an infinite chain of causes is not aware of himself as integrated in such a chain. He is not aware that nature poses or constitutes a threat to his freedom; he is necessarily even less aware that his consciousness of his plight is (that is, would be) *eo ipso* emancipation from his enslavement. He is unaware of these things because he is not a philosopher but a citizen — a fact that remains decisive until it is shown that the deepest thoughts available to an age seep into the average consciousness as *Zeitgeist.* In such a case, average men would have a feeling, perhaps a vague sense of unhappiness or detachment, but certainly not the clear and distinct understanding of their situation that is prerequisite to their enslavement, nor the clear consciousness of their own consciousness that is the condition for their emancipation from the bonds of nature.

Failing a theoretical perception of the nature of things, what remains to a man is life within his horizons as these appear to him through his everyday existence. As far as the issue is freedom and bondage, those horizons are the horizons of the citizen, who as such thinks of his freedom and bondage in direct and immediate terms, which are political: Is he or is he not in thrall to men who wield the state's power? But even if, or rather especially if, there seeped into the average consciousness an unhappiness that reflects a philosophic conception of man as enthralled to nature, it would be folly or wickedness to represent that unhappiness as the product of political formations. Further, it would be absurd to hold out hope of emancipation at all unless there were means, which would have to be other than those of contemplation, for giving the mass of mankind an existence on a plane "outside of nature." But those means do not exist, and every nostrum offered under such a guise proves to be one kind or another of state organization, or political regime. Thus the folly and wickedness are compounded, for the means of emancipation that are offered, being political, are represented to be effective against a bondage that has no political foundation at all but arises from man's inclusion in the infinite chain of natural causes.

The claims and offers that appear so problematical have indeed been made, and with great practical effect. They are directed of course against the system of thought and life engendered by Adam Smith. For the moment we do not know how vulnerable Smith is to the attack. We have seen that he uses the term "natural liberty" with an innocence that is either thoughtless or farseeing, maintaining as it does a total silence about any possible tension between natural necessity and human freedom. I have tried to show that there is a sense in which there is no problem, and also a sense in which there would be no solution if there were a problem. There would be no problem, and if a problem no solution, if the problem and the solution would have to be political or practical rather than philosophic or contemplative. But Smith, in proceeding so directly to the compatibility of nature and liberty, appears to adopt what I have called the average man's posture or the horizon of the citizen. In doing so, has he avoided a spurious issue that has bemused much of modern thought, or has he overlooked a crucial condition that has vitiated much of modern life? If the former, his stature has never been properly acknowledged. If the latter, we can understand only too well the basis for those complaints against our institutions that disturb the celebration of our political bicentennial. Against the background of the issues so delineated, we turn to Smith's formula of the invisible hand.

Smith makes reference to the invisible hand in two places, *The Theory of Moral Sentiments* and *The Wealth of Nations*. Let us look at the two passages.

> The produce of the soil maintains at all times nearly that number of inhabitants which it is capable of maintaining. The rich only select from the heap what is most precious and agreeable. They consume little more than the poor, and in spite of their natural selfishness and rapacity, though they mean only their own conveniency, though the sole end which they propose from the labors of all the thousands whom they employ, be the gratification of their own vain and insatiable desires, they divide with the poor the produce of all their improvements. They are led by an invisible hand to make nearly the same distribution of the necessaries of life, which would have been made, had the earth been divided into equal portions among all its inhabitants, and thus without intending it, without knowing it, advance the interest of the society, and afford means to the multiplication of the species.[1]

> As every individual, therefore, [naturally] endeavours as much as he can . . . to employ his capital in the support of domestic industry, and [necessarily] so to direct that industry that its produce may be of the greatest value; every individual necessarily labours to render the annual revenue of the society as great as he can. He generally, indeed, neither intends to promote the public interest, nor knows how much he is promoting it. By preferring the support of domestic to that of foreign industry, he intends only his own security; and by directing that industry in such a manner as its produce may be of the greatest value, he intends only his own gain, and he is in this, as in many other cases, led by an invisible hand to promote an end which was no part of his intention [p. 423].

It is clear that the invisible hand is not a metaphor for a power by which nature compels men to perform any acts. The invisible hand is a metaphor that certainly presupposes that men are compelled to respond in act to their natural selfishness and rapacity. It presupposes that men may be described as being in bondage to the compulsions of nature. But in contradistinction to what it presupposes, what it says is that something called nature transforms the ugliness and bondage of man into a true human good. Whatever else can be said, it seems obvious that Smith begins by conceding that man is a passive object governed by and immersed in an overwhelming environing force, that he is part of a great chain of causes; then Smith must find a way to extricate humanity from a desperate slavery that, in destroying freedom, threatens morality (what morality has an automaton?). The way Smith finds for achieving these ends is the discovery of nature in its expanded amplitude. Nature is to begin with the inescapable causes of human actions. It then proves to be also the power that prescribes the remote ends of those actions and in addition causes those ends to materialize in fact, according to an intention that must be said to belong to it (nature) and not to the human actors. There is scarcely any way for us to avoid a deep sense of uneasiness brought on by the suspicion that Smith's nature is only too literally just that — Smith's construction: a rationalized wish.

Smith's vision of nature might be defective, but it does not differ from others in being a construction. No one has ever seen nature; what we see is the world, and from it we go on to arrive at nature, which is an explanation of the world. There can be no such thing as an account of the world as *nature* that does not go beyond the mere description of the phenomena as phenomena. But what is the philosopher free to add? Only what makes the world intelligible. And what can that mean? May Ideas be added to the phenomena? May God be added to the world, as if nature, the explanation, is itself a thing to be explained? Does this perplexity not reveal that the world to be explained might have to be seen as the sum of the phenomena and the explanations of the phenomena — with the consequence that not only the intelligibility of the world but the goodness of the comprehensive explanation for man (that is, the goodness of the natural philosophy for man) becomes the criterion that governs the question, What is the philosopher free to add to the phenomena in order to arrive at nature? Whatever might be the answer to this question in general, with regard to Adam Smith it may be said confidently that he added compulsion and benevolent pupose to the world to arrive at nature.

Man in nature is the subject of a benevolent despotism; nature is the benevolent despotism that when added to the world makes it intelligible and, incidentally, good. This comes close to suggesting that natural philosophy can resemble high mythologizing. And it comes close to suggesting that Smith locates within the world, in order to constitute nature, what biblical theology locates outside the world in order to explain what came to be called nature. Smith makes it unnecessary to look beyond nature — to a divine will above it, as Scripture teaches, or to a human will alongside it, as Kant teaches. What Smith achieves is the transposition of an ancient understanding that nature is exhaustive into the theoretical arena in which nature is thought to be wholly mechanical. When I say that Smith achieved this transposition, I do not mean to imply that he was the first to envision exhaustive mechanical nature. On the contrary, the clarity with which Spinoza, for example, perceived both the vision and the threat contained in it to freedom and morality typifies the reason for modernity's insecurity in the embrace of nature. What I do mean to imply is that Smith's achievement gives us the decisive clue to the discovery of the decisive question for his system: what does it tell us about the status of man in nature that is supposed both exhaustive and mechanical?

The figure of the invisible hand brings to light the fact that along with human bondage in nature goes the reconciliation of the selfish impulses with the good of many or all. If the individual and society and the species are fully integrated in comprehensive nature, then nature could be said to be taking care of her own in exploiting greed for the common advantage. But in so doing, nature appears to release every human being from a conscious concern with the happiness or good opinion of the rest of mankind. Certainly it is the intention of much of Smith's work to show the contrary. The invisible hand goes no further than to argue that in matters of preservation — the production and distribution of the means of life — the repellent egoism of men is mechanically converted into actions useful to society and species. But Smith believed that he understood how, in important affairs of life that are not reducible to mere preservation, nature leavens the self-regard of men and converts it into virtue. In making what looks like an act of arbitrary distinction between matters of preservation and of morality, has he in his own way recognized the distinction between what were once called external goods and goods of the soul and in so doing found a means for reconciling mechanical nature with both preservation and morality? It is to *The Theory of Moral Sentiments* that one must turn for an answer. The metaphor of the invisible hand serves its chief theoretical purpose in bringing to light a problem for which the solution must be sought in a different context.

A leading question of *The Theory of Moral Sentiments* is, What is virtue? Smith makes it clear from the outset that he is in fact interested in the questions: What are the grounds of the distinction between right and wrong? What accounts for the human recognition of this distinction? What accounts for the large measure of practical respect enjoyed by the distinction? He begins his discussion in the first sentence of the book by announcing a premise that will bear the weight of much of what follows: "How selfish soever man may be supposed, there are evidently some principles in his nature which interest him in the fortune of others, and render their happiness necessary to him, though he derives nothing from it but the pleasure of seeing it."[2] This is simply a matter of fact. But Smith notes the further fact that there is no way by which one human being can feel the feelings of another, although our response to those feelings plays so large a part in our lives.

The link that proves to join one sentient being to another is imagination. We are forever having vicarious experiences because we are able to imagine ourselves in the other man's position — indeed, because we are unable not to do so. On the fact that men, so to speak, exchange themselves in imagination with one another depends the fact and the force of morality. One observes a human act and puts oneself in imagination in the place of the agent, and if there is a patient, then in his place too. Then one considers whether there is a harmony between the strength of the passion that moved the actor to act and what oneself could have felt in the same case. One judges by the same means whether the gratitude or resentment of the patient was suitable to the good or ill received. Thus human beings come to know approbation and disapprobation, but only because the feelings of one man are transferred to another through imagination. The natural mechanism that produces this transfer is therefore responsible for what is called sympathy — a term that Smith insists be understood in the technical sense of fellow-feeling ("com-passion") rather than in the special sense of kindliness or benevolence. It applies to all the sentiments, gentle or angry.

The mere operation of the sympathy mechanism does not of itself explain morality, although it does explain the approbation that underlies morality. To arrive at a norm that is undistorted by idiosyncrasy in bestowing and withholding approbation, Smith applies the construct of the impartial spectator, an imaginary bearer of the judgment of universal mankind that is infallible because of its impartiality as distinguished from its possible wisdom or virtue. If it is asked how any man can divine the judgment of the impartial spectator, the answer is that the impartial spectator is really none other than that "reason, principle, conscience, the inhabitant of the breast, the man within, the great judge and arbiter of our conduct."[3] We can easily enough find the way to duty by the use of natural common sense in conjunction with an honest desire to do right.[4] A man who forms his behavior on such lines will find by repeated experience that he gains the approbation not only of an imagined impartial spectator but of his living fellowmen. He will find at the same time that he has discovered morality, for virtue is precisely what deserves the impartial approbation of humanity.

Smith sets it forth that men by nature desire or need the approbation of their fellows. We have by nature the strongest desire for the love, the gratitude, and the admiration of mankind.[5] From this irresistible inclination proceed not only the general rules of morality but their strong grip on our behavior. Smith does not neglect the demands of preservation and utility, but he persistently denies that moral criteria or incentives can be derived from or reduced to considerations of mere advantage. Nature apparently does two things for mankind: it implants a powerful instinct of survival in the individual — even a tendency to gross and repellent selfishness — and it endows him with the imagination and gregariousness that unite the species mechanically through sympathy. With the use of an invisible hand, nature cajoles and compels us to society and virtue, to prosperity and humanity.

Smith's work demonstrates that, if one takes nature quite seriously and receives it altogether in its modern acceptation as mechanism encompassing mankind, one need not reject as a premise the impulsive sociality of man or jeopardize morality, abandon mankind to deductions from self-preservation, or jettison the virtues as such. Obviously, it must be asked whether an author may reasonably load or overload nature with this philanthropic freight. We cannot reach that sovereign question in this discussion but must confine ourselves to the meaning of Smith's project as a project.

Smith's thought is an impressive effort to solve, within the limits of mechanical nature alone, the problem of morality: the source and ground of the distinction between right and wrong, virtue and vice. It is a peculiarity of Smith's doctrine that it resolves the central moral questions faithfully to the tacit presupposition that nature is indeed the *comprehensive* mechanism. Smith reasons by abstraction from the question of man's freedom within the grip of that mechanism. Of course, he perceives that men are free to do well or ill, to heed or to ignore the call of conscience. But that fact does not respond to the much more radical question of freedom within nature, as is clear from a formulation of the issue that directly addresses Smith's own argument: Is the man who fulfills all the requirements of virtue as the sympathy mechanism defines virtue preeminently free or preeminently a slave to the strong need that men have for the approbation of their fellows? Evidently, Smith does not regard this as a crucial question.

If one had to guess why he did not attach the importance to it that, for example, Kant did, one might conjecture that he regarded the difficulty as artificial or superfluous. For if one speaks literally of nature as comprehensive or all-inclusive and of man as absolutely articulated in the chain of natural mechanism, then one ought not to speak of man's bondage to or in nature; for bondage is a relation between a one and some other that is capable of being "over against" the first. Two things may both be conceived as included in some larger One that comprehends them; and then either might be "over against" in relation to the other. But as far as the one is contained in the other as a part is in some whole, "bondage" is a misleading figure for characterizing the status of the part; for there is no "over against" in their relation. A wheel in a clock is not in bondage to the clock any more than the clock is in bondage to the wheel. Thus the question of man's "freedom" in the order of nature (under the stated assumptions of comprehensiveness and mechanism) does not arise spontaneously, that is, without stimulation from presuppositions. It expresses the notion that to be part of *the* whole is not different in principle from being part of any limited whole like a family or a city; and in seeing inclusion as assimilated to domination, it appears to envision subjection of the will of the part to the will of the whole. But precisely if the principle of the whole (nature in this case) is mechanism (say the motion of lifeless matter according to mere laws of physics), then will can enter only as a confusing metaphor, and the issue of freedom is a gratuitous intrusion in the context. It is in a sense such as this that the difficulty could be regarded as artificial or superfluous.

I freely grant that Smith's references to the intention of nature appear to expose him to the charge that he imputes a will to nature. Those references would have to be shown very precisely to point to some characteristic of nature that differs decisively from volition, for Smith's abstraction from the question of freedom vis-à-vis nature to be adequately covered by the suggested reasoning. For the immediate purpose I am assuming, but cannot discuss the assumption, that a purely mechanical principle such as evolution through natural selection is compatible with a teleology of nature but does not presuppose a will in nature.

Superfluously to raise the question of man's bondage to nature has effects that go beyond the theoretical. It either prepares the way for despair — there is no escape from the absolutely comprehensive and equally tyrannical grip of the natural All — or it compels men to find, which probably means invent, an enclave inside or a platform outside nature in the form of a state of the consciousness or the will, by which in spirit man will elevate himself to freedom in a most elusive sense. (I speak profanely, of course, and without respect to what may be hoped for through the enlightenment of revelation.)

Articulating man entirely within nature, yet declining to see a question of man's freedom vis-à-vis nature, Smith has adopted an ancient simplicity: man's integration in the order of nature is beneficial rather than threatening to humanity and is concordant with man's sociality and virtue. Smith's project for liberal commercial society is part of his wider project for accommodating man's sociality and morality to the environment of mechanistic nature, although the traditional setting for that conception of man in nature is the older and teleological vision of nature. Evaluations of commercial liberalism that do not consider this fact are to that extent defective. And they deprive one, moreover, of access to a most interesting reflection: modern society, like modern natural science, might be more reconcilable with the moral benefits that we tend to connect with "the tradition" than we sometimes permit ourselves to perceive.

Perhaps the time has come to remind ourselves of the twin bicentennial with which we began. Through reflection on the issues that surround the concept of the invisible hand, we are enabled to see what justifies Smith in restricting the sense of the term "liberty" to contexts that must be called social or political and thus what allows him to use such an expression as "natural liberty" without internal contradiction. If we see so much, we may also see the superfluousness of the vast and popular constructions that presuppose the bondage of man in nature and deduce on that foundation ambitious projects for an imaginary human emancipation, which have carried great masses of mankind into very palpable political servitude. Finally, we may see the sense in which *The Wealth of Nations* illuminates the liberal commercial polity of the United States, vindicating it at least in part against those moral complaints that arise from insufficient thought about freedom in and out of nature.

NOTES

1. Adam Smith, *The Theory of Moral Sentiments* (London: Alex Murray, 1869), p. 163.
2. Ibid., p. 9.
3. Ibid., p. 120.
4. Ibid., p. 156.
5. Ibid., p. 139.

Index